FUNDAMENTALS OF SOCIOLOGY

FUNDAMENTALS OF SOCIOLOGY

Edited by

Sarat C. Joshi

AKANSHA PUBLISHING HOUSE
NEW DELHI - 110 002 (INDIA)

AKANSHA PUBLISHING HOUSE
R-37B, Vani Vihar, Uttam Nagar
New Delhi - 110 059
E-mail: ektabooks@yahoo.com

Showroom
4649/21B, Ansari Road
Daryaganj, New Delhi - 110 002
Phones: 23263193, 9811582579

Fundamentals of Sociology

First Published, 2006

ISBN 81-8370-065-9

PRINTED IN INDIA

Published by M.P. Misra for Akansha Publishing House, New Delhi 110 059 and Printed at Tarun Offset Press, Delhi

Contents

Acknowledgments

I am indebted to many individuals for their assistance, inspiration and support in bringing out this book. While I do not have room to list them all, I would like the contributions of my teachers, friends, colleagues and seniors at the Institute. My family members provided vital support at key stages. Since the book is substantially based on the secondary sources, penned by leading men of letters, I am deeply beholden to all the original contributors. My greatest debt, however, is to my wife whose patience, understanding and support know no bounds. Finally, my publishers deserve all appreciation for materializing the venture superbly and elegantly.

--Editor

Prolegomena

"It is never safe to look into the future with eyes of fear."

--Edward H. Harriman

"We must always remember that knowledge of understanding is not the same thing as the understanding, which is the raw material of that knowledge. It is as different from understanding as the doctor's presentation for penicillin is different from penicillin."

--Aldous Huxley

Sociology is really a late arrival to the university or intellectual community and one of the youngest sciences. Although it is impossible to say, "Here is the beginning!" most sociologists find it convenient to place sociology's origin in the early nineteenth century with the work of Auguste Comte (1798-1857), who was the first one to use the word sociology and who defined sociology as the science of society. Like all perspectives, the development of sociology was linked with social conditions. After all, perspectives are ways of defining what is "out there", and not all societies encourage their members to examine society critically. But nineteenth-century Europe was ripe for self-analysis. Several developments came together to bring about the right climate for the questioning spirit to grow and flourish.

What is Sociology?

In fact, the simplest definition of sociology is "the science of society", but this is no longer adequate, since sociologists differ in their views as follows:

MacIver & Page, says, 'Sociology is a study of web of relationship or a network of relationship.'

In the opinion of Giddings, 'Sociology is the systematic description and explanation of society viewed as a whole'

While P.A. Sorokin says, "Sociology is a generalizing science of socio-cultural phenomena viewed in their forms, types and manifold interconnections"

To quote E. Durkheim, "Sociology is the science of collective representation" and Auguste Comte says "Sociology is the science of social order and progress".

According to Max Weber, "Sociology is the science which attempts the interpretative understanding of social action in order thereby to arrive at a causal explanation of its causes, its course and its effects."

An Analysis

1. Some sociologists a more inclusive view of sociology, seeing it as the study of all *social organization,* from the largest unit -- society -- to the smallest -- a pair of interacting individuals or dyad. The emphasis is on the nature of all organized life.
2. Some sociologists do focus on *society* -- that very abstract and large world that humans share. They are often referred to as "macrosociologists", because they study the largest unit of organization, society.
3. Sociology is increasingly taking a specialized look at *institutions* or institutional systems. The focus is on family patterns, schools, government, the military, courts, religion, and economic patterns. Specialization has created experts who spend their time examining one part of society.
4. Many think that sociology is to study social *problems,* such as inequality or family disorganization or poverty.
5. Finally, some sociologists are more interested in the *micro* world or face-to-face *interaction,* how individuals

act in relation to each other in everyday life. Often they are interested in how individuals shape their society, how society is built on the dynamics of interaction, how the individuals through interaction become human, become a member of society, learn roles, develop personality traits, etc.

Sociology offers fresh insights into what we do. Typically, it does not focus on the individual's personality as the cause of behaviour, but examines *interaction, social location* (position, role, class) and ongoing *socialization*. For example, sociologists try to understand what patterns of action emerge among people in a certain group or organization, what rules develop, what expectations arise. Sociologists understand the power of the "student role", being "middle class", and being a "man" or a "woman" in modern Indian society. We see actors changing as they shift groups or organizations, influenced by the inevitable socialization (attempts by people in the organization to teach their ways) that comes with joining. In nutshell, sociology is an attempt to understand human action in the context of our social life. Humans are to be understood as social animals, influenced by interaction, location, and socialization.

From socio-psychological perspective people may explain the mass suicide of a religious cult as the result of religious fanaticism or a powerful leader or irrational and sick persons. Although this may be a partial explanation, sociologists perceive that a religious cult must also be understood as a society, an organized group sharing culture, as individuals influencing each other in interaction, as a structure with people filling positions and acting in accepted ways, conforming to each other's expectations as in any other group or society. As another example, instead of emphasizing characteristics of individuals who are sent to prison, sociologists might look at factors relating to the position of these people in society: how poverty "position" might influence criminal action, arrest, and imprisonment, and how economic power might influence the definition of crime.

Basically, each perspective has its own bias, in a sense, tending to emphasize certain points and ignoring others. Psychology examines personality, chemistry treats reality as a mixture of chemicals, and biology understands life as largely hereditary. No single perspective can capture every aspect of reality or give us certainty, but a perspective can be a useful guide. To be useful, a perspective has to help us understand a number of concrete situations, solve problems which are important to us, and get through life successfully. For many, sociology is a very useful perspective. Like all academic perspectives it is limited, yet those who understand it often find it to be like a "passion" (borrowing from Peter Berger), for it truly alters their understanding of their own lives in a profound way.

As an Academic Perspective

How do we come to know anything? How can we be sure that what we know is true? How do we know when it is time to change our ideas? Probably all thinking people at some time or other ask these questions. Looking for answers can be frustrating, for the more we do so, the farther we seem to get from certainty. Most of us seek certainty, and, unfortunately, most of us at one time or another think we have it. But as time goes on we become increasingly aware of the problems of knowing anything. Sociology is one systematic attempt to understand the world we live in. It is like psychology, biology, anthropology, astronomy, mathematics, and the humanities in this sense. We call each of these *academic perspectives.* They are "academic" in that they are recognized disciplines in the academic or college community. They are "perspectives" in that each is one way of looking at things, one approach, one set of eyeglasses.

Sociologists may differ on which focus is most important, but all regard the study of humans as social beings to be central to understanding human action. Sociology, then, is an academic perspective, the goal of which is to understand the actions of human beings in the context of their social life, as resulting from interaction, social location, and socialization. It focuses on society, social organization, institutions, interaction, and social problems.

As an Objective Perspective

Sociology is a perspective which attempts to understand people *carefully* and *critically*. Understanding ourselves is difficult, and unless we are careful we may accept an idea without having enough evidence to back it up. Evidence is systematically, objectively, and carefully gathered, and this is done in sociology through empirical testing. Sociologists say, "If the idea is a good one, then show me in a controlled situation (a test) that it makes sense! If you can't do it, I can't believe you!" At first maybe a poor test is tried, when someone else figures out a better one, then the idea is tested in a "super test", but a debate continues back and forth until a number of satisfactory tests support or negate the idea. This process is known as science and it is different from the way opinions are formed by most people.

Remarkably a science, the purpose of sociology must be to *understand* human action. Its purpose is not that of social work, which has as its primary purpose helping people deal with their personal or family problems. Nor is sociology primarily an attempt to change society.

Many of us may care about making a better world by changing things we regard as wrong, but as sociologists we regard understanding the world clearly and objectively to be an important task in and of itself. Sociologists wish to provide information based on generalization and real life knowledge or data. Sociologists, like other scientists, have made important contributions to various disciplines whose job is to work with people in order to bring desired changes in society.

Sociology is a critical perspective; that is, sociologists try to "see through" the ideas many of us take for granted. No idea that humans accept about themselves and their society is beyond investigation. Most people are caught up in the ideas, values, and rules of their group or society and so they cannot easily get away and see things as they are. Sociology is an attempt to break out of society's "truths" and ask basic questions. That is why it is, by its very nature, *critical. Of* course, some sociologists are more critical than others, and some, as in all perspectives, have lost that critical eye, accepting without serious question the "truths" of a certain group of society. However, more than almost any other perspective, the sociological perspective leads to questions about the human condition that are by definition critical. Why does a prosperous society have widespread poverty? Why is there inequality between poor and rich or between men and women? Why is there widespread crime, divorce, dissatisfaction with work? Are these things inevitable? Why do some people seem to try hard to succeed and others just give up? Who really runs society? Are human beings anywhere free? What changes can we expect in society in the next twenty-five years? Why do people conform? Why are some people labelled "deviant"? These questions are themselves critical and make the sociologist the eternal skeptic.

As an Inspired Science

Sociology grew out of a desire by some intellectuals to apply the techniques of science to the study of society. Before sociologists, there were social philosophers, political economists, and religious thinkers who looked at society or its different aspects. In ancient Greece, the philosopher Plato wrote *The Republic,* a fascinating and enlightening critique and a guide to a more acceptable and just society. Machiavelli's *The Prince,* More's *Utopia,* Rousseau's *Social Contract,* as well as the Old and New Testaments are but a few famous works dealing with society and its institutions. Most of these examined the political world primarily, and most were a mixture of an attempt to understand and an attempt to say what the world should be like. Sociologists, however, took the advice of the Enlightenment thinkers of the eighteenth century.

Sociology from its start borrowed from the natural sciences the tools that were being used to fashion new discoveries about the stars, the earth, and the human body. The universe is made up of natural laws; so too society must be governed by such laws, and sociology would discover these laws through applying scientific procedures. Its purpose would be to describe what society is, not primarily to make a statement as to what it should be.

Sociology, then, was born in a time of intellectual excitement. Indeed, Comte was so excited about the future of the "science of society" that he naively predicted that sociology (which he also called as the "queen of the sciences") would be the focus of a new religion, and sociologists, as the bearers of knowledge, would be the "priests of the new order".

Sociology and Political Science

In fact, Political science deals with social groups organized under the sovereignty of the state. This may also be studied as a social institution. The state is a structure within which other lesser societies such as the family, the commercial world or the university develop: but as a social group and as an institution, it is also the object of sociology. From the historical viewpoint, the affinity between sociology and political science is very close; for it was not until recent times that the distinction between politics and sociology was made. Before this the main works on subjects such as Plato's *Republic,* the *Politics* of Aristotle, and other classical works of the East and West were meant to be complete treatises on political science. In accordance with our conception of sociology it would not be accurate to consider political science as a part of sociology; for it has special topics of its own such as the nature and systems of law, the methods of political representation, the sphere of the legislative power etc., with which no other science is concerned directly. But certain political questions such as the relation between law and freedom, or the nature of political allegiance inasmuch as they are related with the whole of social life, may also fall within the scope of sociology. In short, the ground covered by sociology and political science is largely common, but the viewpoints are different; the former looks upon the state as social institution or association; the latter as the supreme regulating power of the community and the source of political law.

Here, it is apt to note what Giddings say, "To teach the theory of the state to men who have not learned the first principles of sociology is like teaching astronomy or thermodynamics to men who have not learned the Newtonian laws of motion."

Sociology and Economics

Generally, economics has been defined as the study of mankind in the ordinary business of life, but more properly, it is taken as the science of wealth in its three phases of production, distribution, and consumption. As the economic process develops in society, it influences and is influenced by the social life of man; the relation between these two sciences is very intimate.

Moreover, many economists like Sombart, Max Weber, Oppenheimer, Pareto, and Schumpeter interpreting economic change as an aspect of social change, held that the study of economics would be misleading and incomplete apart from its social setting--an opinion that has gained considerable ground during the last few decades. Again, as the economic system is embedded in the social structure as a part of it, the study of the former cannot be undertaken but as a function of the latter; that is why a celebrated modern economist has said, 'Economics must be the handmaid of sociology. At the other end, environmentalist writers like Marx or Veblen, by thinking that the social reality is in the last resort reducible to the interplay of economic or technical forces, tend to transform sociology into a part or aspect of economics. The popularity of this view in past years accounts much for the common tendency to confuse economics with sociology. This tendency was popularized by the fact that both subjects were concerned, to the exclusion of any other, with solving the vexed question between capital and labour.

In the context of modern period, hardly any grounds remain for confusing the distinction between economics and sociology. The development of the social sciences has cleared up many doubts and smoothed out many differences. In particular cases, to define the limits of both sciences, still remains a difficult task.

Ethics and Sociology

Ethics is concerned with the moral lightness or deprivity of human actions. It investigates the laws of morality and formulates the principles and rules of morally desirable actions. It cannot be said that ethics is concerned with ends to the exclusion of means, because every human action is capable of morality, not only in itself as an end, but also in relation to other ends which it may subserve. A peaceful strike directed to improve the condition of the working classes, when all other legal men have proved futile, is morally good, or at least not wrong; whereas the same strike, used as a piece of revolutionary strategy, with the object of spreading unrest in the population, is ethically wrong. There are some authors who, while acknowledging the distinction between sociality and morality, seem to imply that morality is exhausted in terms of sociality; or, in other words, that no ethical action is possible unless it is social.

This view seems to be the product of behaviouristic bias, for, setting aside the fact that many actions performed in society cannot be included directly in the category of what is moral or immoral, one must recognize that in many internal and private actions, which, as such, escape the definition of what is social, man is capable of morality. In the total configuration of a complex human action we shall usually find social as well as ethical elements intimately interconnected; their reciprocal influence may be so intimate as to render the task of disentangling them extremely difficult.

Yet, for all this, their value and meaning will be quite different. A situation like this demands for its solution the close co-operation of ethics and sociology. The difference, therefore, between ethics and sociology has more than one reason for it. Firstly, their fields do not totally coincide, for not everything that is social is ethical; nor is everything, that is ethical, social. Secondly, the viewpoint from which they may envisage the same problem is different On the other hand, the moral life of man is developed in society, while the influence of ethical behaviour on social and political life can hardly be exaggerated.

Anthropology and Sociology

In fact, the physical and cultural development of human beings, from their origin to the present time, is the object of the study of anthropology. For convenience of method such a vast field is divided into the following parts: human solution or the study of the foss man; physical anthropology which is concerned with the bodily characteristics of racial groups, their biological reactions and the influence on them of environmental factors; archaeology or prehistory which attempts to reconstruct the social life of prehistory which attempts to reconstruct the social life of prehistoric man; cultural anthropology, called also social anthropology which deals with human culture in the sense upheld by anthropolgists, with its elements, organizations, changes, organs of transmission, etc.; and linguistics which seeks to investigate the characteristics of the various cultural groups and their changes through the study of the languages of mankind both in the preliterate and historical periods. According to its etymology, anthropology (from the Greek anthropos; man) should deal with man as such, whereas sociology should deal with him inasmuch as he is a social being. But in the concrete some restrictions are made for both concepts, and anthropology has also made its adjustments to the other social sciences.

Thus cultural anthropology, to which sociology is more related, confines itself to the study of culture mostly among preliterate peoples. Though the youngest of the traditional social sciences, it has developed and gone ahead of many of them; it has made outstanding contributions to the study of man. By its insistence on field research and on fact rather than on a priori speculations, it has rescued the social sciences, especially sociology, from their hazardous commitments to the theory of unilinear evolution easily adhered to by early sociologists and anthropologists. Anthropologists like Westermarck, W. Schmidt, Malinowski, Boas, Goldenweiser, Paul Radin, Lowie, and others subjected the social sciences to the discipline of the anthropological fact by which it has been possible to make a new and safer start.

As of now too, there is a tendency towards the union of cultural anthropology with sociology and some works on sociology have been written by anthropologists with dubious success. Yet, the distinction between these two branches of the social sciences will continue to be observed as their points of views on the social reality are dissimilar and their fields of investigation do not always coincide.

History and Sociology

Like political science, sociology is becoming one of the most genuine fruits of history, to which it is intimately related, though the overstressing of this intimacy has led some writers as G. von Bulow of refuse to acknowledge sociology as a science distinct from history. On the other hand, the distinction between both subjects was somewhat unduly magnified by some, as Troeltsch, who claimed that history dealt with particular historical occurrences, whereas sociology was concerned with general laws.

This distinction, though exaggerated, is not without some foundation, as the primary interest of the sociologist is the finding of the general laws of society and that of the historian the reconstruction of the order in which historical events have been taking place.

But in reality the sociologist cannot dispense with social facts any more than the historian with historical laws. A deeper distinction between these two sciences lies in the fact that history deals with human events in so far as they are correlated in time, while sociology studies them from the viewpoint of he social relationship involved. Thus while the historian describes the Indo-Pak wars with all the circumstances accompanying them, a sociologist would study their impact on the lives of the people, the role that these wars had on the subsequent development of the nationalistic spirit in Indian subcontinent.

Still other differences, related to those mentioned above, exist between sociology and history. Thus while the historian may deal with the development of the family in different civilizations, the sociologist's task is to investigate into the various forms of this institution; to trace the morphological similarity between them; to find their correlations so as to be able to formulate the laws of change and causality that intervene among those traits and institutions.

Sociology and Social Psychology

Social psychology deals with the mental processes of man considered as a social being. It studies particularly the influence of group life on the mental development of the individual; the effect of the individual mind on the group, and the development of the mental life on the groups within themselves and in their relations with one another. Pickford says more particularly that. Social psychology analyses the framework of social relationships in such a way as to show the interaction of individual and groups now and in the past, and by study of the dynamic of these interactions to reveal how they lead to the establishment of that framework and to the personality patterns of participant individuals. Apart from the distinction between general psychology and social psychology, which some authors quite unjustly consider as purely academical, the relations between the latter subject and sociology, though intimate, leave plenty of room for distinction.

If the whole of social life could be reduced finally to psychological forces, as McDougall and Freud seem to admit, the question between inheritance and environment, with which we have to deal, would definitely be decided in favour of the former and social psychology. But as the causes affecting social behaviour are likewise other than psychological, social life cannot be studied exclusively with the methods of the psychologist.

Though economic, cultural, geographical or biological conditions are essentially different from psychological factors, though there is close interaction among them; nor can the development and variety of social institutions be explained exclusively on psychological grounds. The various forms of marriage and of the family among peoples having presumably the same psychological equipment, as well as the existence of similar institutions like private property or monogamy among psychologically very different peoples precludes once for all a purely psychological explanation. The attempt to ascribe social causation to a single factor, though it be as important as the psychological, is doomed to failure at the outset. In the interplay of forces influencing social change more than one such force is responsible for every single effect.

Sociology and Social Sciences

Not long ago the number of the social sciences like that of the Muses was supposed to be nine. But they have increased so enormously of late that they exceed that number considerably; though the agreement among authors about the exact number of the sciences which may be considered as social is far from unanimous. To those already mentioned, the following may be added: demography, law, education, criminology, social service or social work, and social statistics. The points of connection and differences between them and sociology may be gathered from comparing their concepts, fields of action and objects.

Sociology and Social Philosophy

Social philosophy, as is obvious from the name, is the meeting point of sociology and philosophy, and may equally belong to both branches of knowledge. Its role in the social sciences is the study of the fundamental principles and concepts of social life in their epistemological and axiological aspects with a view to elaborating the higher synthesis of the social sciences and to define their place in the universe.

Sociology, which occupies the central seat among the social sciences, co-ordinates them. Social philosophy, starting from the data supplied by them, rises towards a higher synthesis. With History, Philosophy, Mathematics, Physics, the relationship of Sociology is of one way only it takes the content but it does not give any thing. While the relationship of sociology with other disciplines like psychology. Geography, Political Science, Education ctc. is of two ways.

The present book encompasses all vital information on sociology as a whole Though many recent developments could not be dealt elaborately yet efforts are made to make this an ideal text-cum-reference book.

1

Culture and Society

"To cling stubbornly to old opinions just because we once cherished them is as stupid as to cling to them because they one belonged to our grandfather."

"Culture is not just an ornament; it is the expression of a nation's character, and at the same time it is a powerful instrument to mould character. The end of culture is right living."

—*W. Somerset Maugham*

WHAT IS CULTURE?

Culture requires to be explained, particularly because it is the central concept round which cultural sociology has grown. 'Culture' can be used to convey various meanings. Thus there is the common, literary use of the term when we use 'culture' to convey social charm and intellectual excellence. This is what Matthew Arnold, famous critic and poet, meant when he defined culture as sweetness and light. There are some sociologists also who use the term 'cultural elite' for the intellectual leaders of a society. Then there are philosophers like Cassirer and sociologists like Sorokin and MacIver to whom culture stands for the moral, spiritual and intellectual attainments of man. David Bidney, philosopher-anthropologist, defines it as the self-cultivation of human nature as also the cultivation of natural, geographical environment.

Both Sanskrit and *sanskriti* are derived from *sanskar*,

meaning ritual performance. Right from the day he is born, a Hindu goes through various ritual performances as a result of which he is accepted into various roles, like that of an adult or a husband, in the course of his life, *Sanskriti* stands for that state of collective life which can be attained only after going through the various *sanskars*. It is a process of refinement. It is interesting to note that Sanskrit was the urban tongue of ancient India, The rural speech was Prakrit which is derived from *prakriti,* meaning nature. Man is born as a social being; he attains sociality by going through the *sanskars*.

Tylor was the first anthropologist to define and make extensive use of the term 'culture'. He said that culture stands for the beliefs, ideas, customs, laws, morals, arts and other capabilities and skills acquired by man as a member of society. What is emphasized in this definition is that culture is a social heritage; it is the gift of society to an individual. Others, including Malinowski, have paraphrased this definition to point out that the social heritage may be said to consist of a material part and a non-material, intangible, imponderable part. Or, to put it in other words, culture is a total way of life and the instruments, mental, social and material, of which this way is constituted. On the one hand we have social culture and on the other material culture. This view has been extended and yet put in a summarized form by Bidney who defines culture as the product of agrofacts (products of cultivation), artifacts (products of industry), socifacts (social organization), and mentifacts (language, religion, art and so on). A view of culture as the one outlined above stems from the belief that culture is a substantive reality; a thing which exists *per se*. This may be called the sensate view of culture.

Culture has been defined by Marett as communicable intelligence. Redfield amplifies this viewpoint when he defines it as the sum total of conventional meanings embodied in artifacts, social structure and symbols. This idealistic position arises out of the recognition of the all-important role which symbols play in the communication and acquisition of knowledge. Benedict writes on the patterns of culture, not its content. Then there is the formalistic, aesthetic viewpoint of Ruth Benedict, according to which culture is not so much to be conceived in terms of the content of social life as in terms of its formal ordering and organization.

Malinowski and Radcliffe-Brown take the instrumental, humanistic view of culture. To the former, culture stands for a total way of life which secures for an individual the satisfaction of his bio-psychic drives and the fulfilment of other wants and cravings and, ultimately, invests him with freedom. Radcliffe-Brown regards culture as cultivation, the process of handing down and acquiring traditions, as a result of which society is perpetuated. The functionalists take a holistic view: culture, as a whole, is regarded as the unit of study, and not a culture trait (i.e., an item from a culture), as Tylor supposed, nor even a pattern as Benedict said. There is also a more recent viewpoint espoused by Linton, Kluckhohn, and now very lately by Kroeber, which takes its stand on the plane of the subjective nature of human understanding. Linton says the way of life of a people is one thing, and what we study and write about, another. The former is reality, the latter our understanding of the same. If the former is to be called 'culture', then the latter may be called only 'culture-construct'.

It is an abstraction from the reality which is the actual human behaviour. Kluckhohn describes it as a way of thinking, feeling and action, and Gillin makes the viewpoint even more clear by maintaining that culture is not activity, but its patterning. According to this viewpoint, culture is only a model constructed, not by a people themselves, but by an anthropologist who studies their life. Therefore, it is to be differentiated from the actual conduct of life.

From what has been said above, it is obvious that even though culture has been the most dominant concept used by cultural anthropologists, yet there is no unanimity among them as to what culture is. Each viewpoint has led to useful researches, and it will be the task of future research to give a final definition of what constitutes the nature of culture. It may be pointed out here that none of the viewpoints enumerated above enjoys any special superiority over the others.

Cultural Attributes

Anthropologists have not, of course, busied themselves only with the definition of culture. They have also tried by comparative study to arrive at some generalizations as regards some attributes of culture.

Ethos and Eidos. Kroeber has drawn attention to two aspects of culture, which he calls eidos and ethos. Eidos is the formal appearance of a culture derived from its constituents. Contrasted with the aggregate of constituents is *ethos,* the disposition of a culture which determines its quality, its main themes and interests. Bateson also says that each culture can be said to have two aspects: the first, consisting of the total emotional emphasis of a culture, called *ethos,* and the second, consisting, of the emphases resulting from the cognitive processes operative within a culture, called *eidos.*

Explicit and Implicit Elements. Such regularities as may be perceived with the aid of the eye and the ear are the explicit items of a culture. There may be other items which would be perceived by us only after being specially trained for looking for all that is not obvious, the motivations and impulses underlying human action of which the actors themselves may not be conscious. These would be the implicit items of a culture. A total and representative study of a people's way of life must include both explicit as well as implicit items.

Culture Determinism. Culture, Tylor, said, was acquired by man as a member of society, but the culture determinists do not believe in such a social matrix of culture. According to them, culture is the matrix of everything else, and is itself governed by its own laws of growth and operation. Neither human biology, nor human psychology, nor even human society is regarded as capable of explaining its reality. This view, for long associated with the name of Kroeber, who has lately changed his position, has been called the superorganic view; but it is more than that: it is super-psychic and super-social as well.

With the increasing accumulation of the evidence of the role which individuals play in fashioning and changing culture, it became obvious that, among various other types of causes, individuals also were, at least to some extent, the creators of culture. To accommodate this evidence, cultural determinists said that a culture operates 'as if it were independent of individuals. Leslie White is today the main spokesman for culture determinism, a viewpoint which, it may be said, suffers from the 'culturalistic fallacy' of regarding culture as the essence and the self-moved mover of human life. Human beings, it must be realized, are perhaps equally the creators of culture as they are its creatures and carriers.

Culture vis-a-vis *the Individual.* Linton has pointed out that for the majority of people, who are of the conforming type, culture plays the role of guide. It lays down norms of behaviour and provides the mechanism which secure for an individual his personal and social survival. Without culture, man would have never survived; therefore it is his liberator, it frees him from biological determinism, but only after exacting a price from him. This price is paid in the shape of surrendering complete independence of action. If a person is to benefit from society, he must conform to its accepted ways of life; and that is what the common man does. Thus, culture is man's guide; it liberates as well as enslaves him as all guides do. But for the non conforming few, called 'mystics' by Bergson and 'the creative minority' by Toynbee, culture is the framework within which to try their new ideas. They do not seek to destroy; their non conformity is not negative but constructive; they seek to change culture. Such a view does not espouse Carlyle's theory that heroes make history; it only points out that human beings are always required to save society from stagnation. The ways of doing so are often inherent in a culture; only someone must come along, perceive these and utilize them.

Culture and Civilization. Morgan believed that human society had, since the emergence of man, passed through three stages; beginning with savagery, it had gone through barbarism and come to civilization. This culminating stage of civilization was correlated with the growth of cities, the emergence of writing, metallurgy, science and so on. This use of the term civilization has been generally followed by all anthropologists who contrast pre-urban, pre-literate society with civilized society. Thus civilization represents a particular type of culture.

However, German idealists, and some American sociologists like MacIver influenced by the former, differentiate between culture and civilization differently. Culture is regarded, as the moral, spiritual and intellectual attainments of man. It stands for symbols and values. It is the primary and basic thing; it is inside us, and Is what we are. It may register progress or decline.

Civilization is secondary; it is something outside us and consists of technology, material culture and social institutions. It is the sum total of the instruments of cultural life. It is what we have, and will accumulate and it will never progress or decline by itself.

Culture Trait and Culture Complex. When culture is taken to mean the way of life, it is obvious that within this whole there are elements like, say, prayer, ritual, making of stone tools by percussion and so on. Each of these elements is called a culture trait, or element. If a number of culture traits combine together to produce a meaningful congery, a segment within the total culture, then the same is called a 'culture complex'. A culture complex is not an institution: it is the out-come of interaction between several institutions. Culture complex has also been defined as the pattern of the inter-relation of culture traits.

Culture Growth: Theories

Right from the beginning, cultural anthropologists were faced with the problems of the growth of a culture and cultural parallels, i.e., how do cultures come to be and how do they come to have similar culture traits and complexes? The earlier theories about culture were concerned with these two main problems.

Evolutionism. Sociology as a modern science was born when the star of evolution was shining high and bright. Darwin and Spencer had between themselves sought to establish evolution as the life-breath of all phenomena. Under the impact of the evolutionary bias of the day, early pioneers like Tylor and Morgan devoted themselves wholeheartedly to the study of the evolution of human society and culture. Other contributory forces also were present to goad them on in this venture. Thus there were the widely held belief that, from the point of view of psychic makeup, man was everywhere the same. This was given expression in the phrase 'the psychic unity of mankind'. Consequently, it was believed that, given the same problems, man would think out similar solutions. Variations of environment would, however, register themselves in variations of the same institution as found in various cultures. Thus, cultures were supposed to grow through evolution, from simpler towards complex and differentiated types; and cultural parallels were explained to be the outcome of the psychic unity of mankind. Each institution was believed to evolve independently within the setting of the local culture. If two cultures exhibited similar traits or institutions, the same were referred to as cases of *convergent evolution*. Examples were often cited; thus agriculture had been evolved independently in south-eastern and south-western Asia and in the New World. Zero was invented independently by the Hindus, Babylonians and Mayas; corbelling by the Mycenaeans, Mayas and Eskimos. Writing is believed to have been evolved independently in various parts of the world on half a dozen occasions. Paper-making and printing also were evolved independently in the East and the West.

Illustrious examples of how the evolutionary theorists argued may be taken from the writings of Morgan, Tylor, Haddon and Levy-Bruhl.

Believing that human societies have evolved from lower into higher types, Morgan postulated three stages. To begin with man lived in savage society, which had an older period, a middle period (synchronzing with fishing and the use of fire) and a later period (when the bow and arrow were used). With the invention of pottery, man entered the older period of barbarism. Domestication of animals and cultivation of plants by irrigation ushered in the middle period of barbarism. From the time the process of smelting iron ore was invented and iron tools made use of, till the next change, man lived in the later period of barbarism. Then came civilization, ushered in by the invention of a phonetic alphabet and writing. Civilization, according to Morgan, was as well the contemporary condition of western European society.

Morgan applied the same kind of conjectural reasoning. Assuming that legally enforced monogamy was the highest stage of the martial bond, he supposed the evolutionary process to have started from a hypothetical stage of promiscuity and to have gone through stages of group marriage, polyandry, voluntary monogamy and polygeny. Corresponding to the changes in the nature of the marital bond, various types of family were also believed by him to have evolved out of the clan through stages of matrilineal and patrilineal reckoning into the bilateral family.

Tylor made a similar study of the growth of religions. He regarded animistic polytheism to have been the earliest and the simplest form of religion. Then must have come an intermediary stage of a higher polytheistic ideology which ultimately gave way to monotheism.

Levy-Bruhl also posited the evolution of modern logic from a primitive logic. He asserted that, in so far as the primitives are not conscious of the implications of contradiction and physical separateness--which he asserted they are not--theirs is a mentality undeveloped as compared to ours. He, therefore, chose to call it a pre-logical mentality. Evidence for all these conjectural reconstructions was collected from various cultures spread over time and space without bothering too much about the significance of cultural context. Students of material culture went even so far as to collect various specimens of various artifacts, like bows and arrows for instance, from various parts of the earth and belonging to different times; they then arranged them in order of ascending complexity and made a statement about the evolution of the bow and arrow. Whereas these early evolutionists made significant contributions to our understanding of cultural processes, they often became extremist in their espousal of independent evolution. Their uncritical use of the method of comparative analysis brought them and the method into disrepute. They always spoke in terms of logical sequences, irrespective of whether there was any historical evidence in support of the same or not. They revealed a strange ignorance of the role of cultural borrowing. They were armchair theorists drawing amazingly uncritically upon the accounts of travellers and missionaries. Their preoccupation with building schemes of cultural evolution made them blind to other ways of cultural growth and other explanations of cultural parallels. They also revealed a high degree of ethno centrism, arising directly out of their belief that society and culture had advanced to reach their perfection in 19th century Europe. Their judgements of primitive cultures were vitiated by this ethnocentric attitude.

Many writers developed modified forms of evolutionism. Thus, there is the theory that social institutions do not develop in an upward straight line, but along a parabolic curve. An institution starts in a particular form, develops into its opposite, and then further develops into its original form, but at a new, higher level. Thus, the earliest form of property ownership was undeliberate communal ownership. Later on, the institution of private ownership emerged, but the communistic doctrine has already re-established a rational, communal ownership of property through the agency of the state.

Diffusionism. Remarkably, due to insistence of evolutionists that culture traits always evolve independently, and that cultural similarities are the consequence of parallel or convergent evolution emerged many critics for them. Not that such processes of growth were denied, but the complete neglect of known instances of customs and artifacts being added to a culture by borrowing was resented as an unscientific disregard for history. It did not require special field training to realize that the doctrine of unilinear development of human society from savagery to barbarism to civilization, from promiscuity to group marriage to monogamy, and from hunting to pastoralism, to agriculture, to handicrafts, to industrial life was not tenable in the light of the accumulating knowledge about the socio-economic life of the simpler folk of the world. In the biological sciences, the rediscovery of Mendel's laws of inheritance provided a point of departure from Darwinism; and there was also a corresponding shift from Spencer's position in the social sciences. Nor was special training required to observe that culture traits and also whole culture complexes are passed from one group to another through the agency of communication or migration.

Two people may simply be living in physical proximity; a high frequency of inter-communication would be the consequence. Such inter-communication would be in the form of words, customs, spouses, goods and services, beliefs and so on. It is obvious that if two people, not belonging to the same culture group, are very near from each other, then they must observe each other's dress, ornaments, utensils and outdoor life. They may as naturally talk to each other, and that could be done only after picking up some words from each other's speech. One need not labour any more on the reality of cultural inter-communication through physical contact.

Culture traits may also be carried by a migrating people into an area where they settle down temporarily and may be communicated to the inhabitants there. All this constructive criticism of evolutionary extremism stemmed not from logical reasoning or conjecture but from the knowledge of actual historical happenings. Such transmission of culture, leading to culture growth and culture parallels, was called 'diffusion'.

The Kulturkreise School. Kulturkreise means a culture-circle or a culture-district. Some German-speaking writers, Graebner, Ankermann and Schmidt being the prominent among them, presented a theory of diffusion in the early years of this century and their followers have since been propagating it. Their theory consists of a belief in evolution tempered with diffusion. They said that various culture complexes develop at various times in different parts of the world and later on diffuse over corresponding portions of the earth. Such diffusion is a continuous process and layers of diffused-in culture traits may be identified in a culture. These scholars depended too much upon the evidence of material culture and did not substantiate all their schemes of diffusion of social institutions. However, Graebner, from among them, made an important and lasting contribution by evolving the criteria of quantity and form. He said that when historical evidence is lacking mere superficial resemblance is not enough to conclude that diffusion has taken place. Along with the similarity of form there should be the sameness of the number, and the arrangement of constituent elements of a trait or a complex. Thus, if it is to be seen that the knowledge of the zodiac has diffused from one place to another, one must look for the same signs, same number of signs and same clock- or anti-clockwise way of reckoning distribution. Critics have accused this school of mysticism so far as its view of the growth of culture is concerned. Certainly this theory is at best an attempt at explaining diffusion in certain areas, and the same has" been done better by others. This has also been called the *Kulturhistorische Schule,* i.e., culture-historical school.

Culture Area Approach. Graebner and others were concerned with discovering the facts of a case of diffusion. Boas raised the additional question of 'Why does it take place?' It is this concern with the cause and dynamic effects of culture contact which distinguishes American diffusionists from others. Franz Boas divided the study of diffusion into various stages. Firstly, the facts of the situation must be described. Then, analytical study may be started, proceeding from the particular to the general, making a map of actual distribution in a restricted area, before covering continents and the world. The reasons for the dynamics of contact must be ultimately sought, Boas advised, in the psychic makeup of the individual. Clark Wissler developed these basic viewpoints, and defined the restricted area, to which Boas refers, as a *culture area.*

Wissler also pointed out the need, in fact the compulsion, which necessitates such narrowing down of ambitions. He pointed out that a culture trait, particularly if it is non-material, cannot travel long distances without getting diluted *en route*, partly by losing some of its features and partly by getting associated and mixed up with features that do not belong to it. Further, he demonstrated that in each culture area, consisting of a certain set of culture complexes, a central point of dispersal could be located, and boundaries fixed when the culture-complexes involved become most diluted and the influence of a vague but distinctly alien culture is felt. Wissler also pointed out that geophysical reasons like-- long distances, mountains, oceans, arid deserts prove to be effective barriers to culture diffusion. However, actual experience has shown that discontinuous diffusion (mostly as a result of migration, or as a result of further change in the intermediary area, or the strong individuality and resistance power of this intermediary area) also does take place. Wissler substantiated his theory by mapping out various culture areas in the Americas. Each area of characterization was defined by him in terms of technological, artistic and institutional features; and he showed that a culture area might embrace several distinct populations.

In 'marginal areas' where people who live on the borders of two culture areas share features from both the ways of living.

British Diffusionists. Even before Europeans and Americans talked about diffusion, Tylor had already pointed it out as a process of culture growth. He wrote that civilization is like a plant that is oftener propagated than independently grown. He even traced the diffusion of several culture elements, like the Madagascar bellows which he said had come from the East. But, 'British diffusionists' is a description which refers to Elliot Smith, W.J. Perry and their followers. They were the last of the diffusionists to come on to the world scene and the first to disappear. Elliot Smith and Perry insist on the universal spread of culture from Egypt, but their data have been found out to be inadequate and unreliable.

It is no doubt difficult to prove the simultaneous discovery of similar culture traits of a complex nature, and as Tylor said, unless there is evidence to the contrary, diffusion must be accepted as the generally usual process. But these British scholars, also known as Egyptologists, put forward a queer hypothesis. They said that man is very unimaginative and uninventive and that only very favourable environmental stimuli may result in man making inventions. They further held, and it is here that absurdity was incorporated in their view, that such favourable circumstances were found only in ancient Egypt. Therefore, the Egyptians, the Children of the Sun as Perry called them, were the chosen ones of history. These scholars tried to map worldwide distributions of various cultural institutions, rooting them all in Egypt, cradle of all human civilization. In advocating such a theory they dug its early grave. Hutton pointed out to Perry that it was a commonplace that identical results flowed from very different causes and regions, and in support of his contention.

Hutton mentioned (i) the fire piston independently invented in Asia and France; (ii) the bull-roarer discovered independently by the Australians, N.W. Thomas and whoever else uses it; (iii) the use of adrenalin as an arrow poison by certain Amazonian Indians; and (iv) the use of suggestion in magic and medicine. However, Perry tried somehow or other to belittle the significance of these examples, and similar others. It may be pointed out here that duplication of scientific research is no evidence against diffusion because of the fact that discoveries have been inspired by the same literature. Kroeber thinks that complex traits existing at different places and yet having their elements combined in the same combination are undoubtedly of common origin.

To conclude, cultures grow and cultural parallelism arises from both independent evolution as also diffusion. There are no inexorable laws about sequential evolution, nor about the uninventiveness of man. Cultural borrowing will always make impossible growth stage by stage and upwards in a straight line. Likewise, distance and resistance will always put checks on diffusion. Whether a particular case of growth is the outcome of evolution only or diffusion only is, therefore, a misleading question as both the processes operate.

Acculturation: When culture-traits or complexes have been diffused we talk about diffusion, but when a whole way of life is in process of change under the influence of another culture we call it *acculturation.* Linton, Redfield, Herskovits, Hallowell and Beals have made important contributions towards the development of a body of explanatory concepts relating to acculturation. Thus Herskovits says that when a growing child learns to conform to his own cultural traditions, the process may be designated as *enculturation.* If there is exchange of cultural traits and complexes it may be called *transculturation,* but when one way of life is being displaced by another, it is *acculturation.*

Acculturation may lead to assimilation, but very often it does not. The dominated culture breaks down at first and then recovers to develop a reaction to the loss of its own individuality. Such a reaction is called *contra-acculturation.* For example, after centuries of exploitation and material impoverishment, the Chota Nagpur tribes in India have developed a new-found sense of strength and opposition which has resulted in the *Jharkhand* movement demanding autonomy in cultural, social, economic and political matters. Acculturation studies have been motivated by the realization that there are no 'pure' or 'uncontaminated' cultures in the world today. Secondly, the conjectural studies of diffusionists about what happened in unrecorded history had also to be supplemented by more authentic studies of a scientific value.

Theories of Culture Integration

Functionalism: 'What is the internal structure of a culture?' Is it a loose congery of 'agrofacts', 'artifacts' 'socifacts', and 'mentifacts' having no inner interrelation or consistency? If not, then, What is it that makes culture a meaningful whole?' In this connexion, Malinowski and Redcliffe-Brown put forward the viewpoint which has come to be known as functionalism. They hold that there is an inner consistency in a culture, or in other words, cultures are integrated wholes. Why that is so, they explain differently. Malinowski makes use of Tylor's definition of culture, but does not mean by it a super-organic reality as Tylor did. To Malinowski, culture is an instrument which enables man to secure his bio-psychic survival and, subsequently, a 'higher' mental-intellectual survival. Therefore, since each aspect of a culture, whether it is economic organization or social organization or religion or language, is rooted in the needs of the human being, they are all inter-related to each other through the common ground in which they are rooted, i.e., the human being with his needs. Therefore, Malinowski does not believe in loose survivals. The evolutionists often referred to obviously functionless culture traits as *survivals* or 'hang-overs' from the past. Malinowski ridiculed this as inability to search for the proper place of the so-called survivals in a culture. There is nothing loose within a culture: it is all inter-connected, and no single trait has any meaning by itself unless it is seen in the context of the whole.

Similarly, diffusion was interpreted by him in a new manner. He said that when a trait is diffused, it may retain its original form, but it can perform only such a function for which there is scope in the culture into which it is diffused. Thus, Malinowski emphasized the self-sufficiency and the holistic character of a culture. He pointed out that if one aspect of a culture is changed the whole of it will change. Malinowski believed in *culture pluralism'*, he said that every culture grows in response to localized versions of the bio-psychic needs of a people, and that it is to be judged in terms of these and not in terms of any absolute values. Adequacy in terms of local needs is the characteristic of a well-integrated culture in the light of prevailing knowledge.

Radcliffe-Brown is more concerned with the survival of society than that of the individual only. He, therefore, points out that integration within a culture being the only way to secure the survival of society, such integration is both an ideal as also the reality. If such integration breaks down, there will be no society. And the function of every single institution is the contribution it makes towards the solidarity of the group as a whole--not towards the fulfilment of individual needs, bio-psychic and socio-cultural.

Both these viewpoints are partial in the sense that they conceive of integration only in terms of the content of a culture. Form is not subservient to function, as Malinowski imagined it to be. It has an independence of its own; and integration prevails also on the formalistic level. And to that we will now turn our attention.

Patterns of Culture. Deriving her inspiration as also her models from the field of art and aesthetics, Ruth Benedict said that the integration in a culture is brought about by its content being arranged into a permanent or semi-permanent design or style. Such a design, she called *pattern.* Within a culture there would be the style of each large segment, and these segmental styles would come together into super-style which would be the design of the culture as a whole. This is called *configuration.* She further indicates that all styles are harmonious with each other and blend into a harmonious configuration. This harmony, she says, arises out of a main tendency or trend which every culture exhibits in all its aspects.

This main tendency or trend, she calls the *genius* of a culture. It is this genius or spirit of a people which brings about integration in their culture, the integration of form. She believes that in human society this genius may be of one of the two possible types, the *Apollonian* or the *Dionysian.* 'Apollonian' is derived from Apollo, the benign sun god of the ancient Greeks, and 'Dionysian' is derived from Dionysius, the turbulent Greek god of drink and carnivals. The Apollonian genius represents the principle of calm composure and the same would characterize all aspects of the culture concerned and bring about its integration. The Dionysian genius represents the principle of storm and would bring about integration and harmonious blending of a culture by pervading all its aspects.

Themes. M.E. Opler propogated the concept of *themes* to explain integration. Themes are defined as general motivations which are responsible for various sets of behaviour types in a society. The need for such an enlarged restatement of what is very much like Benedict's theory obviously stems from the limitation which Benedict put on the ways in which the genius of a people may seek self-fulfilment. Opler's themes are not tied down to any types; he leaves that to every field investigator to find out for himself. Therefore, Opler's concept of themes is more elastic than Benedict's concept of patterns. Thames are the specific expressions of cultural integration in each individual case. Opler has illustrated how this concept may be used in his account of the Apache lifeway. The concepts of patterns and themes are both keys to the specific structure and character of a way of living.

Style of Life. The latest addition to concepts of the kind described above is Redfield's concept of *style of life.* He defines it as consisting not of culture but of all that may be regarded as most fundamental and permanent about a culture which has persisted in time. It would include ways of securing a living insofar as these play a role in the shaping of the conception of what constitutes the good life. Style of life emphasizes explicit and implicit judgments about the constituents of right conduct. Also included are those comparatively superficial, though no less significant, tastes and performances which invest a people with their own peculiar individuality. Redfield compares his style of life to

Lionell Trilling's *manners,* which the latter has defined as the implicit, explicit and unutterable expressions of value. Redfield has not, as he himself writes, given a new principle of integration; he only defines the place where it may be said to be located.

REFERENCES

Benedict, R. (1946), *Patterns of Culture,* (Pelican Book).

Bidney. D. (1953), *Theoretical Anthropology,* (Columbia University Press.

Evans-Pritchard, E.E., *Social Anthropology.*

Kroeber, A.L., and C. Kluckhohn, (1952), *Culture: A Critical Review of Concepts and Definitions,* Harvard .

Lowie, R. (1937), *The History of Ethnological Theory,* New York.

Malinowski, B. (1944), *A Scientific Theory of Culture,* University of North Carolina Press.

Tylor, E.B. (1913), *Primitive Culture,* 2 Vols. London.

2

Social Structure and Social Organisation

> "Wild animals never kill for sport. Man is the only one to when the torture and death of his fellow creatures is amusing in itself."
>
> —*James Anthony Froude*

There is no exaggeration in saying that 'Social structure' is one of the central concepts of sociology, but it has not been employed consistently or unambiguously. Though one of the most frequent terms in sociology, this has no specific and universally accepted meaning. Nevertheless, it reveals one of the basic sociological insights: although societies and countless social groups within them are never long composed of the same individuals, their patterns of social interdependence show continuity over time.

Social structure has been defined simple as any recurring pattern of social behaviour. However, for most sociologists such a definition might tend to include trivial behaviours as well as the significant ones. Social structure is based on the working of subgroups and there is always a close relationship between roles and sub-groups because each role occupant is required to perform certain duties towards the members of a sub-group in a social structure.

There are, of course institutionalised norms in every society but what need to be remembered is that in no big society these norms are uniform. In fact the whole social structure has its own characteristics and whether that is good or bad is something relative and not absolute. Every social structure, if it is to get going and serve the purpose of the society, it is essential that it should change with the changing circumstances. If that does not happen, that will make time and society static. When a structure comes under heavy pressures and social institutions do not change, the whole structure get complicated and comes under heavy strains.

Definition

Since long many efforts have been made to define 'social structure' but still there is no unanimity of opinion on its definition. Herbert Spencer was the first writer to throw light on the structure of society. Herbert Spencer was too much fascinated by his biological analogies (organic structure and evolution) to make clear what he meant by the structure of the society. Durkheim also left the term vague. Many later sociologists and social anthropologists have tried to give it a more precise meaning, but their conceptions of social structure diverge widely.

As such Radcliffe-Brown regards it as 'a part of the social structure all social relations of person to person... In the study of social structure the concrete reality with which we are concerned is the set of actually existing relations, at a given moment of time, which link together certain human beings'. But he goes on to say that the object which we attempt to describe and analyse is structural form, that is, the general relationships, disregarding slight variations and the particular individuals involved. It is this structural form which most writers have designated social structure.

A more generally preferred definition is that social structure refers to the enduring orderly and patterned relationships between the elements of a society, a definition which prompted some nineteenth century sociologists to compare societies with machines or organisms. There is some disagreement as to what would count as an 'element' Radcliffe-

Brown, for example, thought of social structures as relationships of a general and regular kind between people. But Radcliffe-Brown's definition is very broad as *Firth* has pointed out, "It makes no distinction between the ephemeral and the most enduring elements in social activity and it makes it almost impossible to distinguish the idea of the structure of a society from that of the totality of the society itself."

According to Talcott Parsons, "The term social structure applies to the particular arrangement of the inter-related institutions, agencies and social patterns as well as the statuses and roles which each person assumes in the group." Parsons has tried to explain the concept of social structure in abstract form. All the units of social structure, that is, institutions, agencies, social patterns, statuses and roles are invisible and intangible and hence are abstract.

According to S.F. Nadel, 'structure refers to a definable articulation, an ordered arrangement of parts. It is related to the other aspect or the framework of society and is totally unconcerned with the functional aspect of society'. So he has emphasised that the social structure refers to the network of social relationship which is created among the human beings when they interact with each other according to their statuses in accordance with the patterns of society.

According to Ginsberg. "The study of social structure is concerned with the principle forms of social organization, that is, types of groups, associations and institutions and the complex of these which constitute societies."

In the opinion of Karl Mannheim, "social structure refers to the web of interacting social forces from which have arisen the various modes of observing and thinking."

MacIver and Page say, "The various modes of grouping together comprise the complex pattern of the social structure." MacIver and Page have also regarded that social structure is abstract which is composed of several groups like family, church, class, caste, state, community etc.

Johnson opines, "The structure of anything consists of the relatively stable inter-relationships among its parts; moreover, the term 'part' itself implies a certain degree of stability. Since a social system is composed of the inter-related acts of people, its structure must be sought in some degree of regularity or recurrence in these acts" of the different conceptions discussed above, the most useful seems to be which regards social structure as the complex of the major institutions and groups in society. There is no great difficulty in identifying these institutions and groups. It can be shown that the existence of human society requires certain arrangements or processes, or that there are functional pre-requisites of society.

The minimum requirements seem to be: (i) a system of communication; (ii) an economic system; (iii) arrangements for the socialisation of new generations; (iv) a system of authority and of distribution of power; and perhaps (v) a system of ritual, serving to maintain social cohesion.

Perspectives on Social Structure

In every society there is a structural system which the society wishes to preserve and is not interested in changing that unless there are sound reasons for the same. The concept of "social structure" has a long history--earlier it was used to refer to the inter-relations between the component parts of the whole. Its extension from anatomy to sociology was a logical corollary of the general use of organic analogies by political philosphers. Different perspectives on social structure are as follows:

1. Levi-Strauss: Levi-Strauss conceived of social structure as a logic behind reality. He insisted that the 'term social structure has nothing to do with empirical reality but with models which are built up after it'. He took Radcliffe-Brown to task for not distinguishing between social structure and social relations. While social relations constitute the raw materials out of which the models making up the social structure are built, the structure itself cannot be reduced to an ensemble of social relations; rather such relations themselves result from some pre-existing structures. The structures exhibit the characteristics of a system and is made up of several elements, none of which can undergo change without effecting changes in all other elements.

2. *Nadel:* Whereas Levi-strauss regards social structure as a model behind reality, Nadel views it as reality itself. He regards the role system of any society, with its given coherence, as the matrix of the social structure. He outlines two specific advantages of structural analysis. These are: lending a higher degree of comparability to social data, and rendering such data more readily quantifiable. Nadel contends that a particular social structure as described at a given moment is accurate only for a particular period of time. Structure and variance are not inherently contradictory; rather the former is defined or built up through taking account of the latter.

Nadel's conception of social structure is based on three criteria; repetitiveness of the social phenomena, durability of the social phenomena and moving equilibrium. Nadel cautions that stability in social process is not uniform.

3. *Murdock:* In defining social structure Murdock's principle concerns are the ethnographic facts and the taxonomic classification of societies on the basis of manifest, readily discernible characteristics. The taxonomy established by Murdock depends primarily on varieties of kinship organisation. In so far as Murdock uses organic analogy, it is that of a dissected model laid out in a showcase; there is no attempt to envisage society as a living entity capable of growth. The taxonomy is based on statistical correlation rather than

the functional analysis. Despite his use of the term 'social structure', Murdock's attitude has been ambivalent. He denigrates the concept as "static" and "sterile".

4. Gerth and Mills: Gerth and Mills defined social structure in terms of institutional orders and spheres. Although institutions are the basic building blocks, social structure is more than mere inter-relations of institutions. The unit and compositions of a social structure are determined by the precise weight which each institutional order and sphere has with reference to every other order and the ways in which they are related to one another. Gerth and Mills distinguish two fundamental traditions--character structure and social structure and assert that the two are united by 'role' which links the 'person' in the former with 'institutions' in the latter.

Character structure refers to the relatively stabilised integration of the organism's psychic structure linked with the social roles of the person. And a social structure is made up of a certain combination or pattern of institutional orders. The role, which is the primary link between the character structure and the social structure is what gives meaning to structure. Moreover, like Nadel, Gerth and Mills also contend that 'social structures and not frozen, they may be static or dynamic, they have beginning, duration, varying degrees of unity and they may disintegrate.

Ultimately, it can be said that sociologists typically wish to use the concept of social structure to explain something, and this usually means that the explanation is a causal one. Such a view can present difficulties in that social structures are not directly observable entities but are rather abstract formulations. This and other difficulties have led to criticism of the use of social structure. Thus it has been seen as a reified concept, as unobservable and therefore unverifiable and as denying human creativity and freedom by suggesting that human action is determined by structures. One solution to these criticisms is to demonstrate as Berger and Luckmann do, the way in which social structures are themselves the creation of active human beings.

Fundamental Elements

In a social structure the human beings organise themselves into associations for the pursuits of some objects. The aim can be fulfilled only if the social structure is based upon certain principles. These principles, which set the elements of social structure in motion are as follows:

1. *Position system:* Position system refers to the statuses and roles of the individuals. The desires, aspirations and expectations of the individuals are varied, multiple and unlimited. So these can be fulfilled only if the members of the society are assigned different roles according to their capacities and capabilities. Actually the proper functioning of social structure depends upon proper assignments of roles and statuses.

2. *Normative system:* Normative system presents the society with the ideals and values. The people attach emotional importance to these norms. The institutions and associations are inter-related according to those norms. The individuals perform their roles in accordance with the accepted norms of society.

3. *Sanction system:* For the proper enforcement of norms, every society has a sanction system. The integration and co-ordination of the different parts of social structure depend upon conformity of social norms. The non-conformists are punished by the society according to the nature of the non-conformity. The stability of a social structure depends upon the effectiveness of its sanction system.

4. *Action system:* It is the object of the goal to be arrived at by the social structure. The whole social structure revolves

around it. The action is the root--cause which weaves the web of social relationships and sets the social structure in motion.

5. *System of anticipated responses:* The anticipated response system calls upon the individuals to participate in the social system. His preparation sets the social structure in motion. The successful working of social structure depends upon the realisation of his duties by the individuals and his efforts to fulfill these duties.

No doubt, social structure is an abstract entity. Its parts are dynamic and constantly changing. They are spatially wide-spread and therefore difficult to see as wholes. Social structure denotes patterns which change more slowly than the particular personnel who constitute them. They are produced and reproduced by the inter-weaving of numerous individual people acting in accordance with their own plans and strategies, yet social structure is rarely planned and intended by them, it results from the unintended consequences of action.

Functional Problems

In every society the people have certain needs and requirements. Some such needs are only individualistic while others are demands of the society. It is very essential that these needs must be met to the extent, possible. An important question is if individuals possess 'free will', how do their separate actions intermesh to produce social structure. In every social structure there are four important functional problems which every group must solve. These are:

1. *Adaptation:* In a good social structure, groups and sub-groups try to adapt themselves to its social and non-social environments. Roles of differentiation cannot, of course, be underestimated but at the same time, it cannot be denied that no one person could perform simultaneously all the tasks that have to be performed by him in society. Thus there is great need and necessity of adaptation in society.

2. *Pattern of maintenance:* From pattern of maintenance we understand that the units of whole structure must learn the pattern and invest them with the appropriate attitude of respect. In the words of H.M. Johnson, 'Moreover, once they are learned, cultural patterns have to be renewed, so to speak, through appropriate rituals and other symbols. "Sometimes pattern maintenance are subject to emotional disturbances and distractions. It is expected of a good social structure system that these must be effectively managed.

3. *Integration:* In a society the people are required to work in close co-operation with each other. They are also required to have good morale because without morale there can be no integration. Without proper integration no social structure or system can smoothly work. It is desirable that in an integrated society, all members must be loyal to the system as a whole.

4. *Goal-attainment:* In every system, every society tries to attain certain goals through co-operative efforts. In our modern society, as we know very little can be achieved through individual efforts. For attaining collective goals it is very essential that all resources must be mobilized in an effective manner, according to specific nature of tasks. But it must be remembered that there is a relationship between adaptation and goal-attainment because unless collective efforts are made, it will become impossible to attain goals.

Levels of Social Structure

The structure of every social system can be analysed in relation to these four functional problems. In any functional analysis, it is important to bear in mind the fundamental rule that partial structures have functions for a system of which they are part. If the only social system super-ordinate to a particular business firm is the total society, then the business, as a partial structure must have functions for the total society as the system of reference; it would be inappropriate to speak of the firm as having functions for one of its own parts.

Relative Nature

In a comprehensive social structure there is a system which includes sub-groups of various types, regulative norms and cultural values. In the words of Johnson, any one of these elements--a type of subgroup, a role, social norm, or a value may be called a partial structure "or what may be called as quasi-structural aspect of the whole social system".

In every big society, there can be no uniform institutionalised norms and deviations are bound to be there. Thus the whole social structure is of relative nature.

Formal and Informal Nature of Structures

Social structure can be both formal and informal. Thus in a factory, formal social structure is represented by the paper plan which outlines the divisions of functions and responsibility, but informal social structure is indicated by informal groupings, the cliques. In the words of MacIver and Page," The factors that give rise to primary groups in industrial organisation are present in all formalised social structures. Thus in governmental bureaus, military organisations, political parties, prisons, schools, labour unions and many others, the complete organisational picture includes the formal blue-print arrangements on the one hand and informal spontaneous grouping on the other."

Change and Social Structure

There is no denial that for a good society it is essential that it should have permanent institutions but at the same time it cannot be denied that without a change every social structure--however sound that might be, will become stationary, stagnant and outdated, such a rigid structure is bound to create social clashes and disharmony. In the words of MacIver and Page," If the conditions of human life were unchanging, then might be the social structure will be unchanging also. But these conditions are always unstable. Accordingly, in a social structure there can be no structure, which is always permanent or stable.

We may thus find that social structure in every society is very complex and complicated. If it becomes elastic, it will create social lags and might even create social stratification.

Types of Social Structure

Talcott Parsons has described four principal types of social structure. His classification is based on four social values, viz., universalistic social values, particularistic social values, achieved social values and ascribed social values. Universalistic social values are those which are found almost in every society and are applicable to everybody. For example, every society value the expert craftsmen as in that case production is both cheaper and superior and thus the efficient craftsmen are selected in every society.

Particularistic social values are the features of particular societies and these differ from society to society. When the statuses are achieved on the basis of efforts, it means that such societies attach importance to achieved social values. When the statuses are hereditary even the society gives importance to ascribed social statuses.

The four types of social structure are:

1. *The universalistic-achievement pattern:* This is the combination of the value patterns which sometimes are opposed to the values of a social structure built mostly around kinship, community, class and race. Universalism by itself favours status-determination on the basis of generalised rules independently of one's achievement. When universalism is combined with achievement value it produces a social structure of universalistic achievement pattern. Under this type of social structure, the choice of goal by the individual must be in accord with the universalistic values. His pursuits are defined by universalistic moral norms. Such a system is dynamically developing system with an encouragement for initiative. On

the one hand, it has to resort to adoptive structures which are in conflict with its major value patterns; on the other hand, it cannot allow the adoptive structures become too important, least the social structure shift into another type.

2. *The universalistic-ascription pattern:* Under this type of social structure, the elements of value-orientation are dominated by the elements of ascription. Therefore, in such a social structure, strong emphasis is laid on the status of the individual, rather than on his specific achievements. The emphasis is on what an individual is rather than on what he has done. Status is ascribed to the group rather than to the individuals. The individual derives his status from his group. Here in such a structure are found the concepts of aristocracy and ethnic superiority. In this type of social structure all resources are mobilised in the interest of the collective ideal. It tends to have a "political" accent as distinguished from the "economic" accent. To sum up, it may be said that the universalistic-achievement type of social structure is "individualistic" whereas the universalistic-ascription type is "collectivistic".

3. *The particularistic-ascriptive pattern:* In this type also the social structure is organised around the relational reference points notably those of kinship and local community but it differs from the particularistic-achievement type in as much as the relational values are taken as given and passively "adapted to" rather than made for an actively organised system. The structure tends to be traditionalistic and emphasis is laid on its stability. According to Parsons the Spanish social structure is the example of such a type.

4. *The particularistic-achievement pattern:* This type combines achievement values with particularism. The primary criterion of valued achievement is found not in universalistic terms such as conformity to a generalised ideal or efficiency but these are focussed on certain points of reference within the

relational system itself or are inherent in the situation. The emphasis on achievement leads to the conception of a proper pattern of adaptation which is the product of human achievement and which can be maintained only by continuous efforts. This type involves a far more unequivocal acceptance of kinship ties than is the case with either of the universalistic types. It is more traditionalistic. Parsons has kept the Indian and Chinese social structure under this category.

Importance of Role in Social Structure

In social structure or system roles are more important than role occupants. Role occupants in turn divide themselves into sub-groups. In the words of H.M. Johnson, "It will be manifestly untrue to say that all the stability, regularity and recurrence that can be observed in social interaction are due to normative patterning, nevertheless we shall say that roles and subgroups of various types are the parts of social structure to the extent that stability, regularity and recurrence in social interaction are due to the social norms that define roles and obligations of sub-groups".

Sub-groups and roles are closely linked with each other because all those who are required to perform certain roles have some duties and obligations towards the group to which they belong. The responsibilities of role occupant are of different types and can be broadly divided into obligatory and permissive. Each social structure has also quasi-structural aspect. In no complex society there can be standardised or institutionalised norms. Though it is good that social institutions should not rapidly change yet it is also unbecoming of a social structure to become stagnant. Every rigid social structure is bound to result in social disharmony.

Social Organisation

The term social organisation means the interdependence of parts, which is an essential characteristic of all enduring collective entities: groups, communities and societies. These inter-dependent part are give different names by different sociologists. The term also has two major uses: (a) to refer to the particular kind of organisation under study and (b) casually, as a synonym for social structure or a related term.

In sociology, the term 'social organisation' is used in a wider sense and wide sense includes any organisation of society. These are, "bodies, persisting over time, which are specially set up to achieve specific aim."

Social organisation indicates that state in which there is peaceful interaction between the different elements of the society. They work according to prefixed and recognized aims. In other words, the existence of definite role and status is necessary for social organisation. Besides there should be uniformity in the aims, goals and programmes among the members of the society.

Definition

According to *Reutar and Hart,* "By social organisation is meant the totality of cultural institutions and their inter-relationship together with the body of unorganised activities and characteristics of the group."

According to *Ogburn and Nimkoff,* "An organisation is an articulation of different parts which perform various functions. It is an active group deviced for getting something done."

According to *Elliot and Merrill,* "Social organisation is a state of being, a condition in which the various institutions in a society are functioning in accordance with their recognised or implied purposes."

According to Broom and Selznick, "social organisation is the patterned relations of individuals and groups" and identify it as one of the two basic sources of order in social life, the other being norms and values."

According to Ernest Jones, "A social organisation is the system by which the parts of the society are related to each other and to the whole society in a meaningful way."

According to Etzioni, "Social organisations are social units which are pre-dominantly oriented to the attainment of specific goals."

According to Auguste Comte, "Social organisation is a general social agreement. The principle which lies at the heart of every scheme of social organisation is the necessary participation of the collective political regime in the universal consensus of the social body."

According to Herbert Spencer, "The term social organisation refers' almost exclusively to social integration and individual regulation through consensus about morals and values."

According to Cooley, "Social organisations are differentiated unity of mental or social life." According to Cooley's analysis, mind and one's conception of self are shaped through social interaction and social organisation is nothing more than the shared activities and understanding which social interaction requires.

Today few sociologists study social organisation in a comprehensive way. Those who do often use the other terms: thus *Parsons and Homans* prefer to speak of 'social system'. The term is so broad as to be synonymous with much of the subject-matter of sociology. However, the necessity for social organisation if any group is to survive and be effective is so universally recognised in sociology that reference to it, implicit or explicit, is to be found in almost all sociological research and all sociological theory.

Social organisation itself is not something static, which once established, will forever remain the same. In one sense, social organisation is a hypothesis, an ideal construct emphasising the relatively unchanging aspects which are always present in every society. Social organisation is somewhat a relative institution. There is no society which may be either completely organised or completely disorganised. Both these conditions are usually found in societies. The difference is only of the degree. Consensus and ability of behaviours are indicative of an absolute social organisation. But these are impossible in complex and dynamic society.

Pre-requisites

The two essential elements of social organization are as follows:

1. *Social control:* In the opinion of B.J. Stern, "The social control which the group imposes upon its members imparts a certain consistency and stability to human activities". Social control becomes very essential in a well-developed social organisation. This control is exercised through traditions, mores, habits, customs and rituals etc. Where the hold through these media is effective, organisation is considered to be sound but when the hold is weak the whole organisation is supposed to be defective and feeble.

We will briefly discuss folkways, laws and institutions.

(i) *Folkways:* Folkways are social habits which are transferred from one generation to other generation and their social importance constantly increases and slowly and gradually they assume the form of social control.

(ii) *Mores:* Elliot and Merrill have placed these in that category of folkways with which is connected the welfare philosophy of the society. These have more social and moral sanctions and beneficial for common welfare.

(iii) *Laws:* Elliot and Merrill have called these as more

clear mores. Laws are those mores which have behind them state sanction and which force anyone to obey them.

(iv) *Institutions:* According to Summer institution is the concept which has structure. Institutions are the representatives of those values which have become parts of society. They are definite and are for the fulfilment of some definite aims. They are instruments of social control.

2. *Consensus:* Elliot and Merrill opine "social organisation is fundamentally a problem of consensus." Social consensus is necessary for society. Without consensus, the physical structure of society is just like a hollow rod. There cannot be complete consensus on matters of social importance. But the consensus of the different parts of society is necessary.

Elements

The following are the essential elements of social organisation.

1. Every organisation is goal-oriented and its members are inter-related to each other by the sense of common purpose, to pursue the goal.
2. It has within it the power centres which control the concerned efforts of the organisation and continuously review its performance.
3. All members in the organisation have an assigned role and status.
4. It has its norms. Every member is expected to follow them.
5. To supplement the norms, every organisation has a system of sanctions.

Factors for Strong Identification with an Organisation

As for factors that makes for strong identification with

an organisation, there is evidence that the following are important:

1. The less the composition within the organisation, the stronger the identification.
2. The greater the extent to which organisation goals are perceived as shared, the stronger the identification.
3. The greater the number of individuals needs satisfied in the social organisation, the stronger the identification with it.
4. The greater the frequency of interaction in the organisation, the stronger the identification.
5. The greater the perceived prestige of the organisation, the stronger the identification.

Various Types of Organisation

There are two types of organisations:

1. Formal organisations: In a society the activities that an individual undertakes fall under two broad categories: those which he himself plans and those which are planned for him by others. In both the cases the activities are goal-oriented in the sense that some special purpose is sought to be achieved. There is, however, a significant difference between the two. In the former, no formal authority is created. In the latter, a formal authority designed to achieve certain purposes is created. The social arrangement in which a group of people plans the activities which others are obliged to participate in is called 'formal organisation'.

Modern sociological analysis of formal organisations began with the works of Max Weber. His propositions about the characteristics of "bureaucracy" are largely based on historical data, which he sought to describe a so-called "pure" type of bureaucracy seems to be a complex hypotheses concerning the institutional characteristics of the most efficient possible kind of organisation.

A formal organisation is distinguished by following features:

(*a*) Once organised and formally registered under the law of the land, the formal organisation acquires a legal personality which can sue and be sued in the court of law. It can also survive beyond the lives of those who brought into being the formal organisation.

(*b*) The organisational pattern is clearly spelt out in a document which, generally, consists of two parts: the memorendum of association embodying the objectives and the rules and regulations embodying the rules of the management.

(*c*) The size and organisational goals change over time. In the societies in which formal organisations are numerous, their specific goals will keep on changing with changes in knowledge, in age and sex composition of the populations and in patterns of economic activity in the social environment of the organisation.

(*d*) Another important characteristic of formal organisation is effectiveness, that is, the extent to which the organisation's activities attain specific goals.

(*e*) Formal organisations are usually planned to some extent as a means for attaining certain objectives. Most formal organisations do use various indicators and indices of their efficiency.

(*f*) Formal organisations are rational in that they are deliberately planned to be so.

(*g*) Organisational effectiveness has three components: (1) Organisational productivity; (2) organisational flexibility in the form of successful adjustment to internal organisational changes and successful adaptation to externally induced change; and (3) absence of intra-organisational strain.

Elements of formal organisations: Three things are generally required in order to plan social activities systematically which are as follows:

(i) The Theory: No formal organisation can succeed in the absence of a clearly defined set of ideas as to how the activities are to be carried out, taking into account the possible changes in the variables in future and the steps to be taken to meet the situation arising out of changed circumstances.

A theory consists of the following:

(a) *A technical-cost theory:* In order to ensure the success of a planned activity, there must be an informed awareness about the required technical resources and the cost to be incurred for having those resources.

(b) *A market theory.* A part of the planning process is not simply to ensure the high quality of a service, but also to be certain that the service in question has a demand.

(ii) Resources: Resources needed for an organisation are of three kinds--men, money and materials. However there may be pulls from alternative uses which may attract these resources away from the organisation. Hence, appropriate measures have to be devised so as to repel or neutralise such pulls. There is also the problem of obsolescence, depriciation and physical wearing out of materials. These must be periodically replenished.

(iii) The authority system: The optimum use of resources demands a well-knit administrative structure providing for supervision, control and discipline. The essential elements are the following:

(a) To fix responsibility or the delegation of authority

(b) Supervision

(c) Discipline

Types of formal organisations: Organisations differ from

one another in terms of variation in their key elements--viz, theory, resource and authority system.

Max, Weber has classified organisations into four types which are as follows:

(a) Organisation with feudal administration: This type of organisation is characterised by traditional pattern of relationship which prevailed among fiefholders and lords during the Middle Ages. Under feudalism, vassals held lands from lords-superior on rendering of military service.

(b) Organisations having charismatic leadership: The underlying principle of such an organization is the charisma of the boss of an organisation in the perception of those who serve there. Charismatic administration occurs whenever people in the organisation behave, in respect to the particular area of activity, that "history is the lengthened shadow of man."

(c) Professional organisation: When the organisational activity is determined in terms of specialised knowledge of the trained members of the organisation, we get a professional type of organisation. Its distinguishing feature is that there is a wide delegation of responsibility to people who are assigned the job after their competence has been certified by a group of peers. Universities and hospitals are typical example of this type of organisation. Further extreme decentralisation of responsibility to men chosen for their competence is a distinctive feature of professional organisations.

(d) Organisation with bureaucratic system: Bureaucratic organisation is basically a rule-centred organisation only the rules, laid down in black and white, count. All the values and principles of the organisation are embodied in these rules. The personnel of the organisation from the top officials to the lowest sub-ordinates hold office under certain conditions for which they draw a salary. Another unique feature of this

kind of organisation is that bureaucrats are organised on a hierarchical basis.

2. *Informal Organisations:* Informal relations inevitably develop. These are sometimes functional, sometimes dysfunctional, as far as they affect the attainment of the goals of the formal organisations.

A common basis for the growth of informal relationships of the clique type is the fact that the members of any organisation are also members of a variety of other groups. In these other groups each have a fairly strong in-group feeling, their members are likely to carry over their prepossessions and antipathies into the formal organisation. A wide variety of social difference often do divide the members of the organisation. Cliques may form on the basis of ethnic groups, religions, castes, regional origins, colleges from which the officials have been graduated, or franternities to which they belong. Such cliques may or may not be dysfunctional for the formal organisation.

In nutshell, salient features of the informal structure are:

(a) There is the dominance of the primary group in an informal organisation: In an informal organisation, the actual authority rests in a primary group.

(b) It is a position system: Among the position holders there are informal relations. The members may meet informally at social functions. It is pervasive through-out.

(c) Individual influence cannot be ruled out: There may also be few individuals in or outside the organisation who may be in a position to exercise influence from time to time on the matters of organisation.

(d) It is the system of anticipated responses: As a result of some particular issue, affecting a large number in the organisation, a large informal group may arise, and mobilise

the public opinion against or in favour of it within the organisation. To anticipate the response it may have, may not be difficult.

Apparently, line between formal and informal organisation is not always clear. While informal organisations may have theoretically high-efficiency value, practical utility and the advantage of cutting down the hard lines of communication and sometimes even the delaying formalities, yet it is common experience that such organisations do not have a scientific manner. These do not function in a mechanical manner. In the interest of proper delivery and successful working of the structure, however, the merits of one or the other cannot be overlooked. The effort should be, in the interest of efficiency, and to make the best of both.

Modes of participation: Some organisations encourage their members to participate in decision-making while others restrict this privilege. So the modes, of participation may be democratic or authoritarian.

The considerations which are taken into account in determining the mode of participation of members are the following:

(a) The principle of democratic participation of the employees and workers may be introduced in a formal organisation like a factory, in which authoritarian controls predominate, in order to maintain high morale.

(b) If a group meets occasionally mainly for purposes of deliverance and discussion, democratic forms are appropriate. If, however, a group is engaged in activities of a long term nature, it usually adopts authoritarian style of functioning. The reasons are obvious. Such a group must have specific goals to achieve. This objective can be attained only when a hierarchical structure is organised in which a few persons are assigned the responsibility of taking decisions and making all other comply with their directions. All large-sized organisations, with small variations, follow this pattern.

(c) Democratic forms are considered to be appropriate in those cases in which high levels of loyality and zeal are required or in which the members of the organisation are expected to take risks.

(d) Democratic style of functioning does not generally be obtained in organisations in which participation is involuntary or in which participation is compensated fully either in monetary terms or in terms of service. In such cases, democratic set-up is not obviously required either to induce or to sustain participation.

3

Social Groups

> "Equality is not a law of nature. Nature has made no two things equal: its sovereign law is subordination and dependence."
>
> *--Luc de Clapiers Vauvenargus*

Man's life to a very great extent is a group life and social interaction takes place in groups. Human personality develops within the group and man is made human by social interaction. There is inter-dependence of members in the group, and the influence of individuals is reciprocal. It is on the basis of interdependence that people come together. Every group is characterised by certain common interests shared by all the members which give rise 'to a consciousness of kind' as is pointed out by Giddings. Common ends are an important characteristic of group life and the interaction among members has to be associative.

Max Weber points out that social relations are established among individuals when they act on the basis of mutual awareness or mutual recognition. The system of social relationships servers as a means to fulfil the common interests. Talcott Parsons has pointed out that culture is the basic element in any system of social relationships. Every group has certain patterns of behaviour which are shared by all its members. These norms define their roles and serve also to differentiate between members and non-members. Many sociologists like Cattle have given stress to the functional aspect of the group. A group has reference to two or more organisms interacting with reference to common goals in such a manner that the existence of many is utilised for the satisfaction of some needs of each. Anderso 'Group are units of two or more people meeting in the same environment, or overcoming distance by some means of communication, who are influencing each other psycholо́gically. The distinctive bond of the group is reciprocal psychological interaction. Friends in conversation, a committee in action, and children playing together are examples.'

Main Characteristics of Groups

(1) When individuals participate in group life they realise that the group is stronger than the individual, and that they belong to the whole which is in some respects independent of their own personal wishes. Group policy emerges from the synthesised wishes of the members. Group policies follow the line of least resistance. Though the leaders may determine policies, in most cases it is the wishes of individuals in the synthesised form which decide group policy. When an overwhelming majority agrees to a certain policy the group is called a cohesive unit.

(2) There are norms governing the activities of the group, and the group could exert pressure on the activities of its members. In some ways group life is frustrating, and if the control is to be successful the mechanism of control should offer rewards and punishments.

(3) *Identification*: The members identify themselves with the goals of the group. As sharing the group interests they are the group personified. It is for the well-being of the group that they live. The individual surrenders himself to the social group, and this view is held by George Simmèl.

(4) *Esprit de Corps:* Every group is characterised by a group spirit. It refers to the idea of well-being prevalent in

the group. Members of the group develop a sense of pride with the ideas, goals, values and sentiments of the group and act in pursuance of the group policies. They feel that their cause is right and this gives them the impetus, confidence and strength to work.

(5) *Reciprocity:* Group life involves interaction and the responses of the group members are reciprocal. The reciprocity is the basis of co-operation which is the foundation of any group. The members realise that their responses are more fruitful if they are reciprocal. For example in a family each member has his role to play and the success depends on how efficiently all the members do their work. Reciprocity differs from group to group.

(6) *Group has its limits:* Members are conscious that there is a line of division which separates them from others. In physical groupings these lines are clearly drawn.

In fact, Social groups are a collection of people brought into social relationships and they imply reciprocity, co-operation and identification. A social group is to a great extent characterised by division of labour. The function of a person in a particular position can be carried out effectively only if the other members do their duties properly. Interaction is a necessary condition for group formation and it is found in the most formal as well as the most primary or face-to-face groups. Interaction must be associative if the group is to be formed and common interests and ends are essential for it.

Major Functions

(1) *Agency of social selection:* Due to the pressure manifest in every social situation people are placed in definite status along the social scale. The basis of differentiation changes with the group. Status is meaningless unless it is associated with roles. The child therefore learns the first steps in the performance of his roles.

(2) *Socialising agency:* The group is an agency of socialisation or enculturisation. As a result of social interaction we learn various traits and we are made human.

(3) *Emotional security and satisfaction of needs:* Every group is characterised by varying degrees of emotional solidarity. It also acts as an agency that satisfies some of the needs of the members.

(4) *Nursery of habit systems:* Our habits are formed in the group, and by virtue of our habituation to the modes of life prevalent in the group we tend to think that they are the best. The habits become the frame of reference by which the members judge themselves and others.

(5) *A school:* The group provides its members with the primary lessons of social life. Certain traits like tolerance, consciousness of roles, accommodation, sacrifice and sympathy are necessary for our participation in group life and these are learnt through socialisation. The value of social relationship also is learnt in the group. The individual in the group realises that it is on the basis of social relations that the existence of the group is possible.

The basic element in social cohesion is lost without it and the ends of the groups will not be fulfilled. It is in the group that we learn discipline and self-control.

In a group the individual is controlled on the basis of certain values of the group. Discipline is the unconditional and rational execution of the orders received, wherein personal criticism or comment is entirely suspended. The evaluation of other people is 'we' and the response is 'I' so that 'I' is controlled by 'we.' 'We' becomes the conscience or super ego and the exterior controls are transferred into interior controls. The looking glass self or what the individual sees reflects in others, controls him. Self-emerges as the result of social interaction. For the individual, others in the group are the generalised 'other'; and it is the subjective conception of the generalised 'other' that makes the individual to realise himself.

(6) Group life stimulates activity among the members. In the group people act more efficiently than they would if they are alone. The status of a person in the group is dependent on his efficiency, and there is an efficient system of rewards and punishments. Problems can be solved better and more efficiently if it is given to the group as a whole. It has been demonstrated sociometrically that groups gain cohesion or are integrated to the extent that the individual members follow the norms. In an integrated group problems are easily solved.

Classification

(1) *Groups based on size:* A simple form of classification is on the basis of size. George Simmel was interested in the way in which the numbers of a group affect its organisation and the social interaction within it. He began with nomad groups where one person is the centre of group relations, as in the case of a teacher in the class. He then pursued his analysis through the 'dyad' and 'triad' and other smaller groups on the one hand and the large-scale groups on the other. Merton has pointed out the distinctión between absolute and relative sizes of a group. A group is large or smaller depending upon our frame of reference. The relative size is important and must be considered in terms of number in any situation.

(2) *Groups based on duration:* Groups may be classified, on the basis of the duration of interaction or relationship, as stable and unstable, or permanent and temporary. Some groups like the crowd are temporary, and the group disintegrates when the common group stimulus is gone. There are other groups like the family which are characterised by a permanent purpose and which transgress the boundaries of any one generation. The family and the village are relatively stable groupings though the membership may change.

(3) *Groups based on status:* Miller has classified groups into horizontal and vertical. Horizontal groups are those which are characterised by similar social status of its members. For example labour unions, association of lawyers, members of a cabinet. Vertical groups are made up of people with unequal social status who are united by a common interest like religious groups or recreational groups. The common set of stimuli binds them together.

(4) Another classification made by Ward is voluntary and involuntary groups. The membership in voluntary groups is largely a matter of choice, for example recreational groups. There are other groups like the family where the membership is beyond the control of individuals.

(5) *Ingroups and outgroups:* The ingroup-outgroup concept was formulated by Sumner, and it is based on the subjective attitudes of the members. The ingroup can be called the 'we group,' and the 'outgroup' as the 'they group.' The members of an ingroup share a feeling of emotional solidarity. There may be several ingroups varying with the standard frame of reference. For example, in a particular city a certain neighbourhood may form an ingroup, and within this neighbourhood a single family may form an ingroup. To this particular family, all other families are outgroups, and to that neighbourhood all other neighbourhoods are 'they' or outgroups.

(6) *Open and closed groups:* Groups may be classified as 'open' and 'closed.' Some groups apply rigidity in membership while others are flexible in accepting new members. Those who place severe restrictions on membership are called closed groups. It is not possible for a person to become a member of closed group like caste. Class is an open group made up of people having more or less similar status.

(7) Based on the degree of cohesion, morale or unity groups are classified. Groups may range from highly integrated

to loosely textured groups. In groups where there is not much internal cohesion the whole group may disintegrate when there is a threat from outside. Sometimes the threat from outside will help the group to gain cohesion.

(8) *Totalitarian and segmentary groups:* This is a classification made by Merton. The totalitarian groups like the family or village satisfy all the needs of a society while segmentary groups like religious organisations satisfy only some needs of the members.

(9) *Primary and secondary groups:* Another classification made by Charles H. Cooley divides groups into primary and secondary. Cooley did not make any explicit reference to secondary or derived groups. However, later sociologists used the word to refer to those groups that are diametrically opposite to the primary groups.

(10) Tonnies has taken social interaction as the basis of a classification of groups and formulated the concept of 'Gemeinschaft' and 'Gesellschaft,' the former signifying a close knit community where the social relationships are personal and informal, and the latter referring to secondary groups where the relationships are formal as is seen in an industrialised urban society.

When we describe any relationship we take into account the quantitative and qualitative aspects. The number of people taking part in the action, their dispersion or concentration, the duration and frequency of the association are quantitative aspects. The qualitative aspect of the interaction cannot be divided so easily as the quantitative aspects. Kingsley Davis mentions five characteristics which when supplemented with the 'physical conditions' concerning quantitative aspects, serve as a criterion for distinguishing primary from secondary groups.

In distinguishing the qualitative aspects of social relationships Talcott Parsons uses a set of five 'pattern variables.' Whenever we act or play a role we are emphasising one or another side of the five basic divisions. The five pattern variables are:

(1) affectivity versus affective neutrality,
(2) self-interest versus collective interest,
(3) universalism versus particularism,
(4) performance versus quality, and
(5) specificity versus diffuseness.

Primary and Secondary Groups

Basically division of groups into primary and secondary is based on social relationships, and C.H. Cooley in his classic analysis of a primary group defined it in terms of face-to-face association and co-operation, sentiments of loyalty, emotional involvement, identification, and concern for friendly relations as an end in themselves, not as a means to an end. Usually the primary groups are small, but sentiment is more important than size. The primary group is the product of long and intimate interaction under informal conditions. We belong to primary groups because we are born into a particular family in a particular geographical area. It gives the individual his first acquaintance with humanity. Cooley wrote, *'By primary groups I mean those characterised by intimate face-to-face association and co-operation. They are primary is several senses, but chiefly in that they are fundamental in forming the social nature and ideals of the individuals.'* The result of intimate association, psychologically, is a certain fusion of individualities in a common whole, so that one's very self, for many purposes at least, is the common life and purposes of the group. Perhaps the simplest way of describing this wholeness is by saying that it is a 'we'; it involves the sort of sympathy and mutual identification for which 'we' is the natural expression.

One lives in the feeling of the whole and finds the chief aim of his will in that feeling. It is not to be supposed that the unity of the primary group is one of mere harmony and love. It is always a differentiated and usually a competitive unity, admitting of self-assertion and various appropriate passions; but these passions are socialised by sympathy, and come, or tend to come, under the discipline of the common spirit. The individual will be ambitious, but the chief object of his ambition will be some desired place in the thoughts of the others, and he will feel allegiance to common standards of service and fair play.

The most important spheres of this intimate association and co-operation--though by no means the only ones--are the family, the playgroup of children, and the neighbourhood or community group of elders. These are practically universal, belonging to all times and all stages of development; and are accordingly a chief basis of what is universal in human nature and human ideals.'

Though the term face-to-face association is used, the stress is on particular qualities of the relationship such as sympathy and mutual identification. It is generally agreed that all groups tend in some degree to possess consensus' which creates a 'we' feeling among the members. Large groups cannot retain their cohesion without this 'we' feeling. Thus primary association is seen in all groups and cannot therefore be used as the means of differentiation into primary and secondary. This quality cannot also be said to be limited to the face-to-face groups. There are friendly and intimate relationships which involve indirect contacts.

Physical Conditions of Primary Groups

Three essential conditions are there for a primary group; close face-to-face proximity; the smallness of the group; durability of the bond. All these conditions are essential and mutually related.

Physical proximity: To have close contacts intimacy

development is necessary which can be achieved by face-to-face association. Meeting and talking to each other makes easy the exchange of ideas, opinions and sentiments. Close contact has come to symbolise good feelings and identity between people. Caressing, kissing, sexual intercourse, eating and living together, playing, studying or travelling together are all regarded as external symbols of close solidarity. Physical proximity provides opportunity for the development of primary groups. The normative order of society regulates the conditions under which physical contact can take place.

Smallness of the group: It is not possible to be sensory contact with a large number of people at the same time and hence a face-to-face group must be a small one. A speaker may address a large audience but this is under special conditions. Other factors being equal, the smaller the group the more intimate it will be. The character of the group changes with its size. As the group becomes larger the individual is counted less as a unique personality but more as a mere unit. The group tends to have a more formal and complex organisation. The rules of association are more clearly stated and the means of control more official. In the case of very small groups even the addition of one person makes a great deal of difference. In small groups people can know each other personally and participate in group discussions, thereby developing a group character. If the group is large more time may be required to establish such a relationship.

Duration of the relationship: Intimacy is determined largely by the frequency and intensity of association. The longer the group stays together, the more numerous and dipper will be the contacts between the members. Through the gradual interchange of habits, social ties deepen. An association that is repeated often becomes like any other experience, a part of one's way of life.

Character of Primary Relations

There is an identity of ends. The relationship is considered by the individuals not as a means to an end but as something good in itself. The relationship is non-contractual, non-economic, non-political and non-specialised but is personal, spontaneous, sentimental and inclusive. In a perfect primary relationship the individuals have almost identical desires and attitudes so that there is no conflict between them. For each person the welfare of the other is significant; but an identity of interests is rarely complete. The fusion of personalities is an important part of the 'we' feeling when the interests of the other person become one's own.

The relationship is an end in itself: In ideal primary groups, the relationship is not a means to an end but an end in itself. For example, if a particular friendship is formed for some economic reason it is not a real friendship. The relationship in a primary group is not a means to an end, not compulsory, but is in itself enjoyable. A close relationship that is forced or pretended with some ulterior motive becomes burdensome.

The relationship is personal, and therefore disappears when the particular person disappear from that relationship. Personal relationships always stand in a class by themselves. The most obvious and inevitable characteristic of a personal relationship is that it is not transferable. Things that seem very trivial in other contexts may become important in personal relationships. The relationship is inclusive. In a personal relationship, the individual is a complete concrete person. His value is related to his whole self and not to any particular aspect of activity. Each person comes to know the other order in all the details of his life. Long acquaintance and close contact are necessary for the development of a primary relationship. In this way the primary relationship differs from all other social relations because in other relation complete personalities are not involved.

The relationship is spontaneous: A purely primary relationship is voluntary and in this sense it dose not differ from a contractual relationship, but in the contract the conditions are clearly laid down. Also the contract is not an end in itself but only a means to some end. On the other hand, the personal relationship which is dependent at all stages on the will of the persons is more voluntary with greater spontaneity.

Concrete Groups and Primary Relationships

Primary relationships do not exist concrete form. In primary group interaction, competition and even conflict may arise. It is seen in families where there may be conflict between husband and wife and between parents and children and the like. In spite of latent hostilities the primary groups present a united front against outsiders. The groups that embody most completely the characteristics of the primary relationships are those that are free from any connection with the social organisation. There is no longer obligations, no fixed status, and no involuntary elements. In some primitive societies friendships are sealed by ceremonies and are expected to continue for life whereas in other societies there quite free. Every society is hostile towards the full expression of the primary association. If society is to exercise control over individuals it must also control their relationships. It must define certain mutual obligations even in the most personal affairs.

It takes advantage of the personal affection or spontaneity or identity of ends to provide organisation for the performance of social functions. In many different ways it limits contacts so that they will develop only in ways that fit into the social organisation. However, society is friendly towards a partial expression of primary relationships. A person cannot develop without close intimate personal contacts and needs the security of stable an familiar group. The process of socialisation is handled by these concrete groups, particularly the family and the playgroups. Such groups are institutionalised and organised because they give the members mutual rights and obligations. In modern society secondary contacts play an important role so that some of the burden of social organisation has been lifted from the primary groups, thereby giving them greater informality and spontaneity.

Ellsworth Faris has pointed out that "the nature of the primary group...lies not in its parts but in its organisation. It depends not upon its spatial contiguity, but upon its functional inter-relation... The primary group cannot exist without memories; it cannot endure without purposes.... It is a changing organisation of functional activities tending toward an end, influenced by its past and guided by its future."

SOME TYPICAL PRIMARY GROUPS

The Peer Group

Peer group is an aggregation of people of approximately the same age who feel and act together. Boys and girls of the same age and approximately the same social background as in a class or in a youth organisation are members of a peer group. Social interaction is the most important quality of the peer group and the peer group helps personality development. Social attitudes are developed in children through their contacts with their peers.

The Army Group

Soldiers from groups with their comrades and thus form an informal relationship within a setup which is highly formal. This kind of informal relationship is an effort to defend themselves against the officers. The primary group defends its members against the arbitrary authority of the officers, and also it sets up standards of behaviour for the soldier.

The Clique

It is a form of close friendship developed between two or more persons which brings them into joint activities and mutual acceptance. It is found among different age groups especially among high school children. According to Hollengshead who wrote Elmtown there are a number of cliques in the town he studied whose members plan to be together, do things together and go places together. The members depend on it for friendship, confidence and emotional support. It is a primary group in the most intimate sense with its norms and values. As in America clique is common among students in India.

The Dysfunction of Primary Groups

Though primary relationship are important, it is not right to imagine that the primary relationship is ideal for all social interactions. At times primary relationships may interfere with other elements in the society. Thus in a complex society many relationships should be non-primary in nature where a purely objective approach has to be taken in making decisions. If a magistrate shows leniency towards a friend for a serious offence or a teacher awards a high grade to a student who does not deserve it or there is any such similar action arising out of primary relationship, such action is dysfunctional. 'Many situations arise in modern society where primary relationships are inappropriate at best and harmful at worst. In large bureaucratic structures, so necessary to contemporary social organisation, impersonality is more appropriate than intimacy, routine more important than spontaneity, and division of labour more necessary than versatility. Societies and subsocieties composed of tight networks of primary relationships are often more intolerant of differences, more resistant to change, and less receptive to freedom than societies where relationships are more casual.'

Some of the dysfunctions of primary group relationships are restriction, conformity and reaction.

Restriction--A family provides comforts, defence and tolerance to its members, but at the same time it imposes many restrictions on its members. The authoritarian influence of the father over other members gives rise to resentment and also leads to emotional problems. The primary group thus may restrict rather than enhance the personality of children.

Conformity--Peer groups help in developing such important qualities as sociability, behaviour patterns and the like. It fosters conformity, complacency and conservatism in the adolescent.

Reaction--Another dysfunction is fostering reaction or resistance to social change. This reactionary spirit is seen among the privileged who do not like their privileges to go, and also among the lower social orders who resist industrial, intellectual and educational changes as such changes may weaken hereditary ties. However, in the modern world due to mass education, mass communication and the like, many changes are taking place in the functioning of primary groups.

The Reference Group

This is a way of looking at the relationship between the individual and any group, primary or otherwise. It is the group to which the individual refers and with which he identifies either consciously or unconsciously. The reference group is 'that group whose outlook is used by the actor as the frame of reference in the organisation of his perceptual field.' The reference group is different from the membership group. A person may identify with groups of which he is not a member, but of which he would aspire to be.

Voluntary Associations

Though we belong to families and other primary groups we interact in various other fields like business, politics, government and religion. The primary group is only part of the larger and more complex reality of life. As modern societies get complex, impersonal behaviour is becoming common, and the secondary groups are less intimate and less personal than primary groups. The relationship in the secondary groups are entered into voluntary and purposely, while in the primary relationships like that of the family the individual has practically very little choice of his own. The secondary group is growing in importance in modern societies with large-scale organisations, impersonal relationships and specialisation of functions. Complexities increase and the average citizen has neither the time nor the skill to face the changing situation.

Differences between Primary and Secondary Groups

In the secondary group relationship we very often interact with people with diverse values because we need their services and we have certain obligations to fulfil. Such obligations may be legal and contractual, and the dealings there is practically no room for affection or sentiment. We get along with them because of our reciprocal needs. In the secondary group the members regard each other as means to ends and not as ends in themselves. The relationship between the trader and the customer is based on the business the former could do rather than on personal friendship. This mentality is spreading in legal, medical and teaching professions. Each member of the secondary group expects something from it apart from the pleasure of the interaction. In the secondary group there is the concept of contract which is gaining strength. The mutual duties and responsibilities of the contracting parties are specified. The personal liabilities of each member in the secondary group is limited according to the contract terms while in the primary group it is almost unlimited.

The city dewellers interact with each other in 'highly segmental roles.' In a society where the secondary interests predominate, the individual's personality gets fragmented. He reacts with one segment of his personality while in a primary group his whole personality is reflected. The development and functioning of an integrated personality will become difficult.

The rigid classification of groups into primary and secondary is difficult and often there is much overlapping of the two. Cooley's emphasis on 'we' feeling cannot be taken as the distinctive element in a primary group as such a feeling to some extent is necessary for any enduring community. In between a primary group like the family and a formal and rigid group like the army there are hundreds of groups, some of which are more primary than others. In modern organisations efforts are made to create a friendly atmosphere among the employees. In order to obtain greater loyalty from its members some religious and educational groups try to inculcate primary group ideas into these groups. This has not always been a success and often the results are dysfunctional than functional. In modern societies both primary and secondary groups are important and it is not easy to substitute one for the other. Some of the modern studies show that the higher the income of the family, the greater their participation in secondary groups. The lower income group has neither the interest nor the money, nor time to spend on secondary groups.

In America a small section of the middle and upper class populations belongs to secondary groups, while the majority of the lower income people do not belong to any secondary groups.

Collective Behaviour

Through socialisation an individual learns to conduct himself in the different situations he has to encounter. In his everyday activity at home, office or elsewhere he has his definite role to play, and clearly defined group norms are followed. His habits, values and attitudes are adjusted for adoption in such circumstances which are known as structured circumstances. However, there are times when people are not prepared to meet situations when group norms are not well-defined. Such a situation, when the individual has no clear role to play, is known as unstructured circumstances. The behaviour of a collective group has as its characteristic 'the spontaneous development of norms and ogranisation which contradict or reinterpret the norms and organisation of society.' Collectivities are human relationship structures and can be defined as 'a number of persons whose behaviour is specifically focussed around a temporary center of attraction that leads to interaction and a unity which exists only as long as the centre of attraction exits.' An event or occurrence attracts people towards a particular spot and this convergence process is the distinctive characteristic in a collectivity. The components of the collectivity are not selected and anonymity is another important feature of collectivity. Very often such anonymity encourages irresponsible behaviour. There is an absence of a previously existing structure, and as the integrating factors are temporary, collectivities are usually short lived. Each type of collectivity determines its own standards of behaviour. Collectivities rarely reappear with the same components once they are dissolved, and these are non-repetitive. If the unifying factors include permanent values to society, the people who compose them may develop organisations to achieve such ends. For example, fire-fighting units in most areas have developed from relatively unorganised collective action groups.

The Crowd

The most elemental of collectivities is a crowd. 'A crowd is a temporary collection of persons who react to a common focus of attention and engage in spontaneous interaction.' It is 'a physical compact aggregation of human beings brought into direct, temporary and unorganised contact, reacting mostly to the same stimuli and in a similar way. It is always a transitory and unstable organisation, an incident, an eruption, therefore integration based upon immediate suggestion plays an important part.'

People who are physically together are also to some extent socially together. They may gather together very casually but their mere presence and awareness of each other starts a lively but silent interchange of mutual impressions. Their faces, clothes and movements reveal a great deal about their status.

Their behaviour pattern makes allowance for the existence of other people. Even their indifference to each other is only a cultivated attitude which changes when there is a change in the situation. The general characteristics of the crowd are physical proximity of the people, absence of any division of labour or system of status, and the prevalence of interaction which is relatively uncontrolled or spontaneous and so uninhibited.

Unlike the family or community, the crowd ceases to exist when it is dispersed. The crowd is thus temporary and has no permanent existence. The crowd may meet at the same spot again but the membership may be different. If the same people meet day after day it is no longer a crowd. The crowd has no permanent identity and is nameless. The crowd is unorganised and though there may be a leader there is no division of labour or status. Every individual in the crowd has the same status irrespective of his status in the larger social system. The members of the crowd gain anonymity as their social position remains unknown. Psychologically the crowd is irrational and emotion and impulse make it active. Individuals have a common interest and respond emotionally to the same stimulus and influence one another by expressions of curiosity, amusement, alarm and the like. Rational response is delayed response where activity is not exhibited until sometime has been spent in comparing the different factors in the situation and the possible modes of reaction. The crowd is irrational and usually responds immediately on the lowest intellectual or emotional level. The crowd is extremely suggestible and ready to believe almost everything at the moment and act in accordance with such beliefs. In crowds individuals often behave in ways which they would consider unworthy of themselves when acting in other situations. So long as the individual remains anonymous and the crowd itself lacks a social responsibility he feels free to let himself go and act as others do. They readily yield to impulses which would be restrained in other situations.

According to Joseph Gittler a crowd may be characterised: (1) by the physical presence of its members; (2) by lack of organisation among its members; (3) by its shortlivedness; (4) by the anonymity and emotional involvement; (5) by the suggestibility among its members which makes for a circular interstimulation; and (6) by the presence of cultural background factors conducive to the formation of crowds. Though there are no tests for the membership of a crowd a common background will help. A person from another culture will be handicapped and have difficulty in establishing rapport with members of the crowd, which is essential for its functioning. The crowd is unstable and what excites it at one moment may not have any appeal on a different occasion. A crowd may easily be broken up if there are other attractions. A simple crowd lacks leadership and internal organisation and this type of crowd is described as a passive crowd whose interests are sympathy, amusement or curiosity. The stampeding crowd which is another form of simple crowd is motivated entirely by fear.

Gustav Le Bon, a French doctor, is the pioneer in studies of crowd behaviour who noted the street behaviour of people at the French Revolution. The street crowd in times of revolution is an acting crowd or mob because it is organised for a purpose. The aim of the revolutionaries is to make changes in the existing governmental structure. The other major type of crowd behaviour is in the expressive crowd which is also known as orgiastic crowd or dancing crowd because the empahsis is on rhythmical movement per se without any goal or purpose in the behaviour. In 1985 Gustav Le Bon defined crowd as, 'whoever be the individuals that compose it, however like or unlike be their mode of life, their occupations, their character, or their intelligence, the fact that they have been transformed into a crowd puts them in possession of a sort of collective mind which makes them feel, think, and act in a way different from what they would were they in a state of isolation. Kingsley Davis, a contemporary sociologist, has described crowd behaviour as follows:

(1) *Crowds articulated with social structure*

(a) Formal audience: Theatre audience, sports audience, religious congregations. These have central focus and like ends but are passive in character.

(b) Planned expressive groups: Dancing crowds, party crowds, religious orgies. These have little focus but pursue a similar end which is the activity itself and the pleasure it gives. They serve the function of providing an escape and a release from the tension of routine activity. The presence of others through group interstimulation is a definite aid in the fulfilment of this function.

(2) *Casual crowd*

(a) Inconvenient aggregations: Collections of people trying to share common facilities, such as a queue at a ticket counter, a group trying to board a public bus, or a number of people caught in a traffic jam. In these crowds the presence of others is a handicap in reaching a competitive goal, and the interstimulation may take the form of mutual antagonism.

(b) Spectator crowds: Groups drawn together to witness a fire or other spectacular event. These resemble the audience mentioned above, except that the occasion is unplanned and the activity largely uncontrolled. The focus is an accidental occurrence; group interstimulation plays a relatively small role except in drawing people's attention to the occurrence.

(c) Panic crowds: Persons fleeing from a building on fire, from a flood, from a battle, or from any other catastrophe. In

these the interstimulation within the group is apt to heighten the sense of panic, to increase the irrational character of the response, and to be a positive handicap to escape from the common danger.

(3) Lawless crowds

(a) Acting mobs: Lynching parties, looting gangs, rebellious crowds. The aim of the group is to achieve some purpose by physical force contrary to the ordinary rules of law and order. The presence of large numbers gives a sense of anonymity, heightens the emotions, and leads to actions that the individuals alone would hardly perform. There is usually the feeling that an injustice is being righted and that basic rights are being vindicated in the face of slowness, inefficiency or inequity of the established system.

(b) Immoral crowds: Orgiastic assemblages, drunken brawls, riotous and destructive celebrations. This type resembles the expressive groups mentioned above, but the release from tension goes so far as to violate the mores. Group interstimulation heightens the sense of release, anonymity provides a feeling of protection from possible punishment, the frustrations of ordinary life, especially sex frustrations, provide the motivation for seeking complete relief. The action of the crowd tends to end when a state of satiety is reached.

Lang and Lang point out the characteristics of the crowd as a form of collective behaviour in the following manner:

(1) *Number of people*--It involves a number of people in interaction. This may range from a few to several thousands. The actual number is not so important, as the type of interaction between the members.

(2) There is heightening of feelings which are translated into a mood shared by all or most of the members. Such emotions can vary between affectionate adulation and blind hatred.

(3) When the heightened feelings give rise to a mood that is shared by the members, people depart from the traditional norms of organised society and do things which they do not ordinarily do. They are aware of what they do but don't bother.

(4) *Redefinition of the situation*--A situation ordinarily not in accordance with the mores suddenly appears just and right and the crowd acts. As there is anonymity action becomes easier.

(5) When the collective emotion is heightened the individual members become a collectivity.

Another classification of the crowd into the acting crowd and the expressive crowd is followed by many writers. In the acting crowd, the action is directed against an outside object that has become the focus of aggression or affection. The crowd may be motivated by love for some person like Mahatma Gandhi or symbols like the cross used by the crusaders in the middle ages. However, very often fear, rage and hatred give rise to some form of aggression. Millions of Jews were killed in Nazi Germany because of the racial prejudice and hatred encouraged by the German dictator. At times we hear of genocide practised in some parts of the world and this shows the depth to which men could sink under certain circumstances.

The acting crowd thinks that it is right and that those opposing it are wrong. Anyone questioning the motives or beliefs of the crowd may be considered an enemy. The members of the acting crowd lack a sense of humour and take their mission seriously. 'Crowd members substitute slogans for clear thinking, utter cliches instead of examining the issues, and treat all opposition as dangerous heresy to be stamped out without mercy.' Ridicule or mockery are destested as these question the rightness of the crowd. The crowd is obsessed by beliefs of its own importance and fears of persecution. Like a paranoid person with his delusions of grandeur and persecution the crowd also shows 'paranoia.' Such confused emotions lead to hatred and suspicion. There is also 'the projection' behaviour when members unconsciously project their own undesirable qualities upon the enemy. An individual who unconsciously wishes to harm another will accuse the other of wanting to do the same thing. For example, the advocate of preventive war may be sure that the enemy is planning to attack him.

The expressive crowd: In an expressive crowd the activities turn inward and the members engage in actions to liberate emotions through the manipulations of self-images and norms of the participants. Once the emotions are liberated the crowd disperses and the people once again assume their individual roles. Though strong emotions are at work, in the expressive crowd the emotions are less aggressive than in the acting crowd.

A football match or a religious revival meeting provides opportunities for a temporary emancipation from the boredom of ordinary life. The stress and strain of modern society fatigues the individual who in turn looks for collective diversions of the type offered by crowd behaviour. There is a longing for change from the daily routine work and the expressive crowd behaviour like dancing, singing, and drinking collectively purge them of emotional tensions.

Expressive crowd behaviour is also associated with the supernatural. The members seem to think that some force stronger than themselves is at work and such an emotional satisfaction is possible only collectively. The behaviour of the expressive crowd is tolerated by society. At times the behaviour may look psychotic as in the case of the participants in some of the religious revival meetings of the pentecostal churches in Kerala, but this behaviour is approved by society, and the individuals can rid themselves temporarily of some of their inhibitions.

Crowd control: Crowd behaviour can be studied only when it occurs. If crowd behaviour is properly studied some of the calamities resulting from it could be avoided. A study conducted by the Chicago police in collaboration with a sociologist has suggested five methods of controlling an acting crowd.

(1) Removal or isolation of the individuals involved in precipitating an incident before the crowd has begun to achieve substantial unity.
(2) Interruption of communication during the milling process by dividing the crowd into small units.
(3) Removal of the crowd leaders, if it can be done without the use of force.
(4) Distracting the attention of the crowd from its focal point by creating diversions at other points.
(5) Preventing the spread and reinforcement of the crowd by isolating it.

Usually crowd behaviour is encouraged by political parties, religious groups and the like, but there is always a danger that the expressive crowd may change into an acting crowd. Crowd speakers and orators have gained considerable importance in modern times and they greatly influence public opinion.

Herd and Crowd

Gregariousness and conformity bring men together. By the institutionalisation of groups more permanent features of social life are formed. Men also have their herd sentiment, an attribute we find clearly in most animals. The migration of refugees from one country to another in times of great distress like war reflects the herd sentiment. Unlike herds, a crowd is short-lived and it is not a mode of life. 'Herd sentiment is the imitative cohesion revealed when men conform blindly to the traditions and beliefs and ways of a group, when they approve of these because they are accepted and disapprove simply because they are divergent from the established norms, when they are moved by the slogans, the stereotypes, the conventions, the 'idols' of their in-groups. In animal society, herd feeling is the manifestation of the gregarious instinct, the simplest form of socialisation. In human society, this feeling is broadened into a sentiment that attaches itself to the socially indoctrinated ways.' Herd sentiment makes people follow the band. Herd sentiment identifies mores and morals, conformity and solidarity and those who differ from it are considered anti-social.

The collective pursuit of some superficial novelty is a manifestation of herd sentiment. Some song, some game or some 'craze' may become popular but may disappear shortly; but the cause of its temporary acceptance can be traced to the social and cultural conditions of a given time and place. Another manifestation of the herd sentiment is the emotional epidemics which occasionally sweep through a country. This may be linked with beliefs or superstitions of the culture. In the middle ages Europe witnessed crusades and religious persecutions which had developed into emotional epidemics. At times a catastrophe or triumph may touch off an emotional impulse of an epidemic character. The threat of a war or a national humiliation may evoke such feelings. Such an emotional feeling spread throughout India on 31st October, 1984 when it was known that Prime Minister Indira Gandhi was assassinated. Normal life came to a standstill and for hours helplessness and gloom spread over the sub-continent. Some wept, some kept silent, and some couldn't simply believe it. In some parts of the country this feeling led to communal violence. It took many days for normal conditions to be restored. Such manifestations of herd sentiments clearly show the gregarious nature of human beings.

The Audience

Etymologically audience means hearers or listeners, but

sociologically it refers to a number of people who act in similar ways due to a common sources of stimulation, but without much communication with each other. Communication tends to be one-sided rather than mutual. There are no bonds among the members and though they may be act similarly they do not act cooperatively. For example, to those who attend a musical performance the common source of stimulation is the music. The only influence the members have on each other is the feeling that there are others also present, and it keeps them following the culturally expected patterns of behaviour.

According to Kimball Young there are three types of audiences: *(a)* information seeking, as in the public lecture or classroom, *(b)* recreation seeking, as in attendance at a play or concert, and *(c)* conversional, where people come to be converted or have their beliefs strengthened. His classification is based on the motivation that brings people together as an audience. There are other classifications of audience. On the basis of the degree of integration Madison Bentley has classified audience into three types; *(a)* heterogeneous or gathered for occasional discourse or event, *(b)* homogeneous or gathered for a common purpose, need or request, and *(c)* primed, or gathered because previous association, common interests, sentiments and needs have existed and are implied. Audience can be defined as 'collectivities of individuals meeting at a particular time and place and unified, in their collective reactions, to a common object or event. Audiences include not only collectivities of listeners, but also groups of spectators of all kinds. The term does not, however, apply to such scattered collections of people as those who are listening to a radio programme, watching a television show, or reading the same evening newspaper. These are particular types of public. Audiences include groups assembled at theatres, concerts, public lectures, formally organised sports events, radio and television studio performance, and congregational church services, to give some varied examples.'

For the members of the audience there is the common expectation of the event and this brings them together. In the integration of the audience there are two aspects. There is the one-to-all relationship between those who perform and those who watch or listen. To make the one-to-all relationship clear those distractions like reading newspapers or talking to friends are not permitted.

Communication among the members is suspended and a one way communication process is made ready. The members of the audience are to be passive recipients of what is to follow. Audiences are usually accommodated into a predetermined setting. The size and shape of the meeting place, arrangements of seating and lighting are all intended to facilitate the all-to-one relationship. The attention of the audience is called for by the lowering of lights, the raising of curtains, the rising of the chairman and the like. Having gained attention, interest has to be built up and various techniques are used for this. Having created the interest, the all to one relationship has to be strengthened. The audience must see and hear what is going on. A pleasing voice, a commanding appearance, and attractive scenery are important. Usually emotional stimulation helps integration more easily than intellectual stimulation. In a heterogeneous crowd to gain attention is difficult and it demands prior preparation.

Very many techniques have developed in this field in countries like the U.S.A. In election campaigns in India also much planning is done to gain the full attention of the audience.

The Mob

Mob is essentially a crowd in positive action usually motivated by joy or anger. Though often mobs are destructive and bad tempered, a mob may also be motivated by friendly emotions. The mob has a leader who serves the purpose of focussing the mob's attention upon certain objectives, and who urges the members to act. The leader may be a professional mob leader or he may appear spontaneously from the group. He must give the impression that he is sharing the experiences of the mob members, and he must be able to phrase his suggestions in terms which strike common emotional chords in the members. He must have vitality and must have a keen sense of the dramatic.

A sense of humour, a fiery emotional way of speaking, a flair for expressive gestures, a knack for concise phrasing are all helpful. The leader builds up emotional tensions by defining for his followers the causes for their unrest. He recommends a line of action which will release these tensions and makes a pretence of justifying such action.

The mob is more emotional than the simple crowd. The members of the crowd are usually motivated by elemental emotions like curiosity, amusement or sympathy. The members of a mob, on the other hand, are restless, feel a vague uneasiness and want to do something about it. Once this has been outlined for them by the leader, the emotional excitement of the mob increases. The anonymity and lack of responsibility which is characteristic of the simple crowd also removes any inhibitions which would be present in other social groups. By means of the rapid exchange of stimuli the emotional tensions of the mob spread like fire and it bursts into action. The use of symbols is important in mob situations. A flag, a slogan, or an individual may serve as a symbol. It tends to focus the attention of the members and to dramatise their emotions. The members of the mob identify the symbol with some vaguely felt emotion which they have never succeeded in expressing, regardless of whether the symbol applies to the particular situation or not.

Like the crowd the mob also lacks internal organisation and stability. Once the objective is achieved it dissolves and the members join the more permanent groups with which they are identified. The emotions which spread through the mob by stimulus and response are frequently transmitted to the official guardians of peace and order. Brutal shootings by police at riots though rationalised as self-defence is no more than mob behaviour. Well-trained officers know that the best way to break up the mob is to remove the leader and substitute him with someone who is capable of awakening the mob to the realities of orderly behaviour.

Public and Public Opinion

In a crowd the behaviour of people is marked by emotion and there is also close physical contact; but in the case of a public theoretically the behaviour is marked by discussion and deliberation. 'A public consists of all those divided on an issue, who, because they take an interest, are actively thinking and talking about it.' Improved means of communications have brought about revolutions in the exchange of ideas. The printing press, telephone and telegraphic systems, radio, and television, communication satellites and numerous other techniques have accelerated the improvement of communication. 'A public is that form of collectivity which includes a number of dispersed and non-organised individuals who are faced with an issue about which there may be differences of opinion. There may often be a desire to achieve collective judgement by the discussion of alternatives.' In the opinion of some there are five developmental phases in each public. When people recognise an issue and show concern about it, it is called problem phase. The next is the proposal phase. This is the preliminary discussion phase when experiences are shared and compromises worked out. The third is the policy phase when there is consideration of plans of action and commitments. The next is the programme phase when decisions are put into action, thereby changing a public into an organisation with specific memberships and definite roles. It now takes the form of a pressure group. It the objectives are not accomplished, an appraisal phase follows. This demands further action which calls the public into existence again. The continuing interest of the issue demands a continuing public when some old members may drop out and new ones join. Each members has his own viewpoints and prejudices and some with strong prejudices become propagandists. It is not necessary for the people to congregate in one place. It is the interest in an issue that is common to the members of the public. At a given time in any society, there may be many issues and these are bound to be overlapping. A person may be a member of many publics at one time. 'Publics are inclusive interest groups, usually with divergent opinions concerning social issues. When the interest of a group of individuals in a social issue or set of social values is more abiding and more national than it is in a crowd, we call the group a public.'

Public Opinion

There is no generally accepted definition of public opinion. 'Public opinion is not the name of something, but a classification of a number of somethings.' It is true that public opinion is a collection of individual opinions on an issue of general interest. Such opinions have influence over the behaviour of individuals, groups and government policies. The public is loosely organised, often scattered and confused while there are different organised groups of individuals who know what they want and try to get it. Some are for power and authority while some are on the lookout for markets to sell their products. They know that for their success they must have the support of public opinion. Public opinion refers to 'action or readiness for action with regard to a given issue on the part of members of a public who are reacting in the expectation that others in the public are similarly oriented towards the same issue.'

Herbert Blumen has analysed the sociological nature of public opinion in the following manner:

1. The society is a functional organisation of groups, institutions, and voluntary associations, whose activities combine to make up the collective life.

2. Public opinion has its setting in a particular society and grows out of the continuous interaction between the members of that society.
3. Public opinion is the product of this process of social interaction. Public opinion thus 'consists of the pattern of the diverse views and positions on the issues that come to the individuals who have to act in response to the public opinion.'
4. These key individuals assess the demands brought to bear upon them by their own members and the members of other groups and then act accordingly.
5. These functional groups respond to the decisions of certain key individuals of high social status.

There are four main approaches to the study of public opinion: the quantitative measurement of opinion distributions; investigations of the internal relationships among individual opinions that make up public opinion on an issue; description or analysis of the political role of public opinion; studying the communication media that disseminate the ideas on which opinions are based and of the uses that propagandists and other manipulators make of this media.

In the 1930s George Gallup, Elmo Roper, and Archibald Crossley made use of the sample survey method in predicting the results of the U.S. presidential election of 1936. The correctness of the prediction has increased the popularity of the sample survey.

Public opinion studies have their uses. They have helped the governments to guide their public opinion and propaganda programmes. It also helps in the formulation of other policies.

It gives an insight to politicians and governments as to the prospects of their success. Industry and business are interested in assessing public opinion in matters like marketing. Public opinion research has become an important aspect of

American industries. Business, industry, labour and government have shared in the development.

During World War II a number of governmental and military research organisations conducted large scale attitude and opinion studies in the U.S. Public opinion is of immense significance in democracies. A democratic government is based on the assumption that on matters of common concern a great majority of citizens will act as a public. It is assumed that the majority will reach their decisions with reasonable intelligence and tolerance, and that they will express these decisions through the periodic elections. However, there are many flaws in this.

Propaganda plays an important role in controlling public opinion. Propaganda is the deliberate use of communication to induce people to favour one predetermined line of thought or action over another. Unresolved issues give rise to different opinions and as opinions represent attitudes, they are subject to manipulation by the propagandists. Sometimes propaganda yields valuable social ends like national loyalty in war time. In India the family planning propaganda is aimed at changing the attitude of people towards family size.

During World War II there were intensive propaganda machineries in Germany and Russia and various new techniques emerged to increase the effectiveness of propaganda. At present propaganda is used in politics, industry, religion and other aspects of social life to promote particular interests. At times conflicting views are presented by opposing groups which lead to confusion.

Rumour

Spreading rumours is another kind of collective behaviour. Though often discredited it has some significance. When information is not freely available, and when things are hidden from the public, rumours spread. 'A rumour is a specific (or topical) proposition for belief, passed along from person to person usually by word of mouth, without secure standards of evidence being presented.' Many factors facilitate the spread of rumours. These are group responses to situations affecting the group as a whole. The situation giving rise to rumours is highly charged with emotion, or with something that is of unusual interest to the group. Rumours are sometimes group responses to complex situations or sometimes act as solutions to problems arising from emotional and imaginative factors. According to Shibutani, 'Rumour is a substitute for news; in fact, it is news that does not develop in institutional channels. Unsatisfied demand for news--the discrepancy between information needed to come to terms with a changing environment, and what is provided by formal news channels--constitutes the crucial condition of rumour construction.'

REFERENCES

Anderson, Walfred A. and Frederick B. Parker, *Society*, D. Van Nostrand Co. Inc., New York, 1966.

Simmel, George (translated by K.H. Wolff and R. Bendix), *Conflict and the Web of Group Affiliations,* The Free Press of Glencoe, New York, 1955.

Tonnies, Ferdinand, (translated by C.P. Loomis), *Fundamental Concepts of Sociology,* American Book, New York, 1949.

Davis, Kingsley, *Human Society,* Macmillan, New York, 1957.

Parsons, Talcott, *The Social System,* The Free Press, Glencoe, Ill, 1951.

Cooley, Charles H., *Social Organisation,* Scribner, 1909.

Faris, Ellsworth, as quoted by Francis E. Merrill, *Society and Culture--An Introduction to Sociology,* Prentice Hall, New Jersey, 1969.

Merrill, Francis E., *Society and Culture--An Introduction to Sociology,* Prentice Hall Inc., Englewood Cliffs, N.J. 1969.

Shibutani, Tamotsu, 'Reference Group as Perspectives, *American Sociological Review,* 27: 19--30 (February 1962).

Turner, Ralph H. and Lewis M. Killian, *Collective Behaviour,* Prentice Hall, New Jersey, 1957.

King. David, C. and Marvin R. Koller, *Foundations of Sociology,* Rinehart Press, San Francisco, 1975.

Lundberg, George A., C.C. Schrag, O.N. Larsen and W.R. Catton, *Sociology*, Harper and Row, 1963.

Eros, J.S. and W.A.C. Stewart, *Systematic Sociology*, Routledge and Kegan Paul, London, 1957.

Gittler, J.B., *Social Dynamics*, McGraw Hill, New York, 1952.

Ross, Arnold M., *Sociology*, Alfred A. Knopf, New York, 1957.

Lang, Kurt and Gladys Lang, *Collective Dynamics*, Thomas Crowell Co., New York, 1961.

Ginsberg, M., *The Psychology of Society*, Methuen, London, 1949. Chapter IX.

Lundberg, George A., A.C. Schrag, O.N. Larsen and W.R. Catton, *Sociology*, Harper and Row, New York, 1968.

MacIver, R.M. and C.H. Page, *Society*, Macmillan and Co., London, 1964.

Young, Kimball, *Social Psychology*, Appleton-Century, New York, 1946.

Bentley, J.M., as quoted in W.A. Anderson and F.B. Parker, *Society*, Van Nostrand Co., Princeton, 1966.

Lang, Kurt and Gladys Lang, *Collective Dynamics*, Thomas Crowell, New York, 1961.

International Encyclopaedia of Social Science, Macmillan Co., 1972, Vol. XIII.

Ogburn, W.F. and M.F. Nimkoff, *A Handbook of Sociology*, Eurasia Publications House, New Delhi, 1966.

Krech, David and Richard Crutchfield, *Theory and Problems of Social Psychology*, McGraw Hill, New Delhi, 1976.

Allport, G.W. and Leo Postman, *The Psychology of Rumour*, Holt, Rinehart & Winston, 1947.

4

Social Institutions

> "Civilization requires slaves. Human slavery is wrong insecure and demoralizing. On mechanical slavery, on the slavery of machine, the future of the world depends."
>
> —*Oscar Wilde*

In this chapter we have made attempt to delineate the outlines of all major social institution, though some of these are given elaborate treatment elsewhere in the book.

In simple terms, social institutions can be defined as culture patterns influencing human behaviour, and it is through these social institutions that human beings obtain a large part of their material, social and cultural satisfaction. Graham Sumner has defined an institution as 'a concept and a structure, the former meaning ideas, notion, doctrine, interest and the latter a framework, or apparatus, or perhaps only a number of functionaries set to co-operate in prescribed ways at a certain conjuncture. Concept and structure are intertwined and form part of a functioning pattern. The objectives and values of life are emphasised in the concept, while concepts are fulfilled through the mechanism of the structure. Social institutions are patterns that direct the behaviour of human beings in their manifold activities. The basic social institutions are the family; the economic institution; religion; and government. In addition there are educational, welfare, military, recreational and other activities which also have ordered forms, but the first four are common in all organised societies. Social institutions function through a complex structure of reciprocal roles that prescribed the behaviour of the individual in his institutional capacity.

Notably, Institutions' are formal and regularised and thus are different from various other common forms of behaviour. 'The needs they answer, the values they serve, and the direction they provide are so important that every society organises institutional behaviour more formally than presumably less important behaviour. The ceremonials by which the institutional functions of the church, state, family and other basic institutions are surrounded attest to this formalisation. The elaborate ceremonies in churches, temples and mosques are formal, solemn and indispensable to their members. The age-old ceremonies are continued which pave the way for the continuity of the institution, and individual behaviour becomes patterned. The Sanskrit *slokas* recited in some of the Hindu ceremonies are reminiscent of the Vedic times when this bad started. The same is true of the Latin or Syriac verses used in some of the ceremonies of the Christain churches. The Catholic and Anglican churches keep up their old traditions in matters of worship. The more they get deeprooted in one's mind, the greater the chance for continuity and survival of ceremonies. In India, the Hindu marriage ceremonies and cremation rites have a very long past and the established forms and patterns continue without much change.

Remarkably also help in the continuity of institutional practices. When rituals become a spontaneous practice, done automatically without much effort or thinking, and when it is associated with cultural values, the behaviour of the individual becomes ritualised.

A number of social practices like the celebration of certain holidays and birthdays have been institutionalised and form part of the social system. According to Talcott Parsons institutionalisation is 'a system of patterned expectations defining the proper behaviour of persons playing certain roles, enforced both by the incumbents' own positive motives for conformity and by the sanctions of others.' Society accepts the rules and considers them binding. It brings about moral restraints on the behaviour of individuals and most people accept them as right though some may violate them.

Though some basic social institutions are dealt with elaborately as separate chapters, here we are presenting them in general way.

MARRIAGE AND FAMILY

Family is the most important primary group and almost all human beings have grown up in some kind of family. It is through families that societies present themselves biologically and culturally. Families have varied considerably in form from one region to another, one generation to another and from one culture to another. According to Le Play, 'The family in its accepted form is like religion and property, an imperishable institution, but its types undergo considerable modifications. Together with religion and property family gives each social organisation its essential character.' He distinguished two extreme types of families, i.e., the patriarchal and the unstable families. He also mentioned an intermediary type called the 'stem family.' The family exists only as a process and a study of the changes gives us a greater understanding of its nature. 'The family is a group defined by sex relationship sufficiently precise and enduring to provide for the procreation and upbringing of children.' Marriage which marks the beginning of the family has concerned people in all ages and in all places. It is by marriage that a couple gains a special social status in society as man and wife. Earliest moral and ethical writings suggest that a society loses its vitality if people fail in their family responsibilities. Confucius thought that happiness and prosperity would prevail in a society only if everyone behaved correctly as a family member.

Some common characteristics of family are there which are universal in nature: (1) a mating relationship; (2) a form of marriage or other institutional arrangement based on which the mating relation is established and maintained; (3) a system of nomenclature which enables a mode of reckoning descent; (4) some economic provision shared by the members of the group especially for the upbringing of children; and (5) a common habitation. In most modern societies family is a conjugal unit where the basic relationship is based on husband and wife and the union is dissolved either by death or divorce. The children born of this wedlock grow in a closely-knit, emotionally bound group. In such a framework other relatives like grandparents, uncles and the like play only a subordinate role. This nuclear family pattern is mainly seen in the industrial nations of the world. Such a restricted conjugal family, comprising husband, wife and children, is comparatively new and it is the smallest family grouping in history. The traditional family in the Eastern world has been the extended conjugal family. A typical extended conjugal family contained in one household three generations whose relations with one another were integrated within a family-centred economy.

Distant kinsmen like cousins, aunts, nephews and nieces rarely lived and worked together but very often met in family reunions. In times of crisis they helped each other and they preserved a widened sense of family solidarity. In the consaguine family, which is another basic pattern, the central relationship is not spouses but of blood-relatives. Those who marry remain with one of the parental families, and thus the family responsibilities are shared. Even in the case of death or divorce the family continues and the absence of one makes no major difference. Consanguine family consists of 'a nucleus of blood relatives surrounded by a fringe of spouses' while the conjugal family consists of a 'a nucleus of spouses and their offspring surrounded by a fringe of relatives.' While in the conjugal family the emphasis is on husband-wife relationship, in the consanguineous system such relationship is given only secondary importance. The newly married person continues to owe his loyalty to the kin group and he is controlled from his or her point of origin. It is not a husband or wife from different families who cooperate in important activities but a brother or sister who have been trained from childhood to habits of mutual adaptation.

As is being noticed, in India the Joint Family System is slowly giving place to the nuclear family. In a joint family the married sons or daughters as the case may be live with the parents under parental authority. When the parents die, either they break up into individual families which eventually may become joint families, or continue in the same family under modified conditions prescribed by customs. In different parts of the world extended families are common. When young people, even after their marriage, live with their parents it becomes an extended family. These kinds of families are common in China, India, Japan, Iran, Turkey, Nigeria and in many other countries of the world. While nuclear families are found in numerous societies there are significant differences. For example, among the Tobrianders of New Guinea, the role of the father is shared by the father and the maternal uncle. In course of time the uncle gets the predominant place and the biological father recedes into an insignificant position. In the days before the communist take-over in China consanguineous families prevailed there: a large number of kinsmen living in one house. The family elders were viewed with great respect. Males dominated. According to Mencius, the ancient Chinese philosopher, 'It does not belong to a woman to determine anything of herself, but she is subject to the rule of three obediences. When young she has to obey her parents; when married she has to obey her husband; when a widow she has to obey her son.'

The family into which a person is born and in which he is reared is 'the family of orientation' while the family with whom he is associated by marriage is 'the family of procreation.'

Descent regulations are mainly of three types: (a) patrilineal descent where the affiliation is with the male ancestor; (b) matrilineal descent where the affiliation is with the female ancestor; (c) bilateral descent where a person claims decent from both parents.

Patriarchal Family

The patriarchal family is a compact family unit under a single head. In a patriarchal family the descent is traced through the father. The father's relatives are of closer affinity than the mother's and children assume the father's name. The patriarchal family is in substance a joint family under the control of the eldest married male. This type of family existed in many ancient civilisations in various forms. In the patriarchal system the family is a closely knit inclusive system in which authority belongs to the paternal side. The head of the family by virtue of his position had to conduct religious rites, and held unlimited powers over the children and the wives. Among the Jews, the Chinese and the early Romans, a wife could be divorced by the husband on certain grounds, but the•wife had no such reciprocal rights.

The Semitic tribes and the Aryans practised it. In Roman days, the Roman family head called 'pater familias' had combined in himself the powers of the priest, the supreme head of his people, and had absolute power over his family. The Roman traditions had influenced the growth of European family systems. In the eighteenth and nineteenth centuries a woman held few rights in England and America. The family was an economic unit managed by the husband. On her marriage her property rights vested in her husband and in the eyes of law she was a ward or minor. It was the duty of a wife to obey and serve the husband.

In France Rousseau wrote that 'the education of women should always be relative to that of men' for they 'are specially made to please men.' The authoritarian mores of the patriarchate was supported by the church also. As time passed the authoritarian pattern began to change and more democratic institutions emerged. Le Play thought that the patriarchal family was suitable only for groups that had not enough social authority, or an adequate political system, outside the family.

Matrilineal System

Remarkably in the matrilineal system a person belongs to a mother's line, which includes the mother, her sisters and her sister's children. A married man belongs to his mother's line, but his children belong to his wife's line. Such a kinship system prevailed in different parts of the world. In India the Nayars of Kerala had matrilineal kinship. Trodrianders of New Guinea preserve the matrilineal system.

Matriarchy is a system in which the control of the family is by the wife or mother. In most cases matrilineal descent is associated with matrilocal residence. The husband holds only a secondary position in the household where he is more or less like a visitor. Within the family group a male member of the wife's kin exerts authority over others. Among the Labrador Indians the mother's father holds authority while among the Omaha Indians the mother's eldest brother has the predominant position. The maternal system tends to join the kin-group together, but lessens the cohesiveness of the conjugal family. The principle of exogamy works in the system, with its different intermarrying groups.

Marital Forms

There are various cultural controls associated with the physiological phenomenon of mating. Mating can take place outside marriage and marriage can occur without mating. Marriage prescribes the rights and responsibilities of the couple and it is governed by customs and norms. It formalises and stabilises the social relationship in the family. It also distinguishes between socially acceptable and unacceptable mating.

Various considerations arise before a person selects his mate. Though affection has its priority, there are numerous conventions in the community which restrict his freedom of choice. No society is completely free from restrictions, though the rigidity varies. Exogamy prohibits a person from marrying within a special category of which he is a member and this practice is prevalent among people who trace descent on a strictly matrilineal or patrilineal basis. Marriage between close blood relations like father and daughter, mother and son, and brother and sister is almost universally prohibited.

There were notable exceptions like those in the royal families of ancient Egypt, the Incas of Peru and the like. In a vast sub-continent like India with its numerous religions, different types of marriages exist. The Hindu lawgivers of the past had discussed about eight modes of attaining a wife, of which four types were according to dharma and the rest non-dharma. The raksasa and paisaca modes were condemned by society. The woman was abducted or captured and seduced while unconscious. The gandharva marriage was based on choice. There was also the selection of a husband by a princess which was called swayamvara. However, this marriage was not always one of choice. It was also customary for the king to arrange a meeting of would-be suitors. They were asked to perform a particular feat and his daughter was given in marriage to the successful man.

In Hindu society, the code of Manu restricted the freedom of women. This was in the post-Vedic period and this pattern has been followed for centuries with slight modifications. Though monogamy was considered ideal some people had more than one wife. In the ceremonial rites envisaged for the royalty, four wives were recognised; Mahisi or chief wife; Parivrkti or influential; Vavata or favourite and Palagali or daughter of the Palagal who was the lowest court official. Very often the desire for a male child prompted a man to marry again. The Hindu practice prescribed marriage within one's own varna. However, union from outside one's varna was not impossible, though not desirable. A Brahmin may marry a woman from his own varna and also from the other three varnas. A Kshatriya can have a wife from his own varna and from other lower varnas. A Vaisya can have only two wives and a Sudra can marry only from his varna. Marrying from a varna lower than one's own was known as anuloma. The marriage of a man of a lower varna with a woman of a higher varna was called pratiloma. Though centuries have rolled by, the marriage pattern in India has not changed considerably, though higher education and egalitarian sentiments have made many modifications.

Prohibition against marriage within a certain social class or family group is also common in many countries. In the U.S. marriage to half-siblings is prohibited by law in 29 states. Twenty-three states in the U.S. prevent marriage between step parents and step children. Thirty-two states prohibit marriage between first cousins. In China it was customary not to marry persons bearing the same surname. Among some people marriage between persons of the same village is discouraged or banned. Among the Indian tribes in America and among African tribes this type of restriction prevails. Among the Masais of East Africa, no two people living within one hundred miles of each other could marry, which was an extreme form of residential exogamy. According to some, exogamy was the result of early man's attempt to prevent the adverse hereditary effects of inbreeding, which he had observed.

Endogamy

Endogamy is marriage within a social unit. This practice of marrying within a particular group was common in many parts of the world, especially in India where inter-caste marriages were not allowed. Marrying from one's own religion or from one's own race is encouraged by society. Very often in the matter of choosing a spouse, parents and other members of the family play their parts. In social and economic matters families are better judges than individuals. Though at one time arranged marriages were customary in Europe it is no longer so, but in countries like India this is still in vogue. Inter-faith and inter-racial marriages are discouraged in America and even inter-class marriages are viewed with disfavour. This is endogamy.

Levirate and Sororate

In some societies the brother of the deceased husband marries the widow, thereby assuming responsibility for her and her children. This practice is known as levirate. There is another practice called sororate, by which if a wife dies, the husband may be expected to marry her sister. Levirate and sororate were prevalent in some preliterate societies which stressed the obligations of a person towards his relatives. This varied from society to society. There are four types of marriages. Monogamy is the marriage of one male to one female. Polygamy refers to a person married to two or more spouses at the same time. Polygamy can be of two types. Polygyny is the marriage of one male to more than one female, and polyandry where one woman has more than one husband. Group marriage involves the marriage of several males to several females. Murdock who studied about 250 societies found that 193 preferred polygyny while 43 preferred monogamy. In polygynous societies only a few could afford to have more than one wife as it involved much expense, and most were satisfied with one wife or none. In Tibet where land was unequally distributed the few who were rich were monogamous or even polygynous, while the majority who were poor with small landholdings practised polyandry.

Functions of the Family

There are definite functions for the family to perform and

these are prescribed by society. The primary function of the family is the procreation of children, and with the task of production are associated maintenance, status ascription and socialisation. For the continuity of society, children are required but it is highly improbable that people get married by the consideration of such an abstract idea, as what seems important is immediate personal satisfaction. The family regulates reproduction and gives training in communication and cooperation. The functions of a family include sexual gratification, protection, affection, cooperative pursuit of the physical necessities of life, satisfaction of gregarious cravings and the like. The bearing of children is an important function attributed to any family.

Maintenance: During the long period of infancy the child is to be fed, clothed and sheltered by parents or others. The health of the child is also to be taken care of and these functions are mainly executed by the family. There is no substitute for parental care even though other agencies do some work in this field. However, the intimacy and personal care so vital to the development of the child's personality cannot be obtained elsewhere. The common saying that 'there is no place like home' testifies to the fine sentiments developed in childhood.

Socialisation process: The family has the complete care of the child in its infancy. Other institutions and agencies enter the field only much later. The attitude of the child towards society will be greatly influenced by what it learns within the family. Out of the intimacy and affection in the family a 'we feeling' is developed among the members. The transmission of habits and attitudes from parents to children takes place. The social ranks of the child is based on its birth and the family, more than any other group, exerts a far-reaching and intimate influence on the attitudes of the child.

Transmission of property: Personal property in the form of land, buildings, money and other assets belonging to a family is transmitted to children. Every society has its own rules regarding property rights. In some societies, land is owned by the clan or tribe but in modern industrial societies there are clear cut rules of inheritance.

Cultural transmission: Family is one of the major agencies for transmitting culture to the young. The ideals and values of society are learnt from home. The family introduces the child to the world of values which enables it to enter into the wider world. Members of the family bound together by blood ties are the closest of the primary groups, and reciprocal sympathies and affections enable them to face many of the problems of life. Living together and sharing the joys and sorrows of the family help them to develop the spirit of mutual affection and sympathy. Social distances are eliminated and this close association of the family members is uinque. The affection among the members of the family continues even after they leave the ancestral home and establish their own homes.

The personality of the individual is greatly influenced by his family. Family members become models for children and their habits of cleanliness, honesty, integrity, kindness, hard work, self reliance and so on are reflected in one's character.

Psychological needs: Family provides the individual with the satisfaction of basic psychological needs. An individual's behaviour in society is moulded by physical urges like hunger and sex, and by acquired desires built on inherited equipment from stimulation of the environment. As W.I. Thomas and F. Znaniecki remarked, 'Every individual has a vast variety of wishes which can be satisfied only by his incorporation in society.' The four fundamental wishes W.I. Thomas and Znaniecki postulated in their work *The Polish Peasant in Europe and America* are: the desire for new experience; for security; for recognition; and for mastery. The sense of security is important to every man. An important function of the family, especially in western societies where there is much tension, is in providing emotional or psychic security. Independent nuclear families are especially associated with intimacy and emotional interdependence.

Marriageable Age

Marriageable age varies from society to society and from age to age. Child marriages which were common at one time are practically unknown in modern societies. The minimum permissible age for marriage is usually the age when sexual maturity is attained. In India the minimum marriageable age prescribed by law is 18 for women and 21 for men, and similar guidelines are followed by societies all over the world. In 1959 the median age for brides in the U.S., was 20.2 years and for grooms 22.7 years. There has been a slight change in the attitudes of people in the U.S. regarding marriage, especially early marriages. Realising this trend Margaret Mead warned Americans of the seriousness of such a change. 'Early student marriage is domesticating boys so early they don't have a chance for full intellectual development.' She said, 'I think it's bad for women, too.' This trend has also led to an increase in broken marriages in young age groups. She pointed out that parents were also to be blamed for this malady--those who had passed through the World War II and years of depression and uncertainties telling their children to 'take some enjoyment in life while you can get it. The future is totally uncertain.' There has also been the growing willingness of parents to pay for the education expenses of their married sons or daughters. One out of four college students in the U.S. is married and this gives rise to very many problems. There are two predominant types of young married couples: both studying in the same institution and cases where the wife leaves school, takes up a job and finances her husband in his studies. This may give rise to problems. The husband may grow intellectually while the wife stagnates. They live in different environments and their interests also may diverge. A feeling of inadequacy may develop in a man who is supported by his wife.

The increase in birth and divorce rates are matters of grave concern in most countries of the world. In densely populated countries of the world like India and China married people and advised to have fewer children and numerous family planning methods are encouraged. In contrast, countries like Sweden and New Zealand encourage parents to have more children as these countries fear a decline in their population. Countries with a high standard of living generally register a low population growth.

The tendency of girls getting married earlier than the boys is prevalent in most parts of the world. In the case of a man late marriage presents no serious problems while with a woman it does. In India women getting married after thirty are few and far between. In many societies a woman cannot propose marriage as this has to be done by the man; though in a leap year a woman could take the initiative in making the proposal. Among the Syrian Christians of Kerala where arranged marriages are common the initiative is taken by the girl's parents or relatives.

In most societies the wife is younger than the husband. Usually men prefer women younger than themselves, and women prefer men older than themselves. If the age difference is much, usually the woman has to pass through a long period of widowhood, as normally she lives longer than the man. There are people who argue that great difference in ages between the married couple may bring about unhappiness, but this has not been proved.

Mate Selection

In practice, mate selection follows two main patterns: arranged marriages and free will marriages. In countries like

India where arranged marriages are common, parents do most of the work and leave the final decision to the individuals concerned. A girl or boy is at liberty to voice frankly her or his opinions and parents generally don't impose their decisions on children. Parents and relatives make extensive enquiries about the people and families involved and then make up their mind. They also make their demands of dowry, ornaments and the like. In rural areas parents still play a dominating role and the dowry system is one of the greatest social evils facing Indian society. Various lagislations have been passed prohibiting dowry, but the age old practice continues under new names like girl's share of family property or presents. Domestic quarrels on this issue are also numerous.

In countries where there is freedom of choice, the children are not completely free. Parents and children alike face many problems. In a rural set-up where primary groups functioned, families knew each other so well that choice of a mate was not a serious problem. On the other hand, in an urban set-up where the relationships are secondary, the contacts tend to be superficial, and a couple making a hasty decision based on psychological and emotional reactions may eventually get into trouble. Parents, and numerous agencies like the church and community groups try to guide the young people in the right direction. Those who work in large establishments, get opportunities to meet a number of people. Universities, colleges and other educational institutions provide ample opportunities for making contacts, and it has been mentioned that some young women in America go to universities primarily for the purpose of finding mates. There is a tendency for people to seek mates of similar culture, educational achievements, social status, religious convictions and the like. This tendency of likes seeking like is called homogamy; while heterogamy is the tendency of choosing opposities. An individual has in his mind the picture of an ideal mate and in this he is motivated by qualities like sexual attraction, physical beauty, temperament, health, attitudes and so on. Attitudes, values and other sublime qualities can be understood only by close contact. In selecting a mate the individual aims at getting the maximum satisfaction. If there is mutual appreciation and like-mindedness, the personal relationship may be healthy. In all societies parents are anxious to see their children happy. They are also anxious about the social status of the family with whom they are going to be linked. Keeping this in mind they often use their influence in creating situations where their children could meet desirable mates. Selected clubs, and other associations help this. Parents take some interest in the courtship proceedings of their children.

Studies undertaken in the U.S. have shown that this influence is more than what it is ordinarily thought to be. Alan Bate has found that fifty per cent of the fathers and eighty per cent of the mothers exerted their influence over the courtship proceedings of their children. Seven out of ten fathers and all the mothers exerted influence over their daughters. Another study by Sussman Marvin called 'Parental participation in mate selection' showed that 85% of the parents expected the children to choose mates from backgrounds similar to their own, and in achieving this, they used various methods like persuasion, appeal to loyalty, and even threat to withdraw economic support if they wanted to marry from unacceptable families.

Very often brothers, sisters and close relatives help in mate selection by arranging contacts. There are numerous marriage service bureaus which help their clients in finding suitable matches. Marriages arranged through computers are also becoming frequent in western countries. In India some of the newspapers carry matrimonial columns which serve the interest of many. There are numerous private agencies engaged in arranging marriages for which they charge a fee.

In western societies marriage is preceded by courtship and betrothal. Courtship involves the association of unmarried men and women who try to explore the possibility of marriage. It starts with dating when the boy and girl take part in common activities which give them opportunities to enjoy each other's company. This period is also known as 'the hunting period' when they meet their opposite members and form judgements about them. Eventually someone is more liked than others and they begin to date regularly, and this is known as 'going steady.' They start learning each other's sentiments, values, aspirations, temperament and the like. Such intimate association leads them to a stage called 'falling in love' which leads to an understanding that they are going to get married. It is followed by betrothal for which the consent of the parents is sought by some while others make the decision and inform the parents. An engagement ring worn by the girl indicates her intention to get married. The engagement period may be brief of long depending on the circumstances of the couple.

In all societies there are ceremonial rites associated with marriages. In some societies these are elaborate and expensive while in others are quite simple and inexpensive. Such ceremonies signify society's control over its members. Among most Indian societies marriage ceremonies are expensive, especially to the girl's parents as they bear the brunt of the expenses. In western societies the ceremony is simpler and less expensive than in most eastern societies where people usually borrow money to meet the expenses. In India the couple are entertained in their own or in their relatives' homes, while it is the practice in most western societies for the couple to go honey-mooning away from home.

In pre-literate societies marriages were usually arranged by the families. In some parts of Africa a 'bride price' is paid to the woman's parents, and this practice is made to protect the interests of the woman. She is properly treated in her husband's home. The cattle or other materials given are to be returned to the kin group in case the marriage is dissolved and she has to return to her parent's home. In some societies the bride price helps to strengthen the mutual economic interests between brothers and sisters. Among the Kwoma of New Guinea an unmarried girl's virginity is guarded by her unmarried brother. If any of her sexual affairs are known, it would lower the bride price to be paid for her. Even if his sister is wrong he tries to hush up the matter. Dowry system is prevalent among many modern societies and this has its advantages and disadvantages.

Dissolution of Marriage

In modern western societies divorce is common. Every day over one thousand divorces are granted in the United States and the divorce rate in the U.S. is twice that of Swedon and four times that of England. In 1962 there was one divorce for every 3.9 marriages in the U.S. Majority of the divorces involve childless couples and they tend to occur in the first few years of marriage. Various studies on this subject have revealed many points. Religious groups generally have a rather uncompromising attitude towards divorce and this keeps the divorce rate low. People of some occupations like clergymen and teachers expected to behave perfectly in their family lives, and divorce may force them even to change their profession. On the other hand, actors, writers and others with many contacts with the opposite sex and almost free from the control of relatives or colleagues, tend to have a high divorce rate. A study undertaken in Sweden has shown the divorce rate of actors and artists as 21%; authors and journalists 16%; athletes 14%; officers 13%; clergymen's sons 6.5%; farmer's sons 6%; judges and magistrates 5%; teachers 4%; clergymen 2%. The younger age group tend to have a higher divorce rate than the older ones.

Grounds for divorce vary from country to country. The grounds usually recognised are adultery, cruelty, desertion, non-support, felonious crime and incompatibility. Many reasons lead to the increase in divorce rates. In the industrial nations of the world employment opportunities for women have considerably increased and thus the economic dependence of women on men has greatly dwindled. It is no longer necessary for most women to endure prolonged ill treatment from their men as they have independent means for their existence. This makes dissolution of marriages easy for women.

Religious attitudes are important in the matter of family adjustments. Among the Christians, the Catholic Church is not very lenient in granting a divorce, while some of the Protestant churches are liberal. In the U.S., in areas where Catholics form the majority, the divorce rates are lower than in other areas.

In almost all parts of the world the traditional family structure is undergoing changes. The patriarchal pattern which prevailed in western countries was authoritarian which allowed little chance of decentralisation, but this type of authority has disappeared. The family which at one time was the centre of economic, religious and educational activities is no more so in western society, and these roles are taken up by other agencies. In some of the Arab countries of the world, the old family pattern continues with slight modifications. The most important cause of the break-up of families is the inability of couples to make adjustments in family life. This may be due to economic difficulties or to undue parental interference. Great differences in education and religious beliefs may also aggravate the situation. Serious personality defects like alcoholism and psychopathic tendencies may foster the break-up of families. Personal disappointments in the marriage may also worsen the situation. Above all, the sanctity of married life is not given much significance as was done in the past, and this leads to divorces. Some of the functions of the family like the education of children, looking after the sick and the old are done today by other agencies and some of the special agencies perform these functions efficiently.

The economic responsibilities are fulfilled by the factory or office which provides the individual with his salary. The sick are treated in hospitals much more efficiently than they could have been in homes. Education of children is given much importance all over the world, and in countries like Russia and Sweden the government spends much money on it. When women go for work children are looked after the efficient teachers and this gives much peace of mind to the mother. In the factories and offices there are canteens providing food to the workers at prescribed times. The cradle-to-grave services provided by some governments greatly reduce some of the main functions of families. In the traditional family, old age was not a serious social problem. In most parts of the world aged parents live with their married sons or daughters who consider it their obligation to look after them. In western countries such sentiments are not in vogue and the responsibility of looking after the old is mainly fulfilled by the state or other private agencies. In some cases children occasionally visit them but neither the parents nor the children expect too much from each other. The expectancy of life also has increased in modern times.

The changing family structure of modern times reflects the attitude and values of the society where it exists. As Ernest Burgen wrote: 'The family is historical times has been, and at present is, in transition from an insituation to a companionship. In the past the important factors unifying the family have been external, formal and authoritarian as the law, the mores, public opinion, tradition, the authority of the family head, rigid discipline and elaborate ritual. At present, in the new emerging form of the companionship family, its unit inheres less and less in community pressures and more and more in such interpersonal relations as the mutual affection, the sympathetic understanding, and the comradeship of its members.'

RELIGION

At all times and in all ages religion has been a strong force in the affairs of man, and his inability to explain many of the mysteries of life has made him all the more aware of a power beyond his comprehension. Different people have given different interpretations to these questions, and the world moves on. Religious beliefs have found expression in different forms and practices. In some societies religions are simple cults with very few rituals or ceremonies, while in some other societies it is associated with elaborate forms of ceremonies conducted by professionals like witch doctors or priests. A religion like Christianity has become highly organised, while many others are not so well-organised. Some of the religions like Christianity and Islam, in the course of their growth, have brought about drifts within the group resulting in disharmony and even wars. There had also been religious wars like the crusades which had resulted in misery and hardship for many. Dawson has pointed out, 'Whenever and wherever man has a sense of dependence on external powers which are conceived as mysterious and higher than man's own, there is religion, and the feelings of awe and self-abasement with which man is filled in the presence of such powers is essentially a religious emotion, the root of worship and prayer.' Under such a liberal interpretation animism and magic could be brought under religion. Most religions have common characteristics like: *(a)* belief regarding an ultimate power in the universe which can be called metaphysics, *(b)* beliefs regarding the proper mode of behaviour or ethics, and *(c)* ceremonial ways of expressing the beliefs. A religion must be a social tradition rather than a pure personal philosophy.

There is much of emotion and devotion in religious behaviour. 'Religion is a system of beliefs, emotional attitudes, and practices by means of which a group of people attempt to cope with the ultimate problems of human life.' Some anthropologists have made extensive studies of religions in primitive societies. Edward Tylor, the 19th century anthropologist, considered religion 'as a belief in spiritual beings.'

In primitive societies religion has often been mixed with superstitions, magic and the like. Edward Tylor thought in terms of social evolution. According to him, animism was the beginning of all religions. The next stage of progress was polytheism, which was eventually superseded by monotheism. Though this type of animism-polytheism-monotheism change took place in Judaism, many other ancient civilisations had no such trends. Moreover, some of the primitive societies, un-influenced from outside, have developed pure monotheism. Thus social evolution as seen by Tylor is only partially true. Man's life in primitive China corresponded with the annual rhythm of nature. 'Human life was an aspect, a mirror, an imitation of the mysterious process of nature.'

In all societies superstitions of some form or other exist. In most parts of India the sight of a black cat, especially if it crosses one's path when one gets out of one's home, is considered a bad omen, and some even postpone their travel if such inauspicious signs occur. Similarly if one meets some low caste people when one sets out a journey, it is considered a bad omen.

Animism: In animism, the belief is that the spirits of the departed exist in some places or things and that they can communicate with human beings. There is another belief that the spirits are not of the dead, but are independent and inhabit trees or plants and are supposed to have special powers.

Fetishism: A fetish can be any object believed to have mysterious powers of good and evil, and those who possess it do so for bringing in good fortune or toward off any evil ones. Charms, amulets, images and the like belong to this category and wearing them is common all over the world. In the Second World War many soldiers carried charms in the hope that this would protect them from the dangers surrounded them. How fetishism originated is unknown, but it is probable that when two things happen in succession or together, the cause for one may be attributed to the other. Very often people seem to think that wearing of a particular dress or ornament may bring them good fortune and thus some kind of magical effect is attributed to them. Beliefs that have originated in the past still continue. Comte considered fetishism as the most elementary form of religion; but there are some who think that fetishims need not to be considered as a from of religion.

Totemism: Generally, it is a belief prevalent among some people , especially among some tribes, that they are connected with some animals or plants by descent. Thus totem animals, birds or plants are revered and well looked after. In some parts of north Africa lizards are well cared for by some tribes as these are considered totems. The totem animal is not killed or eaten, and the same is applicable to plants also. very often the name of the totem animal or bird is also accepted by its members. The writer, who has spent about eight years in Central and West Africa, was struck by the totemism followed in these countries and the efforts to please the totem. In the Buganda region of Uganda, mangoes are not eaten by some tribes as mango trees are totem trees for them, and when others eat the mangoes, they are viewed with suspicion. Thus mangoes in thousands are left to rot, though they could be exported to other countries. Clan totemism is only a variety of totemism. In Australia a number of types of totemisms prevailed. In some places there was sex totemism in which men and women were associated with two animal species. In some parts of New South Wales in Australia, the bat is the totem for men and tree creeper for women. 'In some parts of Australia the tribe is divided into two exogamous moieties, patrilineal in some regions, matrilineal in others. In some instances the moieties are named after species of animals, generally birds.' According to Freud totemism as the earliest form of religion was an effort to deal with guilt and repression.

Magic: 'Magic is a pseudo science, based on a false conception of causality, assuming a control over powers not understood, by means of which these powers are not subjected to the test of objective exploration. It is magic to sing an incantation over a wound. It is magic to stick a pin in a waxen figure in order to injure the person it represents. Magic pretends to control.' Magic is a technique by which certain things are supposed to be achieved by the administration of certain medicines. The operation of such medicines is a magic rite, and is usually accompanied by a spell. Evans Pritchard has mentioned, 'Witchcraft, oracles and magic are three sides to a triangle.'

Magic and religion are closely connected, and some even think that magic is a special form of religion or an aspect of it. There are a few basic differences between the two. In magic, the practitioner is trying to get things done by forcing the unseen forces to do it and at times even ordering them to do things. In religion the individual worshipper is seeking the help of God through prayer and supplication. In religion, apart from a man's relationship with God, there is also a relationship between man and man as is reflected through religious teaching, while such ties are absent in magic.

Magic is a pseudo science based on a false conception of causality. Like in religion, in magic also there is the idea that people can get in touch with forces beyond and the world of senses, and techniques are devised to get things done by these forces. According to Malinowski people generally resort to magic when they lack the practical ways of controlling the environment. He cites the example of the Tobrianders of Western Pacific to whom magic is a matter of everyday life. In safer places like the lagoon where fishings was comparatively easy magic was not used, while fishing in the open seas with its hazards demanded the use of magic.

Spiritism: Spirits are thought of as definite personalities. When people did not know much of the working of nature, they imagined that spirits existed which controlled the destinies of men. Evil spirits were often associated with neurotic and psychotic behaviour. There were attempts to please the spirits, and as the spirits were supposed to know what was happening, it was not possible to cheat them. This type of belief was common among the pre-literate societies, and still exists in various forms among some of the primitive people. For example, the Chaga of the Kilimanjaro mountain of East Africa worship ancestral spirits. Any calamity is attributed to the wrath of the ancestors.

Demon worship: People in different parts of the world had their beliefs about demons. The Siamese thought that apart from the demons in hell there were other sorts of demons diffused in the air. They thought that calamities were brought about by such demons who appeared in different shapes.

The ideas and images of a religion are to a great extent influenced by the culture in which they emerge. For example, in the African kingdom of Dahomey (now Benin) the religious hierarchy was somewhat similar to that of the administration of the kingdom. At the apex was the sky goddess who had divided the universe into many parts and entrusted her sons with them.

There are four basic elements underlying the functioning of any religion. Man realises that there are external forces which influence him and over which he has no control. He has very little knowledge of these external forces which some call god while others call the work of god or even mysteries. Then there is man's adjustment to supernatural forces and he becomes dependent on these beliefs. He is only happy to obey these forces. This results in a form of worship, which makes engage in singing hymns, praying, reciting the creed and other actions which may please the supernatural force. In primitive societies conformity was essential, while in modern societies those who stay out are not reprimanded. The concept of right and wrong develops and religion teaches as to what is acceptable to God and what is not. For example, the prophet Micah tells his followers: 'He hath showed thee, O man, what is good; and what doth the Lord require of thee, but to do justly, and to love mercy, and to walk humbly with thy God?' As man advances in age he becomes more and more aware of his impending departure from this transitory world and his craving for salvation develops. The Buddhist aims at the attainment of eternal bliss called Nirvana, the Hindu aims at the release of the bondage of Karma, the Muslim aims at heaven, and the Christian for salvation through Jesus Christ.

Emile Durkheim (1858-1917) in his *Elementary Forms of Religious Life* has pointed out that group life is the generating source of religion, and that religious ideas and practices symbolise the social group. Like Plato, Durkheim has emphasised the importance of religion as a source of social integration at a time when social dissolution was feared. Durkheim studies from secondary sources the Aruntas of Australia who had a very simple form of religion, namely totemism. The Arunats had their secular duties when they were scattered in small groups, when life, was dull, uniform and languid. However, when they met together for periodic sacred meetings of the clan, there was much emotional feeling and group euphoria. Participation in religious rituals and ceremonies gave the people a special social prestige. The participants in the religious gatherings get a sense of unity. Only when men meet together the systems of metaphysics and ethics gain meaning. Individual selves are transformed into collective experiences. Durkheim, considers this as communion with society. Some physical objects like an idol, cross or crescent become indentified as the material symbols of the supernatural power.

The recurring gatherings like that in prayer meetings give a feeling of group unity. The celebration of festivals in temples and the eucharist in the Christian churches develop this group feeling. Religion cannot be practised by individuals in isolation and it gains strength when done collectively. Durkheim defined religion as a 'unified system of beliefs and practices relative to sacred things uniting into a single moral community all those who adhere to those beliefs and practices.'

Herbert Spencer (1824-1903) suggested that the cult of ancestors is the basis of all human religions. 'Anything which transcends the ordinary, a savage thinks of as supernatural or divine; the remarkable man among the rest. This remarkable man may be simply the remotest ancestor remembered as the founder of the tribe; he may be a chief famed for strength or bravery; he may be medicine man of great reupte; he may be an inventor of something new. And then, instead of being a member of the tribe, he may be a superior being bringing arts or knowledge; or he may be one of a superior race predominating by conquest. Being at first one or other of these, regarded with awe during his life, he is regarded with increased awe after his death; and the propitiation of his ghost, becoming greater than the propitiation of ghosts less feared, develops into an established worship.'

George Simmel (1858-1918) developed a thesis that religion is the heightening and abstracting of various human relations exemplified in social life. Simmel mentioned that faith is basically a relationship between individuals which is an essential element in group life. Reinhold Niebuhr, a twentieth century theologian, has pointed out as to why religion persists even after three centuries of scientific development. He says that the basic trust in human relationships develops from the family where there is warmth and care. 'But life is full of ills and hazardous natural and historical evils, so that this child-like trust will soon be dissipated if maturity cannot devise a method of transmitting the basic trust of childhood, based on obvious security, to a faith which transcends all the incoherences, incongruities, and ills of life.'

Levi-Strauss had pointed out that the essence of religion is embodied in its symbol system (i.e. myths) which expresses the basic qualities of social reality. The German philosopher Rudolf Otto considered religion as the experience of the 'holy' which engenders a dialectic between two contrasting attitudes, awe and dread. Joachim Wach has mentioned that despite diversities all religions are characterised by systems of beliefs, worship and organisation. He referred to these as theoretical, practical, and sociological expressions of religion. Religion played a predominant role in all the civilisations of the world, and a historian like Arnold Toynbee has stressed the significance of this fact. The decline in religion in twentieth century Europe was considered by him as 'the supreme danger to the spiritual social health and even to the material existence of the western body social.' In primitive societies, religious observances were indispensable on all important events of a man's life like birth, marriage, illness, hunting, harvesting and planting, constructing houses or canoes, setting out on a journey, death and so on. Evans Pritchard has pointed out its significance among the primitive tribes.

A number of Marxists have developed the social interpretation of religion based on the theory of class struggle. Karl Marx's (1818-1883) remark 'religion is the opiate of the masses' shows the aversion he had towards religion. Communistic philosophy which is materialistic says that all phenomena are reducible to concrete and quantifiable elements. It is atheistic, and considers religion as an instrument used by the governing class to perpetuate their power by promising the downtrodden and oppressed a better life in the world to come. The Marxists implied the disapperance of religion in a lossless society. In their view early religion reflects ignorance of natural causes which could be explained animistically. They argue that religion both consciously and unconsciously becomes an instrument of exploitation. Religion has been a unifying force in all societies which made Durkheim say, 'Is it not, then, that God and society are the same thing?' In a society religion is the foundation upon which social values rest, and religion trains its members to accept them. There are moral obligations in a society, and the individual controls his own and other people's actions. Such social values are neither scientifically demonstrated nor rationally explained, but they are accepted as they are. Some of the social norms like respecting one's parents, honesty in ones dealing, are accepted in all societies, while abstract sentiments like 'truth alone triumphs,' 'do unto others what you expect others to do unto you' serve as guiding principles.

Religion provides a sort of peace of mind to the practitioner. When man is surrounded by all kinds of dangers and filled with all types of anxieties, he seeks the comfort and solace of God. Man tries to get this by various means like prayer, offerings and fasting. In times of extreme grief when others fail to console, his trust in God and the belief in God's providential care keep him reassured. The feeling that there are others also sharing his grief, and the consolation extended by them works as a shock absorber. In many ancient societies, the eldest member of the family performed religious functions like offering sacrifices to the gods and conducting religious rites. Elaborate rituals were to be conducted by priests specialised in their work usually after many years of studies. In some societies such priests were not allowed to marry, and were expected to be fully absorbed in their divine mission. The priests enjoy privileges and status in proportion to their duties and responsibilities. Usually monks and nuns devoting their lives entirely to their religions have been able to organise broad philanthropic, aesthetic, educational, and social activities.

Some of these activities can be called 'recreational' as it is an end in itself rather than means to an end. Music and other arts provide rest, refreshment and emotional experiences to the participants, and religious institutions provide these opportunities. Perplexities and mysteries exist in different societies at different times and in different circumstances, and hence the diversity in religion. However, all religions seem to have one common element--belief in the unknown.

Religion usually supports the society, but there have been instances when religious leaders have been critical of the secular powers. The prophets of the *Old Testament* spoke out what they thought right without fearing the wrath of the secular authorities. The history of Christianity is full of persecutions most of which came from the secular powers when they were either criticised or discredited by the religious authorities. In England the murder of Archbishop Becket and Cardinal Wolsey are classic examples of such punishments inflicted by kings for speaking out the truth. The church in Uganda faced persecution when it questioned some of Idi Amin's actions. In recent years bishops in some of the South American states have been faced with threats from the military authorities as they were championing the cause of the oppressed. When Hitler was in power in Germany, the Nazis believed that he was sent by God to save Germany.

In other parts of the world, especially in the western countries, a secular society is considered most desirable. In a secular society the laws are made by the legislatures and not by the divine will of God. Religious freedom is allowed. The theocratic or sacred society on the other hand, considers all the customs and institutions as of divine origin. Ritual observances are strictly adhered to and failures and misfortunes in life are attributed to one's own failure in observing the divine rules. In such a society religion regulates every aspect of human activity and even the lives of those who belong to other religions are to a certain extent regulated by the religious laws. Punishments also tend to be severe in such societies.

George Murdock, the anthropologist, remarks: 'The sociologist will do well to remember that for ninety-nine per cent of the approximately one million years that man has inhabited the earth, he lived, thrived, and developed, without any true government whatsoever, and that as late as a hundred years ago half the peoples of the world--not half the population but half the tribes or nations--still ordered their lives exclusively through informal controls without benefit of political institutions.'

Apart from the manifest functions of religion hitherto discussed, there are a few latent functions. In some parts of the world like Africa some of the pioneer explorers like David Livingstone were missionaries. They have opened the way for traders and later empire builders. For example, the Church Missionary Society which sent missionaries to Uganda in the 19th century paved the way for the establishment of the British empire in Uganda. The example of the English East India Company in India illustrates that the flag followed trade. In some parts of the world, missionary activities have unknowingly brought about changes in social structure.

Robert Merton who developed the concept of latent function cites the example of the Puritans of the 17th century England who played a prominent role in the development of science and industry. Francis Bacon (1561-1626) urged that scientific studies be encouraged in England as new knowledge meant new opportunities for invention. In 1662, the Royal Society was started by a royal charter, and it was directed not only to study things mathematical, philosophical and mechanical, but also to direct their minds to the improvement of all useful arts, engineering, manufacturing and the like. The Puritans who were a predominant force in the Royal

Society argued that the study of nature will result in the greater glory of God and the good of man. The aim of the Puritan scientists was the promotion of science which was latent function of religion. This led to new ideas about the universe which contradicted the teachings of fundamentalists who blindly believed in everything spoken of in the Old Testament. New knowledge also paved the way for the secularisation of modern societies.

Max Weber (1864-1920), in his work *The Protestant Ethic and the Spirit of Capitalism* deals mainly with the latent function of religion. Weber who studied different religions pointed out that modern capitalism in Europe emerged not only by inner economic necessity, but also by another motivating force--the religious ethics of Protestantism, especially Calvinism. There is a system of maxims of human conduct prescribed to the Protestants which he called 'the spirit.' The Calvinists believed in predestination which means that God has his plans for every individual and He knows beforehand as to what is going to happen to man. God's plans about the individual is not alterable and is kept unknown to man. Thus salvation is by the grace of God, and reserved for his chosen people. The attainment of salvation is sought after by all, but no one is sure as to what is going to happen to him. An individual is expected to conduct his life in an orderly and disciplined manner which is acceptable in the sight of God. In his secular life the Calvinist is expected to follow the principles of hard work, honesty thrift and trust in God. These virtues help one to succeed in life. He who is trustworthy and honest is small things is worthy to take charge of greater things. The parable of the talents illustrates this point: 'Well done, my good and trusty servant!' said the master. 'You have proved trustworthy in a small way; I will now put you in charge of something big. Come and share your master's delight.' The Calvinists thought that success in one's secular calling was an infallible indication of what is going to happen to one in the life after death. Max Weber pointed out that such an ethic helped the rise of capitalism in Europe, and this is a latent function of religion.

Religion and Science

All the major religions of the world originated before the time of Nicholas Copernicus (1473-1543) when their cosmology centred around the earth. The stars were considered as objects providing beauty to the earth at night, and not much was known of the sun or the planets of the sun. The rain or wind, thunder or lightning, hurricane or drought, sunshine or darkness and all such phenomena were explained in terms of the activities of gods. The god of thunder, the god of wind, the god of war, the god of plague and pestilence and numerous other gods were supposed to be active. The Hindu Puranas, the ancient literature of the Greeks and the Romans are full of accounts of the activities of various gods. Gods often interfered in the affairs of man and some even took sides. For example Poseidon, a Greek god, had been harsh towards Odysseus the renowned warrior of the Trojan war, while some other gods sympathised with him. Much of man's time and energy were spent in pleasing the gods through the performance of music, drama, dance, rituals, festivals and the like. To exalt the name of God, temples were built and wars fought. The quest for truth and scientific knowledge led to numerous scientific discoveries. The Renaissance in Europe was associated with a renewed interest in the pursuit of truth. When Copernicus said that it was earth which move around the sun and not the sun moving around the earth as was popularly believed, it created a sensation among the people of that period, as it was contrary to the prevalent cosmology.

Galileo (1564-1642), the famous Italian scientist, reiterated the Copernican theory that the sun was the centre of the universe and that the earth and other planets revolves around it. This theory was in opposition to the church which believed in Aristotle's view that the earth was the centre of the universe. The church reprimanded him, but he published a book supporting his beliefs. The Roman Catholic church found him guilty and sentenced him to imprisonment. However, some of his influential friends interfered and instead of imprisonment Galileo was restrained in a friend's palace in Florence. Whenever new theories unacceptable to the church have emerged the church has resisted them. The theory of evolution was discredited by the theologians though eventually many churchmen were able to modify their points of view. In this respect the Protestants were more liberal than the Catholics. 'Throughout Protestant intellectual history it had been widely though not consistently assumed that the results of independent scientific inquiry would tally, when properly interpreted, with Protestant teaching.'

Bishop Barnes of the Anglican church wrote: 'Man is the outcome of Nature's process. He is a product of the general scheme of the universe. No one of his faculties is entirely independent of his ancestry and environment. Without exaggeration we can assert that man's spiritual experience is as unreal as a dream unless the God to whom it leads him is also the God whose nature is shown in the universe as a whole.'

To say that religion has been an impediment to scientific truth is not right. As has already been an mentioned, one of the latent functions of the Protestant church in Europe, especially the Puritans in England, was the encouragement given to the pursuit of knowledge which resulted in new theories some of which were not acceptable to the fundamentalists. The Nestorian Christians of Persia were well-known for their contributions to the development of science.

The *Bible* contains the creation story and accounts of numerous other miracles are given. Other religions also have their numerous stories some of which may sound fantastic and unrealistic. However, it is to be noted that 'that religious, language is not scientific language, but with different concepts and necessarily more metaphorical; its aim is not the scientific aim, for it seeks after interpretation, not description. In short science and religion are incommensurables.' In the nineteenth century when there was a rapid scientific advancement and when many churchmen found it difficult to conform to scientific views, Dawson wrote, 'The Bible recognised progress and development in nature. At the very outset we have this idea embodied in the gradual elaboration of all things in six creative periods, rising from the formless void of the beginning, through successive stages of inorganic and organic being, up to Eden and to man. Beyond this point the work of creation stops but there is to be an occupation and improvement of the whole earth by man spreading from Eden.'

The scientist through observation and experiment tries to reach the truth but what lies outside his field of study remains unquestioned. Many new discoveries are made and many things which were mysterious at one time are no longer so. For example, in the field of food production scientific technology has brought about radical changes and the increased production is the result of man's effort. Diseases like plague, cholera and small pox are no longer considered as the wrath of gods as they once were. The causes of the diseases are known and remedies are discovered. Some of the mental diseases were attributed to the evil spirits. A hysterical man was considered as one 'possessed by the devil', but medical science has found out remedies for such mental diseases. 'Where science forges ahead, the supernatural recedes, becomes more vague and "symbolic."

Individual religious beliefs originate from personal convictions, and are also based on the belief that religion is revelation. Fascinated by the superb blending of language and style of the *Authorised Version of the Bible,* Newman has remarked that it can be nothing but revealed writing. Such convictions make a person a firm believer in religion.

Religion is not unscientific. It is non-scientific. It deals with a supernatural world which lies outside the realm of scientific observation and analysis. 'Man and society have been proved capable of surviving without science. That man and society can survive without religion is unproved.' The supernatural world in a sense is more important than the realm of science. History has shown that the role of religion has been of great significance throughout the ages. It is not possible to find God by scientific searching, though science need not stand as an impediment to religious belief. Arthur Thomson remarked: 'Science has come to mean so much to man--as torch to illumine and as rudder to control--that we cannot wonder at his desire to have it also as an aid to his faith. But this way lies disappointment. We cannot by scientific searching find out God. Science is impersonal and unemotional. We cannot base transcendent inferences on concrete data in regard to Nature. It is not by science that we can pass from Nature to Nature's God. The pathway is that of religious experience, just as the pathway to the vision of beauty is that of aesthetic discipline. It is possible, however, that science, with its disclosure of the order of Nature and all its wonder, may suggest and enhance the religious view.'

THE ECONOMIC SYSTEM

Man in the course of his life on earth has passed through various modes of economic life and the basic necessities like food, shelter and clothing were met in some form or other. In the food-gathering economy he was engaged in collecting products of nature like fruits and roots and also absorbed in hunting and fishing. He sheltered himself in caves or under shady trees and protected himself from cold weather by the hides of animals. There were practically no tools, and he likes other animals around him, was completely at the mercy of nature. The techniques of securing food varied, but fell into two major divisions: gathering and production. Gathering technique involved the utilisation of the resources of the environment as given, without any methods to improve or increase the available supply. When man began making tools, his life became easier as he could defend himself more efficiently and procure food faster. The knowledge gained was also transmitted from one generation to another. In some parts of the world progress has been very slow while in some other parts this has been much swifter. Agriculture and domestication of animals made changes in the life pattern of man. This led him to settle in places where there was grass and water and the fertile valleys of rivers became centres of organised life.

The Indus, the Ganges, the Yellow river, the Nile, the Euphrates, the Tigris were some of the important rivers which gave rise to the ancient civilisations of the world. The hoe, the plough, making woollen and cotton clothes, building of canoes and store-houses, use of stones and bricks in construction and numerous other inventions made life easier. Horses, dogs, cattle, donkeys, buffaloes, reindeer and numerous other animals were domesticated and so were birds, especially poultry. The invention of pottery and the use of fire to cook food made life more pleasant. Tools and animals became indispensable to agriculture as they reduced the physical fatigue of man. In fact some animals like dogs and horses have become very useful to man. In some of the societies where agriculture was predominant, hunting also existed, thereby effecting a sort of mixed economy.

Social anthropologists note that some of the pre-literate societies of the present day practise both hunting and agriculture. Settled life paved the way for progress, and social organisations developed. Property ownership also emerged and the possession of land was either on an individual or collective basis, but in most cases the fruits of one's labour was not enjoyed by oneself. For instance, among the Buganda tribes in Uganda sharing the meal with other tribesmen is a way of life and as such starvation is not experienced unless there is some serious drought, or some great calamity like the one that occurred during Idi Amin's reign of terror in the 1970s. Sharing of fish or flesh by all the members is common among many tribes in different parts of world.

In the hunting stage, when much of the hard work was done by man while the woman was engaged in less strenuous jobs, there was male predominance in society. In the pastoral stage also this predominance prevailed, as pastoral life more or less resembled the life of hunters. The pastoral people were highly mobile and their housing was also light and portable like tents. On the other hand, agriculturists lived in permanent homes looking after their land and animals. The ways of the pastoral people were associated with marauding expeditions when horses and camels enhanced their mobility and this was specially true of the desert dwellers. Some of the tribes like the Tuaregs of the Sahara still lead a wandering life, while a pastoral people like the Fulanis of Northern Nigeria have undergone many changes in recent years. Life has been rather harsh to the pastoral people as drought may decimate their animals and men.

The mode of life and mode of religious beliefs depend on the environment and the type of occupation one is engaged in. Max Weber points out that farmers who are subjected to the vagaries of nature which affect their economic life tend to believe not in a rational theology but in magic. On the other hand, traders and craftsmen develop ideas of honesty which proves beneficial to them.

Agricultural Revolution was a major leap forward. Thus in the last three thousand or four thousand years the life of man has changed more radically than in all the preceding millenniums. Before the agricultural revolution there would have been great anxiety among men as to the availability of their daily bread, but as man learned to produce food instead of gathering it, and storing it in the bins the mode of life of man completely changed. This enabled him to settle in large communities and the leisure helped him to follow non-agricultural pursuits.

When settled life was made possible a kind of mixed economy emerged. In the early economy there was no room for profit. Goods were produced in sufficient quantities to meet needs, and along with it some of the non-agricultural products like baskets, wooden implements, metal works, pottery works and the like were developed. In the early economy, goods were exchanged as gifts and there was much emphasis on hospitality. Entertaining of guest was known in all societies, and this was reciprocal. There were ceremonial occasions when entertainments were lavish, and usually these were at the harvesting season when there was plenty to eat. Both the giver and the receiver were happy about the exchange of gifts and entertainments. Conspicuous consumption prevailed in societies where there was an economic surplus, and a study of this provides profound insight into the psychology of prestige economics.

The spending spree at the wedding feasts and festivals in Indian societies is to display one's economic position and social status. Among the tribals such display was common, and a person who practises the potlatch gets nothing back except the satisfaction that this would impress others. In some societies, for example during the Kwakiutl potlatch, thousands of valuable blankets were burned, several canoes broken and a slave killed to establish a chief's prestige and importance. At the funerals of some African chiefs the goods placed on the grave were either given out to the visitors outside the family or destroyed and there was much display of wealth on such occasions. Such practices are prevalent among many societies in India. On ceremonial occasions the Ashanti chief of Ghana wears and expensive silk cloth while the commoners wear cotton clothes. The potlatch institution which aims at lavish display of material wealth has been prevalent among tribes in Africa, America and elsewhere. In some places the hospitality extended towards strangers is not for getting back anything, but for the satisfaction of the giver. Thus the financial decisions of many were not motivated by the desire to get back what was spent, but to gain distinction. As Kroeber points out, 'All in all the array of cases is significant in showing that the actual historical behaviour of cultures cannot be predicted from an a priori notion that practical utility--economic motivation--is invariably determinative.'

When men began a settled life and organised forms of society emerged, there also arose the need to protect themselves from eternal aggression. Those who lived in the fertile regions with economic prosperity were vulnerable to attacks from outside, and history is a record of such occurrences. In an agrarian society land ownership was the basis of wealth and the desire to increase one's landed property by purchase, marriage or force prevailed. In different parts of the world different types of land tenures emerged. In most societies land belonged to a few while cultivation was carried out by their agents who had their duties and rights. In the feudal set-up there where the few who enjoyed at the expense of the toilers. Slavery and serfdom were characteristic features of the early agrarian societies. The discovery of America and the opening of colonies there by the Europeans paved the way for slave trade. Slaves and indentured labourers were employed in the development of the colonies. For example, for the building of railways in South Africa and East Africa, indentured labourers were sent from India.

Large scale agriculture motivated by profit led to the exploitation of the weak and the ignorant. It was in 1833 that slavery was abolished in the British empire. In course of time this great social injustice was blotted out from most parts of the world. The agrarian revolution of the 18th century which was a prelude to the Industrial Revolution brought about improvement in the production of food and this had its effect on the health of the people. The enclosure system brought much of wasteland under cultivation and food production increased. In England 'the age of enclosure was also the age of new methods of draining, drilling, sowing, manuring, breeding and feeding cattle, making of roads, rebuilding of farm premises and a hundred other changes, all of them requiring capital.'

Before the Industrial Revolution, agriculture and handicraft economy prevailed in most societies. In pre-industiral economy, activities like cultivation, tool-making, house-building, cloth-making and so on were done by different people and were beyond what a single family could handle. Specialisation and division of labour emerged and these services were paid for in goods or money. The processing of raw materials into finished goods was done by craftsmen whose work required many years of practice and learning. The Industrial Revolution hit hard the craftsmen who possessed highly specialised skill whose work was now superseded by machines. 'This is a real loss; but it is a limited one which must be set off against the general gain--to the consumers in cheapness and to the labourers generally through the subsequent expansion of trade.' In India crafts like carpentry, masonry and weaving were hereditary occupations making use of simple tools. A tool is a comparatively simple instrument for aiding or augmenting the natural powers of man, and is used directly by the worker. Hammer, sickle, knife, spear and the like are simple tools the power which gives them force is the human muscle. With the rise of the Industrial Revolution, muscle power was replaced by machines.

The Industrial Revolution made drastic changes in English economic and social life. Hergreaves' spinning jenny, Arkwright's flying shuttle, and Crompton's mule for spinning thread revolutionised the textile industry. In 1769 James Watt made as steam engine which marked the beginning of a new era of progress. MacAdam, a Scottish engineer, made better roads and the macadamisation of roads, as the new process was known, enabled wheeled carriages to move smoother and faster. Stephenson made the first railway engine. The invention of steam ships, motor cars, telegraphic system, printing press and numerous other devices paved the way for revolutionary changes in England. 'Thanks to a series of remarkable mechanical inventions, England, which had for centuries been a granary and a sheepfold, was suddenly transformed into the workshop of the world. Parallel to the manufacturing revolution, and practically coincident with it, there had taken place in agricultural methods changes which revolutionised the rural economy of England.' Other European nations like Germany, France, Holland, and Sweden and the United States of America also benefited. The Industrial Revolution gave rise to competition within the state among capitalists, and outside between nations trying to sell their goods. 'The industrial revolution gave this competition a new focus--wealth through industrialisation--and turned it into a chase. There was one leader, Britain, and all the rest were pursuers. This lead has since changed, but the pursuit goes on in what has become a race without a finishing line.'

This period also witnessed an increased activity in scientific research, which had its beginning at the time of Roger Bacon (1214-1294) who insisted on the importance of experiments in science. He made discoveries in optics, explosives, engines and mechanical flight. In the 18th and 19th centuries many scientific discoveries were made in the field of medicine which improved the health of people. Edward Jenner (1749-1823), an English country doctor, discovered vaccination as a means of preventing small pox. Sir James Simpson (1811-1870) was the first to use chloroform as an anaesthetic. Sir Ronald Ross (1857-1932) discovered the parasite that causes malaria. Modern nursing system originated from the time of Florence Nightingale (1820-1910).

Alfred Nobel (1833-1896), a Swedish scientist, invented

dynamite which brought about drastic changes in construction works though it happened to be a dreadful source for lethal weapons. Thus a new era of science dawned which led to large-scale exploitation of non-renewable resources of the earth. It also led to the establishment of colonies by major European power like the British, the French, the Portuguese, the Germans and the Dutch. The prevalent notion in England was that the colonies served to take off our product and manufactures, supply us with commodities which may either be brought up here or exported again, or prevent fetching things of the same nature from other places for our home consumption, employ our poor and encourage our navigation.' Another important result of the Industrial Revolution was a gradual shift of population from the rural to the urban regions. Heavy industries were concentrated in some of the large cities like London, Birmingham, and Manchester and this gave rise to numerous problems. In India, Calcutta and Bombay began to emerge as important industrial cities. The development of international trade triggered the growth of seaports some of which like London, Liverpool, New York, Rotterdam, Antwerp, Marseilles, Bombay, Colombo, Singapore and Hong Kong, became important entrepot cities.

There were regions which were practically unaffected by these developments and where people still use the barter system. In the regions around the Sahara traders used caravan routes linking commercial centres like Kano and Timbuctu. Economic activities took place in the oases of deserts. Similarly many other parts of the world which were unaffected by the industrial growth carried on their economic activities in their own convenient ways. There are some important factors connected with the production process. The basic requirements are raw materials, land, labour, capital and organisation. Very often industries are started where raw materials are readily available, but this is not always the case. Britain and Japan import most of the raw materials from other parts of the world and sell manufactured goods to other countries.

United States has or produces most of the raw materials required for her industries, while India, though it has most of the raw materials, is heavily dependent on other countries for oil. Some of these countries like Kuwait, Saudi Arabia, Oman, Venezuela and Nigeria are mainly dependent on oil for their income. Some other countries are dependent on their agriculture. Land is an important factor in production and the farmer and the miner depend on it. Factories, offices and numerous productive agencies rest on land. Similarly, water is also an important source of wealth and in modern times the drilling for offshore oil, and fishing have added to its importance. For example, North Sea oil forms an important aspect of British economy. Each nation zealously guards its territorial waters and international law prescribes the limits of such claims.

Capital is another important feature of modern economic system. As large investments are required for companies, money is collected from the shareholders and some of the pioneers in the field were the English East India Company, The Hudson Bay Company, and the Royal Africa Company. When the liabilities of the shareholders were limited to their shares, it was possible to attract more capital. Modern industries require much capital for buildings, machinery, and payment of wages. Worn-out machinery has to be replaced and other commitments have to be met.

Managerial system is an important aspect of modern industry. Unlike cottage industries where a few managed the whole work, modern complex industries require highly skilled professional staff to manage them. They need not be shareholders but they are selected and trianed to become managers. According to Professor Galbraith this powerful group is the technostructure. The shareholders elect the directors who have the ultimate control of the affairs of the company, but the highly skilled professional take care of the administration. Some of the modern industries like the General

Motors with six hundred thousand employees or the Shell or Caltex or Unilever with branches in different parts of the world need efficient administrative machinery to run their gaint industrial organisations and this is met by an efficient bureaucratic system. In the years following the Second World War, there has been a tendency for an equitable distribution of shares and at present the number of shareholders in some of the large companies in the U.S. reaches a million. Employees are also becoming shareholders and this trend is found to an appreciable degree in Japan.

Labour is necessary for the production of goods and a fair portion of the value of the commodity can be attributed to it. Labour can be defined as 'any exertion of mind or body undergone partly or wholly with a view to some good other than the pleasure derived from the work.' Alfred Marshall adds that 'It would be best to regard all labour as productive except that which failed to promote the aim towards which it is directed, and so produced no utility.' Like other commodities, the price of labour is determined by the principle of demand and supply. Usually the supply of labour is greater than demand and this is particularly true of agricultural countries of the world with large populations. Mobility of labour from one country to another is restricted by various regulations and the rights and liberties of labourers differ from country to country.

Adam Smith believed that if there were no trade restrictions each country would specialise in industries which are most profitable to them. He did not favour the idea of government supporting any industry as free competition was the right path to success. Adam Smith (1723-1790) was not in favour of the theory of mercantilism which dominated the thinking of the 17th and 18th centuries Europe. The mercantilists thought that wealth meant an increase in the supply of a nation's gold and silver, but Adam Smith argued that money was a medium of exchange and what was significant was its power to produce goods. Production was to increase with specialisation and for this it was necessary to have capital and market. He favoured free trade instead of protectionism. The state was not to regulate the economy, but it should allow the economy to regulate itself. In a free economy the price was determined on the basis of demand and supply. In a competitive market the entrepreneur undertakes many risks, and he is answerable to the shareholders for his actions. Thus for the risk he undertakes and the skill he commands, he is entitled to a large percentage of the profit, while the labourers' share is little. Adam Smith thought that labourers without much skill and with no risk to undertake were to be provided with subsistence wages only. He believed that 'laissez-faire' (to let alone), without any governmental interference in industries, is conducive to industrial expansion.

Two other Economists of that period were David Ricardo (1772-1823) and Thomas Malthus (1766-1834) whom Thomas Carlyle referred to as the respectable professors of the dismal science. Malthus tried to reduce population variations to a simple principle, that whereas food supplies rarely increase faster than in arithmetic progression, population tends to increase in geometric progression. Ricardo favoured the 'iron law of wages' which stated that if the labourers got much money, they may not work hard and may have more children who when they grow up may not have sufficient jobs. David Ricardo and the physiocrats of the 19th century thought that in natural society there was a horde of unorganised individuals who thought in terms of self-interest and self-preservation.

In Britain and other parts of the world individualistic capitalism began to grow. The steam engine had a major impact on production and it freed manufacturing from the limitations of water power. Steam power when used for water and land transport increased the market and enabled greater distribution of labour and wealth. Karl Marx was so much impressed by this transformation that he wrote 'the handmill gives you the society with the feudal lord; the steam mill, society with the industrial capitalist.'

Capitalism is based on profit motive and profit is considered as the reward the capitalist gets for his services, especially in taking risks. If the capitalist thinks that labour is only the cost of production which should be kept at a minimum level, labour becomes depersonalised. Some of the capitalists justified their stand and as London *Economist* wrote in 1848, 'Suffering and evil are nature's admonitions, they cannot be got rid of; and the impatient attempts of benevolence to banish them from the world by legislation, before benevolence has learnt their object and their end, have always been more productive of evil than good.' The Industrial Revolution brought about a new class structure. The old Monorial system by which the tenants were bound to the Manorial lord by customs and traditions disappeared. They became free and independent workers and the traditional occupational patterns also underwent changes. People were at liberty to choose any work they liked, so long as there was demand for them. The workers gained a new dignity which they never had under the Manorial system. The guild system also had lost its significance and a new order of society was in the making.

Karl Marx made a distinction between the economic structure of a society and the superstructure. The technology of production and the social relationship which arises when people work together to produce goods make the economic structure. The economic structures are basic and they determine everything else, and the superstructure also falls within its purview. It is through the social classes, the bourgeoisie and the proletariats, that the economic structure gives rise to the superstructure. The superstructure comprises institutions like law, educational institutions, church, the army, and the government. In capitalism the superstructure serves the interest of the bourgeoisie and they invariably control the institutions. The armed forces, the judiciary and every other institution aims at keeping the workers under submission. Those who have power and authority can keep the workers under submission. Laws are passed for the advantage of the bourgeoisie and the police put down strikes and demonstrations. Economic forces of society control political force. In a competitive economy the machinery undergoes improvement and productivity increases. As Simmel points out, 'Countless times it fulfils that service which besides itself love alone fulfils, for it discerns the inmost wishes of another before they have become conscious even to himself.' Marx argued that with the improvement in machinery the capitalist benefits. 'Eventually an hour of each worker's labour yields several times as many products as it did before.' However, the miseries of the workers increase and they agitate against capitalists. Ultimately the capitalist system is overthrown and the workers themselves manage the affairs. The improved machinery makes the lot of the worker easier and he gets more leisure. It is only through political force or revolution that the economic system is destroyed.

Unions eventually began to feel their strength and the union representatives were allowed to gain a fair place at the negotiating table where they bargained with their employers over various issues. At times when the different unions join together in a strike an entire nation is paralysed. Apart from better working conditions and wages the unions have gained benefits for the workers like grievance procedures, seniority regulations, non-discriminatory employment policies, sick leave, vacation pay and in some cases old age pensions.

Apart from factory workers there are organisations of employers, farmers, teachers, doctors, engineers and so on, some of them very influential. Professional associations are found in almost all societies and they try to promote the interests of the practitioners of a particular profession. Farmers Union in India are gaining strength but are not so powerful or organised as in the United States where they exert their influence over the government. There is much lobbying when pressure groups try to exert their influence in matters of legislation affecting them. 'A pressure group is a formal organisation composed of people with common interests or occupations who seek to secure desired legislation by improving their communication with their legislators'. The employers, merchants and businessmen have their associations, and some of them like the Chambers of Commerce are influential in most countries.

In the pre-industrial-revolution era workers were considered as a source of energy, but the introduction of steam engine made vast changes and 'the workers became adjuncts in the new factory system.' In some parts of the world, especially in Soviet Russia and China, the economic system is that in which all producers' goods and services are owned and controlled by the government. However, in these countries also changes are taking place in matters of production. For example, individual farmers are allowed to cultivate wheat and other grains which is a deviation from the orthodox theory of state farming. Efforts were made by some to find out the psychology of workers and owners as to production in factories. An American engineer named Fredrick Taylor brought out the concept of scientific management in industry. It envisaged that if a work is more specialised, workers would become more efficient, thereby increasing the production. Taylor and his colleagues thought that in factories workers were motivated by material benefits only and that if material rewards were closely linked with work output, the workers will gladly respond and production will increase. They tried to find out which physical motions were the least tiring for a person to do his work in the prescribed time, and these came to be known as time and motion studies. They developed ways of reducing the number of physical motions performed by factory workers in carrying out their work. Many industrialist welcomed the Scientific Management idea, but it was eventually found that the workers' response was not so cheerful as

Taylor thought, though they learned many new devices for improving production. It was found that the amount of work done is not determined by a worker's physical capacity as was suggested by Taylor, but by his social capacity.

It was also found that specialisation was not always the most efficient form of division of labour and that workers' response to the norms and rewards of management was not as individuals, but as members of groups. Such qualities like group interest and group loyalty were predominating characteristics and these were demonstrated by Elton Mayo and his associates who researched in the Western Electric Company's Hawthorne plant in Chicago (1927-1932). The researchers stressed the human aspect of labour as against the physical and mechanical aspects stressed by Taylor. They pointed out that fatigue may result from boredom and that increase in the production rate was the result of social factors. In a factory the workers are under the supervision of a foreman who tries to carry out the plans of the management. A foreman is a formal leader, but in every group there is an informal leader whose opinions carry greater weight than that of the formal leader. The social norms of production are decided by him. The members who produced more or less than the socially accepted norm lost the friendship and respect of other workers. Elton Mayo stressed the personal and informal aspects of the organisation while the classicists reviewed this on rational economic terms.

Peter Drucker, after an elaborate study of the human relations approach came to the conclusion that the social function of enterprises is very important. 'They (the workers) placed the fulfilment of their demands for social status and function before and above the fulfilment of their economic demands.

One of the schemes followed in modern industries is the profit-sharing device by which the workers get a fair share of the profit of the company based on their salary structure through bonuses. Bonuses are either paid in cash or deposited into funds meant for pension and other social security schemes. In some cases bonuses are converted into shares, thereby making the workers share owners of the company. This practice is found all over the world, and especially in Japan, where industrial labourers are getting a fair share in the control of industries. In some companies the son of a worker is allowed to take up a position on the retirement of the father.

There is also an increase in the profit of the company as the workers become more responsible. Industrial expansion has given rise to numerous problems, one of which is the business cycle. During periods of prosperity there is full employment, while depression is associated with unemployment, and though some of the states provide unemployment benefits to the workers the amount is just enough to keep the wolf from the door. Living on doles hurts the feelings of the receiver and constant unemployment leads to despair. In modern times inflation has become another threat in many countries. One of the greatest economists of this century, John Maynard Keynes (1883-1946), had many suggestions regarding full employment and general prosperity. Keynes was not in favour of the law of markets expounded by J.B. Say (1767-1832). Say's law held over-production to be impossible. Keynes was of the opinion that the government should control the economy and should regulate, where necessary, free enterprises. The imbalances resulting from the capitalist economy could be corrected by government action.

Unemployment and depression bring about calamities and he treats unemployment as a symptom of technical fault in the capitalist mechanism. He wrote, 'The state will have to exercise a guiding influence on the propensity to consume, partly through its scheme of taxation, partly by fixing the rate of interest and partly, perhaps, in other ways. Furthermore, it seems unlikely that the influence of banking policy on the rate of interest will be sufficient by itself to determine an optimum rate of investment. I conceive, therefore, that a somewhat comprehensive socialisation of investment will prove the only means of securing an approximation to full employment, though this need not exclude all manner of compromises and devices by which public authority will co-operate with private initiative.'

'The problem of want and poverty and the economic struggle between classes and nations is nothing but a frightful muddle, a transitory and unnecessary middle.' He found that individual savings can have the effect of slowing down the economy if it is not reinvested for productive purposes. Such a state of affairs may lead to depression. However, new discoveries or other sources of new investment could alter the situation, or a war with its wasteful expenditure could solve unemployment. The second alternative is frightening while the first is uncertain.

Keynes argued that the solution is for the government to spend money in large quantities, if necessary by deficit financing, to escape from the calamity of depression. Keynes' ideas were appreciated in many parts of the world, especially in the U.S. at the time of the great depression. The industrial system in its quest for greater production result in the rapid exploitation of resources. In some countries forests have been devastated resulting in ecological imbalance. Water pollution and atmospheric pollution are constant threats to industrial societies. The dumping of industrial waste, especially waste from nuclear plants, is a major problem.

Capitalism has its flaws and often it has met with a crisis of some form or other. The Russian Revolution took place before the First World War ended, and it led to numerous economic changes in Russia. The collectivisation of farms brought about a thorough change in the ownership of land. The depression after the First World War brought about untold miseries to many in Europe, and taking advantage of this the Nazis came to power in Germany and the Fascists in Italy. India was agitating for independence. In the 1930s the Indian economic structure was capitalistic. Except for the Post and Telegraph and a few other governmental agencies, the main industries were privately owned. The railways, shipping companies, city bus and tram services, cotton mills, iron and steel industries, banks and numerous other enterprises were privately owned.

The World War II which began in 1939 was followed by many changes in the post World War years. Europe was divided into two camps. In the Russian dominated Eastern Europe state-owned enterprises prevailed while in the rest of Europe free enterprise along with state enterprises continued. The latter economic structure is called mixed economy. Some of the major essential services were brought under the control of the government. For example the post-war Labour government of Britain nationalised some of the industries like steel, and airlines, and similar tendencies were found in the rest of Western Europe.

In North America too governmental control over industries increased and mixed economy emerged. Australia and Japan too followed a mixed economy. Some of the social philosophers like Joseph Schumpeter predicted the displacement of capitalism by socialism in the years following 1949. Europe devastated by war was on the brink of collapse when the Marshall aid programmes were introduced in West European states. This brought about a dramatic recovery of European economy which led to her political stability. Even some of the problem states like Greece, Austria and Spain progressed under mixed economy.

Countries like India, Taiwan, Maxico, Singapore, Hong Kong, Thailand, South Korea follows mixed economy. The prophesied time table of inevitability--savagery to feudalism,

feudalism to capitalism, capitalism to socialism, socialism to communism--has not so far materialised. The newly emerged independent nations like India, Burma, Sri Lanka, Malaysia, Ghana, Nigeria, Algeria, Ivory Coast and Indonesia have devised various schemes to develop their economy. India has adopted her five year plans and accepts a socialistic pattern of society. Some countries like Ghana and Nigeria had a good start but stumbled in their economic experiments which have led to changes in the form of government. Ghana under Nkrumah, Indonesia under Sukarno and Argentina under Peron were noted for corruption and nepotism.

Political changes in Afghanistan, Ethiopia, Cuba and so on are associated with changes in economic institutions. A comparatively new state like Israel, through hard work and economic assistance from the U.S., has come to prominence. Invariably all the states in the world are striving for economic prosperity, though some through lack of leadership, lack of dedicated workers, corruption and nepotism are lagging behind other countries which are striving forward with determination to achieve progress. The main characteristics of a socialistic pattern are the government ownership of productive resources like railways, and of coal, steel and other mineral deposits. In some countries the enthusiasm for nationalisation is dwindling as production in such industries is not up to expectations like in the U.K., Sweden and West Germany. Instead of allowing the free play of profit motive as in a laissez faire market economy, co-ordinated planning is introduced. Sometimes there may not be a profit motive in running some of the industries which are essential for man. There is also a redistribution of income. Social security schemes like unemployment and old age pensions, free medical services are administered.

Cradle to grave welfare services are aimed at. In socialism the stress is on peaceful and democratic evolution. Political changes are by ballot and not by bullet. Another important change taking place in the economic structure is the change in the mode of production. Automation and the computer are bringing about tremendous changes in industries and even in the everyday life of man. Such innovations had taken place in the past also. Electricity was such an innovator. When electricity was used for industrial and household purposes the demand for electrical appliances greatly increased. For example in Germany in 1882 the number employed in this industry was insignificant but by 1895 the number increased to 15,000. By 1902 the number increased to 50 thousand, by 1910 to about hundred thousand. In 1927, one single electrical concern in Germany employed more than 110 thousand workmen. It showed the tremendous demand for electricity in Europe and elsewhere. Lenin was so very fascinated by the potentialities of electric power in the transformation of society that he adopted the slogan 'Soviets plus electrification equals socialism.' In automation the human control of production is replaced or improved by some type of automatic process.

According to Samuelson it is the 'automatic handling of parts between progressive production process.' When computers are fully used in automation the word 'cybernetics' is used. Very complicated mathematical calculations which may take hours for a man to do are done in a matter of minutes by computers with precision, and order are accepted and carried out promptly by the silicon chips. The landing of man on the moon, the control of satellites from the control stations, automatic landing devices in aeroplanes, controlling the working of machines in factories, and numerous other works are made possible by computers. Its potentialities are felt in education, medical science, engineering, industries and even in everyday life. There are marriage bureaus working on computers. Personnel management, banks, and library administration have been made easy by the introduction of computers. In industrial countries children are taught computer languages and how to operate computers. In the field of agriculture also its effect is felt. In the U.S. and Canada, for example, large combine harvesters or ploughing and sowing machines are operated by computers so that the farmer can, from his farm house, control the operations of these machines through remote controls.

Such technological innovations have their effects on the economy. Production increases and the need for labourers decreases. This has given rise to alarm. For example, in the United States in the past few years there has been a loss of 435,000 railroad jobs, 265 thousand in textile mills, 310 thousand jobs in coalmines, and 3,600,000 jobs in agriculture. This gives rise to numerous problems especially in absorbing them in other industries. In countries where there is a high degree of unemployment, automation may aggravate the unemployment situation, but it could be used in industries which are difficult to be properly managed by human beings.

The rising population of the world and the introduction of sophisticated computer machines may disturb the existing equilibrium of the economy. However, such fears have been prevalent ever since the industrial revolution started. It was feared that new technologies would create unemployment. The new technology has made many traditional skills redundant, reduced employment in the old industrial centres, and generated fluctuations in the rates of growth and unemployment. These are very costly social consequences of technological innovations. However, the bright side of the innovation is the reduction in hours of work and consequent availability of leisure to the worker. Labour per unit is substantially reduced. Reduction in price or improvement in quality may increase the demand for goods thereby generating employment. There is also the need to earn a reputation for the high standards of goods produced. Japanese electronic goods are in demand all over the world as they are of a high standard. The Japanese have earned this name by their dedication and hard work.

In the developing countries of the world where more and more sophisticated machinery is used, the number of direct production workers like mechanics, bricklayers and farmers is steadily declining. They are being replaced by 'knowledge workers.' They are people 'who are paid for putting knowledge to work rather than using brawn or manual skill.' They from the largest single group in the American labour force of the present day.

EDUCATION

Education is a training of the young for the adoption of adult roles. In modern times education means formal training by specialists within a formal organisation like a school. 'In one sense, education is the total experience of the infant, child, and young adult as preparation for full membership in adult society. Anything that happens to the child, any experience he may have, is thus educational.' It is also an important factor in socialisation. The early years of one's life is the period when one learns most from others and thus 'educational can be viewed as including all communicating of knowledge and shaping of values; in this sense it is synonymous with socialisation.' In pre-literate societies education was enculturation which is the process of cultural transmission. In such a society, a man has a fixed sense of cultural continuity and timelessness. As for the members in such a society with limited horizons, the mode of life is comparatively static and absolute and transmission of culture undergoes no change.

In pre-literate societies parents and elders taught art or craft, folklores and religious beliefs, making of various utensils and numerous other things to the youngsters. When they hunted animals they were taught the use of bow and arrow, how to detect an animal from its scent or sound of movement, and when an animal was caught how to skin it and preserve the meat. It took years for a young man or woman to learn the ways of life of the elders, but they learnt them well as these were of immense significance to them. In some pre-literate societies young men and young women had their separate dormitories where they got graining for their future life. Institutionalised learning was thus made possible which helped the youngsters to fit in well as members of their society. For instance the Amphlett islanders of the Western Pacific whose women were good in pottery were trained in this art by their elders. To the Argonauts of the Western Pacific fish was an important item of food, and they were good in canoe building. Canoe building was a communal labour when the young learnt the trade from their elders. In tribal societies there was great stress on training for citizenship which centred around communal life. Private property was limited to a few things and most of the activities were to be conducted in groups. Tribal loyalty was important, and tribal chief's orders were implicitly obeyed. In some of the African states, where there are numerous tribes, the tribal chiefs still exert influence over their members. Even where democratic elections take place people vote as the tribal leader says. In a pre-literate society 'a continuity between one generation and the next is preserved; for unlike modern formal education, it does not drive a wedge between generations, to create discontinuities.' Through education, the accumulated wisdom of generations is transmitted from one generation to another with modifications. The new generation takes up the process of culture which the old generation has left off, and this perpetuation and accumulation of social heritage is very important. Either through formal or informal education, many generations of accumulated knowledge is passed on to the young in a much shorter time than was required for its accumulation. Education in literate societies is entrusted to teachers as most parents have neither the time nor knowledge required to teach. Teachers are trained to teach various subjects at various levels in a formal way. There is a special curriculum for each course, and students and teachers are bound by various regulations. There are examinations where assessments are made in the most formal way. Such an objective kind of education which is prevalent in modern societies is called formal. The curriculum of education is designed to achieve the desired results. Rapid changes taking place in society require new approaches in education.

Early education in India was the monopoly of the upper caste Hindus who developed Sanskrit language and literature, Hindu religion, medicine and the like. The study of Vedic literature was indispensable to the upper castes. Formal schooling began with the Upanayana ritual. Hindu education has been dominated by religious beliefs and caste system. It also aimed at preparing one for the life to come. The spread of Buddhism was associated with centres where Buddhist monks spent their time in scholarly pursuits. The best-known education centres of ancient India were Taxila and Nalanda. Similarly Sree Sankaracharya established various mathas which attracted bright students from different parts of India.

In other parts of the world like Egypt, Mesopotamia, China, Greece and Rome there were formal educational institutions meant for the teaching of theology and liberal arts. In ancient Egypt young, aristocratic boys were trained for court services and to govern the country. Religious education was meant for another category of selected pupils whose training lasted for a longer period. The priests held the key to education, and an almost similar pattern was followed in Mesopotamia in the training of scribes and priests. In China the emphasis was on classical scholarship and the administrators were trained in classics. In ancient Greece the youth were trained to serve the state. The Athenians got training in a democratic form of government and a few engaged in philosophical discourses.

The great teachers like Socrates, Plato, and Aristotle had gathered numerous desciples in Athens who believed in simple living and high thinking. Aristotle taught Alexander, prince of Macedonia who later came to be known as Alexander the Great. Aristotle widened his mental horizons and during his military expeditions in Asia, Alexander behaved in a humane was especially towards his foes. In ancient Sparta the stress was on military training to the young who led a highly disciplined life. In ancient Persia too the stress of education was on military training. 'Persian education aimed at the strength rather than the refinement of culture. The predominant aims of its education were practical rather than literary or scholastic. The Persians wished to produce no great body of science and literature; they wished to produce a nation of soldiers, physically fit and brave, with all the virtues implied in the term 'a good soldier'. In Rome there was a privileged nobility known as the Patricians, while the rest were Plebians who had inferior social status. In addition there were slaves as well. Education was mainly for the Patricians who held all the important positions in the state.

The great Roman writers and thinkers whom we know were all Patricians. Roman law, art and sculpture, Latin literature all developed because of education. Similarly the pre-Columbian civilisations of the Mayas, the Aztecs and Incas had developed formal education for the training of nobility and priests. In medieval Europe the emphasis was on the training of youth for the service of the church. The monks and friars were engaged in useful and productive work like agriculture, preserving the ancient manuscripts, copying the Bible, and teaching the young. With no family commitments they were able to devote their full time for the sake of education and religion. Some them turned out to be scientists of great eminence like Roger Bacon, a Franciscan friar of 13th century England, who stressed the importance of experiments in science.

The Nestorian Christians of Persia had also done much for the development of science, medicine and literature in the Arab world. In Europe universities like Paris, Oxford and Cambridge emerged which were residential institutions. Monks and friars were the early scholars in these institutions, and they devoted their time to biblical studies and eventually some of them engaged in scientific studies. In those days such an education was privilege of a few while the masses were living in ignorance. After the 15th century there have been changes in the pattern of European life which have affected education also. The Renaissance emphasised the importance of the individual and his role in the secular world. The lay scholars also began to gain a place along with the clerics.

The Reformation also was of great significance as it encouraged individual study of the Bible. It implied education for the average individual to read the Bible. As Protestantism spread to different parts of Europe it was necessary to translate the Bible into different languages. In the Protestant churches prayers and Bible reading were in local tongues instead of Latin. There had been a revival of trade which led to modern capitalism and the emergence of middle class merchants who required formal education to carry out their mercantile activities like keeping records of their business. The Industrial Revolution which followed brought about tremendous changes in education.

Remarkably, one of the greatest merits of education is socialisation which is the process of interaction through which the individual learns the habits, skills, beliefs, and normative requirements for proper functioning in social life. This process starts at home but extends beyond it to schools. Children absorb the social values, beliefs and norms of society. By acquiring the skill of reading and writing children are able to learn things easily and quickly. The values and social norms are inculcated in children, and they learn what is right and wrong. To achieve socially accepted goars rationally accepted behaviour is pursued for which education is important. 'The process of education should be directed towards social ends, that is, towards the perpetuation, progress, and welfare of the group of which the individual is a member. Through education the culture of the group is transmitted from one generation to succeeding generations, and the beliefs and practices which characterise a particular society are perpetuated. As new ideas and practices develop and are advanced, changes are made in social practices; then progress is made in that the changes can, within limits, be directed toward humanly established goals.' Education, especially higher education, develops the spirit of enquiry among the young. The pursuit of truth has been the aim of education in all the ages, and through diligent study man has been able to reach the truth. Scientists through prolonged enquiries and studies have been able to achieve great things, thereby enriching humanity. 'Science paves the way for value realisation by giving man a surplus of power over and above what he needs to supply his physical wants.' Thus the pursuit of truth is a basic quality in higher education. Very often this pursuit of truth is based on the cooperation of many. The experiences of many are shared, and criticisms and constructive suggestions help the scholar immensely. In modern societies great emphasis is laid on competence and achievements in education. The rat-race starts from the school level. As children are endowed with different intellectual abilities and as the environments are different, differences are bound to occur in student achievements. Except in communist countries, there are schools owned by the state and private bodies. From time immemorial private authorities, especially religious bodies, have been associated with education.

Education was imparted mainly by priests and instructiion centred around religion. For example in the University of Oxford, one of the oldest in the world, as a rule most of the heads of colleges and fellows were ordained priests and it took a long time for others to gain entry. When the Governor-General of India in Council passed a regulation in 1800 for the founding of a college at Fort William in Bengal it was resolved that 'that provost of the college shall always be a clergyman of the Church of England.' Similarly theology was given great importance and it was known as the queen of subjects. The interference of the state in education is of recent origin. A 19th century thinker like Herbert Spencer never liked the interference of the state in education which he thought should fall within the purview of private agencies. The famous public schools in England like Eton, Rugby and Harrow are church establishments, and so are some of the public schools in India owned by private agencies. In the U.S. some of the best schools are run by churches while the state run schools are known as public schools. Though expensive, there is keen competition for places in private schools, and this trend is noted in India also.

In schools and colleges there is keen competition for grades, prizes, scholarships and so on. Opportunities are more or less the same for all, but only a few come to the forefront. Such students are held in esteem. For example, in Oxford colleges there are scholars, exhibitioners and commoners. Scholars are distinguished from others by a special type of gown and enjoy certain privileges along with the monetary benefit of scholarship. Commoners form the majority. Similarly, in schools and other institutions of higher learning there are students who excel in games, sports, debates and other activities and gain the esteem of their fellow students. All these help a student in gaining a good start in life. In India there is keen competition for gaining entry into medical and engineering colleges, because medical and engineering professions are financially attractive. Thus in most parts of the country there are tuition centres where special coaching is provided to those who are trying for such entries. Children are encouraged to work hard and very often it damages their health. In most cases, the parents too bear the brunt. The academic achievements of their children is usually one of the most important topics of conversation when people meet. In Japan, the strain of overwork is felt among students and cases of nervous breakdown are on the increase. Merry I White wrote, 'The single most important contributor to the success of Japanese schools is a consensus that education is important. Across the population, among parents, at all institutional and bureaucratic levels, and highest on the list of national priorities is the stress on excellence in education.' Healthy competition is good as it encourages people to develop their talents. Where the assessment is fair and just it is appreciated by children, but when there is favouritism and unfair methods children feel very badly about it. Fairness and justice are the guiding principles in most of the well-run educational institutions. The ranking system in schools makes the less successful take it as personal failure.

It usually happens that those with high academic distinctions excel in the race of life. Similarly those who excel in debates, sports and games usually get a better start in life than their less fortunate classmates. A chairman of the debating club of the Oxford University, or a cricket captain is rated much higher than others, and his chances of getting a good position are also high. Such competition is found to a higher degree in a non-communist country than in a communist country. Parents in India are much worried about the tough competition for employment and hence are anxious to provide their children with the best education they can.

Critics point out that keen competition for gaining distinctions makes the less talented pupils lose their confidence and that too much competition will given way to rivalry. The schools act as a sieve where the talented are separated from the rest-separating the sheep from the goat. Apart from intelligence which is the main criterion for screening, other factors like, good teachers, good teaching aids and other environmental factors also matter. A good university degree is usually a measuring rod for the status of a person and it helps the individual to have a good start in life. In most advanced countries of the world there are employment opportunities for women also, and as such looking after children is a real problem, especially when both the husband and wife go out for work at the same time. In countries where the joint family system prevails this is no serious problem as there are always people to look after the children. Domestic servants and governesses are rare in western societies, and these are luxuries which only the rich could afford while conditions are different in most of the Asian and African countries. Thus in western societies teachers in infant and primary schools take the role of baby sisters. Children are supervised by their teachers who are paid a fee. Children in the group learn many valuable things and the socialisation process continues. All these are gained much cheaper than what it could have cost the parents had private teachers been provided for their children. Indian cities and towns now have numerous creches and nursery schools where the employed parents leave their children during their working hours. This trend is found in other parts of the world too with variations.

Writing about education during the pre-World War II years in Japan, Theodore Hsi-en Chen remarks: 'The Japanese people are known to be well-organised and well-disciplined people. They obey authority and follow their leaders. They can endure much pain and hardship. They are intensely loyal to their emperor and their state and show great courage in self-sacrifice and self-abnegation for the cause they believe in. They are efficient in group action and conform to group standards. This national character is the result of a planned programme of informal and formal education. The process of conditioning beings early in life.' A few educational institutions are run by the United Nations aimed at fostering international values. The United Nations Educational, Scientific and Cultural Organisation (UNESCO) came into being in a spirit of idealism and internationalism and acts as a global organisation for intellectual collaboration. In higher education, the projects listed with most pride by UNESCO are those which led to the establishment of teacher training colleges in many parts of Africa, and the efforts in tackling illiteracy in Latin America and Africa. In the area of certain sciences, particularly those concerned with the oceans, climate, the solid earth and the biosphere, the UNESCO programmes help to achieve international co-operation. There are also various private agencies like the Ford Foundation and Carnegie Foundation which give assistance to various research programmes. In a pluralistic and heterogeneous society social integration is an important function of education, and for achieving this some kind of cohesion and integration is important. Education gives people many shared experienced. A strong feeling of cultural identity is an important element of nationalism. Along with nationalism come patriotism, another important ingredient of the modern nation state, and this can be the result of living together and sharing experiences over a long time. Different ethnic groups having different languages and different colour usually belong to one state. In such a set-up there are both centrifugal and centripetal tendencies working together. If a sense of deep national feeling has to be felt the training for it has to begin in school. This can be done in many ways.

A study of the culture of the country is invariably a part of the curriculum in schools. In addition, the history of the country, accounts of political leaders and their achievements, the significance of the national flag, national anthem and so on are taught to the youngsters. National holidays make children aware of the important events of national history. In India the Independence Day, the Republic Day, Mahatma Gandhi's birthday and such important events are remembered annually, and children become conscious of them from their schools. The national flag which has a great symbolic value is hoisted on such occasions and those assembled show their respect to it. Patriotism is kindled in the minds of the young. Schools are the most effective places where such an important function can be effectively carried out. In countries where different languages are spoken one language is accepted as the national language though other languages are not discarded.

By studying the national language children become aware

of the oneness of the nation. Thus a student, apart from his own mother tongue, has to master one or more languages including the national language. Educationists stress the importance of the role of education in achieving social and national integration. The Radhakrishan Committee and the Kothari Commission on University Education in India have emphasised the importance of education as an agent of social and national integration. 'Indian society is hierarchical, stratified and deficient in vertical mobility. The social distance between the different classes and particularly between the rich and the poor, the educated and the uneducated, is large and is tending to widen. Our people profess a number of religions; and the picture becomes even more complicated because of caste, an undemocratic institution which is still powerful and which strangely enough seems to have extended the sphere of influence under the very democratic processes of the constitution itself.

The situation, complex as it was, has been made critical by recent developments which threaten both national unity and social progress. The growth of local, regional, linguistic loyalties tend to make the people forget 'India.' The old values, which held society together have been disappearing and as there is no effective programme to replace them by a new sense of social responsibility, innumerable signs of social disorganisation are evident everywhere and are continually on the increase.' Higher education can do a lot in effecting national and social integration, and this has been repeatedly and strongly emphasised by educationists and politicians alike. Establishing social relationships is another important aspect of education. Friendship and associational ties developed in schools and colleges continue, and in later life this may yield good results. Most educational institutions have their associations of old members which enables them to renew their contacts and in some cases this may help them in their social advancement. Education has become 'the society's gate-keeper determining who will advance and who will be left behind.' In the matter of obtaining a job, industries and government prescribe minimum educational qualifications. A university degree is insisted upon as the minimum qualification in competing for all India services like the I.A.S. and I.P.S. A secondary school teacher requires a bachelor's degree in education to start teaching, and a doctor needs a medical degree to treat patients. Engineers require engineering degrees, and lawyers legal qualifications.

One of the greatest developments in the post World War II years is the stress on specialise education. This has become apparent in the U.S., U.S.S.R., India and most of the countries of the world. Technological changes have been rapid in Japan. Europe, America and Russia while most other countries of the world are lagging behind them. Technology consists of the practical arts of producing goods and services. Technology cannot be equated with science. The former is eclectic and concerned with making specific artefacts work, while science is concerned with making generalisable theories. 'The two overlap when focused theories help predict or understand the working of artefacts (e.g. Chemistry and the properties of materials), and when they actually enable the development of a new range of artefacts. (e.g. chemical and biological synthesis, electromagnetism, solid state physics).' Work in modern society has changed from primary industry to secondary industry (agriculture to manufacturing), and in recent years to tertiary industry (service work, professional labour retail trade, finance), and along with this shift in occupational structure there have been changes in education also. In such a society the expert is indispensable and important while the non-expert is usually without work. Such an expert-hungry society which Michael Young calls 'meritocracy' is 'a society in which the people with the highest technical qualifications will form new elites and replace those based on money, power or inherited aristocracy.'

This change has affected not only high-skill jobs but also those which at one time required only ordinary skill. For instance, an American farmer at one time was expected to know of the uses of a few tools only, but his modern counterpart must know about mechanics, agricultural science and chemistry. In field after field technical skill is becoming significant and the lowest level of education required to enter a field is rising, and the less skilled and static are becoming technologically and educationally obsolete. In India too, though at a slower pace, the farmer is learning the use of fertilisers, and of operating farm machinery and other implements which require some training. For more than two thousand years the only method of teaching was the teacher in direct contact with the students. The invention of the printing press by Gütenberg had a profound impact on all aspects of life, especially on education. However, books did not replace the teacher, but became a partner in education. At the present time, the development of modern communication technology is having a profound impact on society, and it can bring about a renaissance in education. 'The range of media available to teachers is rapidly expanding. Video and audio cassettes, cable and satellite television, viewdata and teletext systems, and above all the microcomputers, between them provide a bewildering range of choices.

Each has strengths and weaknesses, but in suitable combinations they can lead to radical changes in education.' In the western countries computers and microcomputers are becoming increasingly popular in universities, schools and homes for learning, entertainment, storing information and data, and performing tedious calculations. 'There are an estimated 3.5 million microcomputers in Birtain: 98 per cent of schools have at least one (the average is nine per secondary school and two per primary school). More than half of these run courses on computing: over 80 per cent have computer clubs; and nearly half of all teenagers have the access to a computer in thier own homes.'

The Commonwealth Standing Committee report has

remarked: 'In the developing countries the potential for distance education is immense. It can be used to extend higher education opportunities to people who would otherwise be denied them. It can also help to alleviate the paucity of teaching skills in rapidly expanding educational systems; indeed the use of new technologies can materially improve the quality of teaching even in conventional education.' The distance education programmes enables people of all ages to study at any period of their life. A good example of distance education implemented is the Open University system in England.

The new technology in education is not going to solve all educational problems, nor can it effectively replace the direct contact of the teacher with the student in the learning process. However, the new communication technologies are likely to open myriads of opportunities in the field of education in the coming years.

The American society, and to some extent the Indian society, is becoming a credentialed society. To enter a particular occupation, a person must have the proper credentials. There is a craze for the display of appropriate signboards with the qualifications of the practitioner whether he be a doctor, an engineer or a teacher, and in every nook and corner of an Indian city one comes across such display boards. Letterheads of Indian professors usually list the numerous qualifications they have, and their membership in various societies. These impress their students and colleagues, and differentiate them from their less fortunate colleagues. There has also been a credential inflation in recent years. As more money is required to live in an inflationary society, it requires more credentials just to get the same job now. This craze for credentials has led to an increase in malpractices in obtaining degree certificates, mark lists and so on, and this is giving rise to great concern among the universities. In the modern competitive society educational institutions aim at training manpower. Education is one of the crucial factors deciding whether a young a man can get a reasonably good post and go ahead in life. 'In fact the more education people have, the more likely they are to have a prestigious job, to earn higher average yearly and lifetime incomes, and to achieve better job positions than their parents.' It has been pointed out by critics that credentials are not always necessary for jobs like those of salesmen, policemen and farmers.

Due to lack of credentials many capable and talented people are not even considered for jobs. This is particularly true of the less privileged communities whose social and economic backgrounds are not congenial to gain distinctions. At present the Indian government is doing much to help the traditionally backward classes to find reasonable positions. The shift in importance from liberal arts to science, engineering and technological subjects is evident in the U.S.A., U.S.S.R., India and other countries of the world. 'In the educational system in America a great deal of lip service is paid to the importance of humanities--literature and other so-called cultural subjects--particularly at the college level. The fact is, however, that the overwhelming majority of male students, and a good many of female students concentrate on useful subjects. They know that graduates with specialised training get the better jobs sooner, and their parents know it too.' In the American society, where the stress is on success, even religious institutions lay emphasis on economic activities. Thus a parish priest who is a good business man and who could raise sufficient funds for the running of the parish school and other institutions, gets wide acceptance among the parishioners.

It has been pointed out that 'the U.S. is probably the only country in which a biography of Christ depicting him as a successful businessman could be a bestseller. The parable of talents is interpreted to mean that a man is morally obliged to use his abilities for economic and material advancement.' Dr. Bennet, the American Secretary of Education, in a recent statement has pointed out that there has been a considerable decline of interest in humanities in the U.S. since the 1970s. The number of English majors has dropped by 57 per cent, history by 62 per cent, philosophy by 41 per cent and modern languages by 50 per cent. A study undertaken by the University of California at Los Angeles revealed that materialism is the motivating force of this decline.

Innovations are important in the modern complex technological society, and innovations are associated with progress. Much of the research is carried out in university laboratories where professors get absorbed in their research work. America, the research laboratories are mainly funded by the government and industries. Basic research is not concerned with any immediate practical result, but it will eventually be applied in industries or elsewhere. New designs of jet planes, communication satellites, application of laser beams and so on are revolutionising the world. Much research is also done about the psychological and sociological problems of man living in a modern industrial society, which help in alleviating the distress of many. In Soviet Russia in 1962, about 75 per cent of Russian Ph.D. candidates were in science, engineering, medicine and agriculture compared with 40 per cent in the United States. It has been pointed out, 'The Soviets gear their system almost exclusively to the production of specialised high-level manpower required for a highly industrialised society which is determined to make its voice heard throughout the world and to spread its ideology. Education and national purpose are inseparable.'

The achievements of Soviet Russia in her rocketry and space satellite programmes is a tribute to the devoted work of her scientists. The competition between the two super-powers in the mastery of space had led to the increased importance of physicists, instrumentation engineers, computer scientists and numerous other specialists, and academician's play a major role in this race. There are people who point out that too much involvement of professors in technical and social innovations impairs their ability to perform their normal duties like teaching their subjects, and in aiding cultural transmission. However, research is one of the main functions of university teachers, and in a knowledge-oriented industrial society, this type of innovation is important for social viability. The students, though not involved in most of the research programmes, benefit from the atmosphere of increased intellectual stimulation. Occasionally some distinguished scientist may be visiting them and may have discussions with them. The funds available for the research project may be used for additional courses of instruction, appointment of new instructors, better laboratories and libarics, better student accommodation and so on. For centuries the traditional attitude of the university scholar was openness, a willingness to investigate and consider new ideas, the ability to compare and examine conflicting opinions.' The academic life is deliberately designed to encourage this. The flexibility allowed to the professor in framing lecture programmes, courses of study, time-table of work and so on are a privilege which is usually known as academic freedom. This flexibility enables him to put in more time for research work which eventually leads to greater achievements. In India the University Grants Commission (U.G.C.) has been consistently trying various methods to improve the quality of scientific research in the universities. In their 1980 report it was pointed out: 'Realising the importance and value of a well-defined science and technology policy as well as an action plan, the commission has prepared a plan for the development of science education and research in the universities in the sixth plan period. The object is that science education and research should play an effective role in national development in future.' It has been pointed out by some sociologists that one of the functions of educational institutions is to keep away the young from the employment market. In some countries compulsory education is prescribed to youth below a certain age. Those who pursue higher education in colleges and universities continue their education up to the age of 23 or 25. A few spend some more years for obtaining higher degress. It means keeping away millions of young men and women from the labour market. In India and the U.S.A. it means a significant percentage of their population.

It has also been pointed out that education in high schools and universities serves as a preparation for family life. Instructions regarding sex, care of children and the like are provided in some schools in some parts of the world, though this has not become popular in many countries. Where there is co-education in colleges it enables young men and women to develop mutual interests which may eventually lead to marriages. Parents try to send their sons and daughters to institutions where youngsters of similar backgrounds study, thereby making the selection of mates easy. As marriages between people of almost the same age are common in countries like the U.S., this type of selection is easy. However, in India where men usually marry women younger than themselves, this type of choice is rather difficult. Moreover, there are numerous other social barriers which one has to overcome before a final decision on marriage can be taken. However, education paves the way for a better understanding between the opposites sexes.

The habits developed in educational institutions may have a life long effect on people. Routine practices like rising up early in the morning, or taking daily baths and so on are usually acquired from homes and boarding schools where there is compulsion in doing things at the right time. Similarly, reading habits, interest in sports and games, extra-curricular activities and the like are developed at school and have life-long effects. There are also numerous hobbies like philately, numismatics and so on which are developed at schools. In this age of increasing leisure when much of the monotony of work is eliminated by machines, man should have sufficient interests to keep him active, and schools play a major role in this. One of the important aims of education is to make children aware of the importance of health and of preventing diseases. Through textbooks and instructions they learn quite a lot about diseases, malnutrition, balanced diet, value of cleanliness, fresh air, regular exercise and so on. All these enable them to face life in a much more efficient manner than they otherwise would do. This is a matter of immense importance to a nation like India, and efforts are made in a limited way to improve the health of school children. However, what is most important is to create an awareness among the children as to the importance of health. 'The school must imbue its pupils with a profound concern for the promotion of a their own health and that of the community, and must inculcate an earnest desire to eliminate disease and defects and privation from the life of man.' However, proper medical examination for students in lacking in most of the educational institutions in India, and children of poor parents are at a great disadvantage as medical examinations and medical treatment are expensive. Students in colleges and universities also suffer from want of proper facilities for accommodation, and their social activities are few. This is particularly true in large cities where hostel facilities are limited and private accommodation very expensive.

The manifest function of mass education is to enable all to share the knowledge and skills once confined to a privileged few. All the newly independent nations of the world are trying to attain the aim of full literacy. Universal education is of special importance in a democracy. The report of the 'Secondary Education Commission' under Dr. Lakshmanaswamy Mudaliar has quoted James Madison to illustrate this point: 'A popular government without popular information or the means of acquiring it is but a prologue to farce or tragedy or perhaps both. Knowledge will forever govern ignorance, and the people who mean to be their own governors must arm themselves with the power which knowledge gives.' The Commission in Addition to Madison's view pointed out, 'We should, however, like to add that it is not only knowledge that is acquired, but also the right kind of social training and the inculcation of right ideals without which knowledge by itself may be sterile or worse. Training for democracy postulates a balanced education in which social virtues, intellectual development and practical skill all receive due consideration and the pattern of such an education must be envisaged on an all India basis.' One of the functions of education is that it creates a demand for further changes. Modern technical devices have fascinated backward societies. For example, as Raymond Firth points out, 'Among the Malay peasantry or the African peasantry, the bicycle, the motor-bus or motor lorry and the sewing machine have come to stay, just as steel tools have replaced those of stone and shell in all but the remote parts of New Guinea.' Technical schools were required to teach how to repair the machines and maintain them. The demand for more schools, more doctors, more roads and so on have come from the African peasants who were fascinated by the innovations. One of the latent functions of education in the colonies was the stimulus it created in nationalistic feelings. The missionaries who started schools and other institutions of higher education in India had in mind the spread of Christianity as their main aim. The worship of God and instruction in religious ideology were the main objects. Similarly when the British started the universities of Madras, Calcutta and Bombay in 1858 they had in mind the creation of university graduates who would help them in the administration of the country.

However, higher education widened the horizons of the scholars who came to know of the developments in other parts of the world. The concept of political liberty, and events like the French Revolution and the American War of Independence fascinated them and kindled their spirit for freedom. All these eventually led to the agitation for freedom. Similarly, the schools started in Africa produced leaders who eventually agitated for freedom. This was not the intention of the missionaries. 'The stimulus of the nationalistic feeling was a latent result of the training received in mission schools and the need to treat potential converts with some measure of equality. The manifest function was simply to produce Christians but the latent function has often been to train nationalist leaders who became enemies of colonial rule.' In the last few decades there has been an increasing tempo in student agitations in educational institutions in the different parts of the world. In the colonies this was against the colonial powers, while in the post-colonial era the agitations were mainly against the existing societies. Many revolutionary ideas had their influence among the student organisations which had been expressing their dissatisfaction of the establishments. Sorbonne university in Paris, the London School of Economics, Harvard university and many other reputed educational institutions were shaken by student upheavals. Some of the universities of Africa like the one in Nairobi had to remain closed for years because the authorities thought that these educational institutions are the breeding ground for revolutions. The Makerere University in Uganda, one of the oldest institutions of higher education in Africa had been run badly under the rule of Idi Amin and was looted during the war which threw him out of the country. Examples like these are numerous.

Many universities had their set-backs while a mushroom growth of universities was found all over the world. Conditions in Indian universities are also deteriorating due to various reasons. Reflecting on the changing educational scene, one of the eminent educationists C.P. Ramaswamy Aiyar remarked: 'While every university should jealously preserve its autonomy and while the students, especially of the universities, should have the fullest right to debate and express their opinions not only upon intellectual and cultural topics but also on matters of politics, nevertheless, their activity should be confined to the university campus and should not extend to public or political demonstrations, or agitation outside their place of learning.

Furthermore, it is positively wrong on the part of political leaders to enlist the assistance of students in political campaigns or to involve them in political controversies and agitations. This principle was strongly advocated by Dr. Besant and others including myself even in the days of the non-cooperation movement.'

Different political parties have their youth wings in educational institutions, and elections to college unions and other student organisations are keenly contested. Political parties spend money on elections and students feel their importance. Students of the different political organisations are trained by political leaders who guide their activities. They go on strike whenever important issues are involved and get the support of the political parties. It doesn't follow that all the students are active members of student organisations; but very often the silent majority are helpless. Students in secondary schools, who are of a lower age group, are equally disturbed as those of the colleges and universities who are of a higher age group.

Education in India is such a complex and gigantic task that it could be handled effectively by the central government only. In 1975 Mrs. Indira Gandhi wrote, 'I wonder if any contemporary society is satisfied with its education system. The developing countries face special problems, however, for the colonial education systems which most of them inherited have proved wholly inadequate for a developing nation.' She also pointed out, 'The basic issues of educational reform are clouded over by a preoccupation with unemployment. The sole purpose of education is not to enable young people to get jobs, or even to know more, but to help them become better human beings, growing in awareness and compassion, so that they can grapple with the problems of today and be prepared for the challenges of tomorrow.' The rapid changes taking place in the educational pattern of developing countries have made the authorities in India, especially the Prime Minister Mr. Rajiv Gandhi, think in new directions. Mr. Pant, the education minister, said that Mr. Gandhi was interested so much in higher education because he wanted to look ahead. Mr Pant mentioned that he wanted the centre to spend more money on education in the new seventh five-year plane (1985-1990). The proportion allocated is 2.6 per cent but he wants in nearer the 6 per cent called for by the education commission in 1968. In his first broadcast to the nation after he had been sworn in as Prime Minister Mr. Gandhi promised a new emphasis on vocational and technical education, and revealed plans to create a nation-wide Open University 'to bring higher education within easy reach of all.' There are also plans for nonformal education to reduce adult illiteracy, modernise the courses, and introduce new technology like the use of satellites in education. There is also a desire to delink degrees from jobs, and it is thought that in future only those who are really very keen and need to go into higher education should do so while the rest be channelled into taking vocational training.

Like India, China also is undergoing rapid changes in its education. For more than two thousand years until the end of the 19th century poets, writers and educated men were also officials selected by the Imperial Examinations, and as long as they served the interests of the emperor they prospered. After the opium war there was an awakening of national spirit, and there was agitation for constitutional monarchy. In 1905 the Imperial Examinations system was abolished. China has passed through various changes in the 20th century like the long years of civil war and the establishment of the People's Republic of China in 1949. The intellectuals were expected to participate fully in the development activities and work regularly in factories or farms. Those who were less enthusiastic were branded as untrustworthy and some were even dismissed from their work. 'We want flowers, not weeds in our socialist garden.' Mao Zedong gave the leadership for the Cultural Revolution (1966-1976) and Mao was deeply concerned about the education of youth which he said took a long time and was divorced from reality. 'In seeking to create a new system of education that would eliminate differences between town and country, workers and peasants, and mental and manual labour, Mao struck a responsive cord within the youth; it was their response that later provided him with his best storm troopers. The cultural revolution was launched with the principal purpose of revitalising revolutionary values for the successive generations of young Chinese people.' The cultural revolution was associated with a fierce attack on intellectuals who were dubbed as 'class enemies.' 'The more knowledge you acquire the more reactionary you become' was a slogan which was spread.

Surprisingly, the revolutionary spirit disapproved of romantic love. The objection was not to sex but the scandalous activities as lovers 'chasing and kissing each other.' A large number of intellectuals like heads of educational institutions, professors, scientists, artists, writers and so on suffered, but with the end of the cultural revolution in 1976 conditions began to change. China with about 100 crores of people has fewer higher education institutions than India, and the political leaders of China are much concerned about the inadequacy of higher education in their country. In 1949 there were 205 full time colleges and universities in China and this had risen to 598 in 1978, and at present it is over 700. The number of students in these institutions is about 1.35 million and this number falls short of China's requirements for her development. There have been numerous to bring changes.

There are also workers' full and part time colleges attached to and run by factories, peasants' universities, correspondence courses, and universities 'over the air.' These are similar to the open university system adopted in some countries. Adults whose education was interrupted by the cultural revolution could make use of these facilities. There are also proposals for the development of short-term vocational colleges.

Taking into consideration the importance of education attempts are made to attract better teachers into this profession. The various university commissions appointed by the Government of India and the University Grants Commission (U.G.C.) have urged the government to offer better scales of pay to the teachers, but as education is to a great extent controlled by the state governments various difficulties arise as to the implementation of the schemes. Private agencies also who run educational institutions give rise to numerous problems. In the matter of selecting teachers and students they are given some freedom which gives rise to criticism. Though there are numerous research scholars in each university, very few of their findings have received international acclamation. Serious research and intensive study is on the decline in most institutions of higher learning, and lack of motivation is apparent everywhere.

Teachers in many institutions are anxious to make money by doing additional jobs like teaching students privately, or having petty businesses like running a printing press, keeping book shops, stationary shops, engaging in banking business and doing insurance agency work. Contact between teachers and students is on the decline. The old view of a teacher being a friend, philosopher and guide is a thing of the past. The respect for teachers is also on the decline India, and this is especially true in cities. Within the teaching community itself values have undergone changes. Modern politics in India is reflected among the teachers too who are in most colleges divided into rival factions. But there are exceptionally good teachers dedicated to their work, who are seldom recognised by society which is easily influenced by false propaganda and publicity. Usually those teachers who give the greatest publicity to their work are those who do the least.

THE STATE

Aristotle has mentioned that man is by nature a political animal and that his innate traits led him to establish government. When societies are small and simple the relationships are mainly informal, but as they increase in size and complexity, it becomes necessary to have more formal relationships. 'It is the habitual association of human beings in communities or local groups. It is this principle that apparently underlies all forms of politico-territorial grouping, from the informal and amorphous local group to the highly organised modern state.' A local group is an aggregate of human beings characterised by a common residence within a continuous and more or less well defined territory. There is like-mindedness amongst its members which distinguishes them from outsiders. Local groups from the starting point in studying organisations, but it is not necessarily a political unit. A political organisation is wrought by a leader or leaders who command the respect and allegiance of its members. The leaders maintain peace and order within the group, organise and direct community enterprises and conduct group activities within the political organisation and when necessary mobilise their men to fight against the enemy.

Many political organisations are voluntary alliance of families and clans who in addition to acknowledging the same political leaders, work together in economic enterprises, social and ceremonial affairs and participate in defensive and offensive wars. The simplest form of political organisation may comprise essentially a local group plus a leader. Another type of political organisation is when some groups organise into tribes or confederacies, thereby extending the group organisation to cover a number of local units. Among pre-literates, groups, bands, tribes and confederacies appear to represent the common types of political organisation; some such people have never developed warfare for conquest.

'Political organisation comes into being wherever societies

are segmented on the basis of kinship, economics, religion, sex, fraternities, or community. Where there are sub-groups, there are discrete entities within the social entirety, there is political organisation--a system of regulation of relations between groups within the society at large and between one society and another.'

A political organisation may use one or more of three major units of social organisation as the basis of its structure: (1) genealogical or kinship units, (2) geographical or territorial units, (3) associational units. It has been found that primitive societies generally rest most heavily on the kinship principle.

In most cases the king or the chief exerts great powers over other members. For example, the paramount chief of the Hehe tribe in East Africa performed judicial, legislative, administrative, military and economic functions. He was the interpreter of law and keeper of peace. Serious offences like murder and treason were tried by him. In most parts of the world the tribal leader known by different names exerted immense powers. The state which is a large society has to carry out many duties and responsibilities and the agency that does these is known as the government. Government is the overall control system of a society.

The state is a politically organised body of people occupying a definite territory and living under a government entirely or almost entirely free from external control and competent to secure habitual obedience from all persons within it.' The state holds both internal and external sovereignty. Ernest Barker has defined a state as 'a juridically organised nation, or a nation organised for action under legal rules.' In expanding this definition he states, 'A modern state is generally a territorial nation, organised as a legal association by its own action in creating a constitution, and permanently acting as such an association, under that constitution, for the purpose of maintaining a scheme of legal rules defining and securing the rights and duties of its members.'

State has a definite territory which may be either natural or not. The boundaries are recognised by the neighbouring states and the violation of boundaries leads to disputes between states. Many wars have been fought on boundary issues and hence modern states demarcate their boundaries in the best possible manner. Entering a foreign state requires travel documents and each state has its own rules and regulations regarding it. Another important characteristic of the state is that it possess both external and internal sovereignty. The state punishes those citizens who violate the rules and regulations prescribed by it, and it also protects its citizens from external aggression, by its defence arrangements. Sovereignty represents the authority of the state, liberty and freedom of the individual. 'Whether the individual or the state is the more important unit, and which should be given precedence at the expense of the other when interests conflict, is a controversy that affects many aspects of human life.' There are people who argue that the state is a necessary evil and that it should do nothing except maintain law and order while there are others who say that the state should exercise large powers and subordinate the individual to the interest of the state.

The modern state is invested with immense powers. In times of war it can order the mobilisation of all resources for war and introduce conscription. It can inflict any type of penalty on its citizens as the situation demands. Most citizens who are law abiding are not directly affected but are indirectly affected as such laws protect them. Thus 'the state exists within society, but it is not even the form of society. We see it best in what it does. Its achievement is a system of order and control. The state in a word regulates the outstanding external relationships of men in society. It supports or exploits, curbs or liberates, fulfils or even destroys, the social life over which it is invested with control--but the instrument is not the life. In the earliest phases, among hunters, fishers, root diggers, and fruit gatherers there have been social groups which knew nothing or almost nothing of the state.'

In a state people are politically organised. In modern societies there are elaborate institutional arrangements whose main function is to formulate and administer laws that deal practically with every aspect of social life and are backed by legitimate force. The rules are the laws and the institution that exercises authority is the government. The state possesses coercive powers. 'The state, therefore, as 'the determinate superior,' having in its hands not only the majesty of law, but the ultimate weapon of physical compulsion, has been singled out and set on a pedestal apart from all other forms of association, and treated as the social institutional excellence, beside which all other associations are merely corporate or quasi-corporate individuals, which the state and the law can only recognise at all by pretending that they are individuals, although it is perfectly plain that they are not.'

'Sociologically, laws are formal prescriptions that direct the citizens' role and spell out expectations that define the relationships of citizen to citizen and governor to governed' In modern times law has gained precedence over all other forms of social control such as religion and custom and 'the legal order is the most conspicuous and most effective form of social control' There are differences between state and society. Society is a wider term than the state and it suggests many social relationships which cannot be expressed through the state. The state is concerned with those social relationships which are dealt with through government. Society comprises all human communities, whether they are organised or not; but for the state, organisation based on law is essential. Though the state is not synonymous with society it provides the framework of social order and it holds society together.

According to Ernest Barker, 'The area of society is voluntary co-operation, its energy is goodwill and its method is elasticity while the area of the state is mechanical action, its energy is force and its method is rigidity.' There have always been thinkers who doubted whether the law was always right and just. Thrasymachus in his dialogue with Plato said, 'Government lays down laws for its own advantage--a democracy democratic, tyrannical laws, and so on. In laying down these laws they have made it plain that what is to their advantage is just. They punish him who departs from this as a lawbreaker and an unjust man.'

Government may be defined as the agency or machinery through which the will of the state is formulated, expressed and realised. 'Properly speaking, therefore, the term includes the sum total of the legislative, executive and judicial bodies in the state, whether of the central or local government, of all those who are engaged in making, administering and interpreting law.' Government is a narrower term than the state, being only one part of it. The state includes both the government and the governed. Government is only the machinery to realise the purpose of the state. Sovereignty is one of the most important characteristics of the state and not of the government, though it may be exercised by the government on behalf of the state. The government of a state is liable to change in some cases frequently, while a state remains unchanged though rarely, through wars or negotiations, the state may change. State is the edifice on which the shifting government is built.

Government administers laws which are rules regarding individual and community activities. Laws are of universal application irrespective of wealth or power, and those who violate them are punished. The sources of law are constitutions, legislation, written and acknowledged words of legal experts, customs and moral norms that have been passed on from one generation to another and so on. Common law is of this type which is unwritten folk law that originated from mores. It was accepted and enforced by courts but not enacted by any government.

Laws are enforceable through courts of law and strict impartiality is meant to be followed. The judges are expected to interpret the laws which are impersonal in nature. Plato's remark 'Man, when perfect, is the best of all animals, but, when separated from law and justice, is the worst of all,' has relevance in modern times also. The rapidly changing societies of modern times require new laws. New types of development in the field of science, engineering, medicine and so on have led to the emergence of changed social relationship.

Development of the means of communication, growth of industries and cities, the rising population of the world, emergence of trade unions, and industrial disputes are a few examples to illustrate this change. Various legislations are required to regulate the activities of people and this has become an important function of the government. In addition to state laws there is the international law to regulate the inter-state activities. A very large machinery is required to regulate the legal implications of human activity. The need to regulate the lives of people has been a concern of the people in all ages. Some of the great lawgivers of the past like Hammurabi of Babylon and Napoleon of France had codified the laws of their countries. Even the wisest ruler cannot dispense with law because law has an impersonal quality, which no man however good can attain. Modern states have their constitutions in the light of which the countries are governed. They state the rights and duties of the citizens and various aspects connected with the state.

The Indian Constitution is the most comprehensive constitutional document in the world. It consists of 395 articles and 10 schedules and it represents a triumph of parliamentary democracy. The constitution was framed by a constituent assembly comprising some of the most brilliant men in India. It provides for a parliament with a prime minister and cabinet, and the president is the chief executive authority of the Republic. Each state has its governor and legislature. The Indian Constitution is more unitary than federal in nature and the Supreme Court is the chief interpreter of the Constitution. Modern states are broadly divided into two: unitary and federal. In a unitary state we find 'the habitual exercise of supreme legislative authority by one central power while the federal state is a political contrivance intended to reconcile national unity and power with the maintenance of state rights.'

In a dynamic society occasionally the need arises for alterning some articles of the constitution, and bearing this in mind most constitutions make provisions for amending them. In most cases such amendments require more than a simple majority in parliament; very often a two-third majority is insisted on. In some cases, this has to be ratified by the units of the state. Such procedures are meant to make constitutional amendments difficult. U.S.A., U.S.S.R., France, Australia, Switzerland and numerous other states have their written constitutions, while in Britain instead of a written constitution they are guided by different conventions and precedents. About the British cabinet W.E. Gladstone, the well-known prime minister of 19th century England, wrote, 'The cabinet lives and acts simply by understanding, without a single line of written law or constitution to determine its relations to the monarch, or to parliament, or to the nation; or the relations of its members to one another, or to their head.' In some states like Switzerland the citizens take great interest in the functioning of the government, while in most states once the representatives are elected the citizens become inactive.

The state has to protect the country from external and internal aggression. The government as an institutional agency of the state has three major roles to play: the executive, the legislative, and the judicial. In modern societies law making is a complicated process as compared to an ancient city state like Athens where the citizens met together and elected their representatives and framed laws. Modern states are large and complex, and law making is a skilled work which is left to the elected representatives of the people and the specialists advising them. The chief legislative body in India is the parliament and the states have their respective assemblies. The British parliament is the chief legislative body in Britain and each country has its own parliament. Various types of organisations try to influence the legislators and this type of influencing is known as lobbying. There are also pressure groups who try to create favourable public opinion and influence the representatives. These strategies are widely adopted in parliaments and as it happens powerful vested interests are able to influence the government.

POWER AND AUTHORITY

Power and authority are closely linked. Power is the ability to make and enforce decisions, and authority is legitimate power. 'Power is the extent to which a person or group can control the behaviour of another person or group, along with the possession of means to enforce this control. There are the civil servants who hold public office while there those who are elected into office. In the case of the latter they cannot take impartial and unbiased decisions as they will be influenced by those who have brought them to power.

Max Weber was of the opinion that the state is the organisation that has a monopoly on the legitimate use of violence in a given territory. The state can use force whenever it thinks it right to do so, while the individual citizen has no such right. This power of the state is legitimate and legitimacy is conferred on the state by the citizens. Usually the legitimacy of the government is not questioned, but if the people question it there arises a dangerous situation as the one the British Government in India faced at the time of 'Quit India' movement. Authority is power plus legitimacy, and in a democracy a government that loses its legitimacy does not last long, while in a dictatorship or military government even if it does not have the authority it does possess the power. It has been pointed out, 'Some men aspire for power over their fellow men and derive satisfaction from the exercise of power aside from the purpose to which power is put...It follows ideally that the democratic constitution provides for free expression of political view, rights of assembly, habeas corpus, and other basic protections of the individual as he confronts government and law;--the actions of government should be subjected to regular scrutiny, criticism, and debate by the people, their representatives, and by an unmonopolised press;--the majority will of the individuals should, in the end, determine the scale and incidence of the inputs to government and the balances struck in allocations to the three abiding tasks of government.'

Max Weber mentioned three types of legitimate authority with distinct characteristics. There is the rational legal type whose distinct characteristic is the adherence to accepted rules or norms in an impersonal manner. In legal-rational type of authority there are clear cut rules and regulations at work along with the rule of law. This type of authority prevails in modern democracies. There is another type called traditional authority as is the case of hereditary chiefs and kings. Sanctity of traditions and legitimacy of status of those in authority are accepted principles in such authority. The other type is charismatic authority where a leader is exalted for his qualities like heroism, patriotism self-sacrifice, honesty and so on.

The executive function of the government is carried out by the officials of the state. In India this is done in the name of the President who is the chief executive authority. The administration is carried on by the civil service which has a high record of efficiency. The present civil service is in many respects similar to the one created by the British for administering India. About the British civil service Felix Frankfurter remarks, 'In Great Britain the traditions of public service are as yet powerful enough to enlist the best brains of the country.' The creation of this service according to Graham Wallace 'was one of the great political inventions in the nineteenth century England, and like other inventions it was worked out under the pressure of an urgent, practical problem.' The ministers have their portfolios and departments and they are advised by the bureaucrats who carry out the administration.

The judiciary carries out the judicial functions of the government. The supreme court is the highest judicial body in India. Interpreting and enforcing law is an important function of the judiciary. Apart from the supreme court each state in India has its own high court and subordinate courts. An impartial judiciary insisting on fairness and justice is a source of strength in any democracy. Every society has its law breakers and criminals who are punished by the judiciary. Modern societies with their complexities need specialists to practise law. Law is broadly divided into two categories: civil and criminal.

Aristotle (384-322 B.C.) made an extensive study of the governments of his day, and classified them as monarchy, aristocracy and democracy. In a monarchy the rule is by one man, in aristocracy by a few, while in democracy it is by many. Aristotle mentioned that a debased form of monarchy may become a tyranny, aristocracy may change into oligarchy and democracy into mob rule. He pointed out that the economic revolution had been largely responsible for the deterioration of Greek political life. There numerous forms of government and different classifications. Some of the kings claimed absolute rights while some had only limited powers.

After the Glorious Revolution of 1688 England became a constitutional monarchy and the pattern has been continued there, ever since. John Stuart Mill (1806-73) mentioned, 'It has long been a common saying that, if a good despot could be ensured, despotic monarchy would be the best form of government.' According to Mosca, 'All governments are oligarchies since they are dominated by an elite to whom the majority defer and who rule because they control the means through which governments operate.' In a totalitarian government the power is vested in the hands of a few persons who take all major decisions which are to be obeyed by the people. Actions are quick and implicit obedience is expected from the subjects. Such speedy decisions have their dark sides also and as Ernest Barker points out, 'The bright initial speed of non-democratic methods has its attraction. But speed is not everything, even in an age so bemused by speed, and so enamoured of speed as our own. There may be a price to be paid for speed which men will not readily offer.' Fox once said that he would not barter English trade for Irish liberty. 'That is not the price I would pay, nor is this the thing that I would purchase.' Fascism proposes a barter of civil liberty for executive speed.'

Dictatorship is nothing new. In ancient Rome in times of major crisis dictators emerged who held immense powers for short periods. Once the crisis was over the dictators were not of use, but modern dictators are of a different type. Once they saddle themselves into power it is rather difficult to throw them out. They govern in a despotic manner though some dictators like Peron of Argentina tried to give a colouring of popularity but he also had his problems. One of the main differences between democracy and dictatorship is that, 'In the democracies what is not forbidden is permitted; while in the dictatorships what is not forbidden is compulsory.' Governments in democratic countries while insisting on the observance of rules and regulations are not much concerned as to the forms of precise behaviour of people. In totalitarian states individual freedom is restricted and expression of resentment is suppressed.

Twentieth century witnessed the waning and waxing of numerous types of governments in different parts of the world. Many monarchies became republics and some states have adopted military form of government dictatorships. A nation like Germany became divided into two with two different types of ideologies. U.S.S.R. and the East European States have become totalitarian states with a rigid pattern of social organisation. In such states implicit obedience to decrees is expected, and enforced, by law. A state like Czechoslovakia with a democratic tradition has been transformed into a one party communist state. China, Cuba, Ethiopia are other examples of such governments. The defeat of Japan was followed by a promulgation declaring it to be democratic republic. In 1949 Mao Zedong formulated a constitution for China largely on the model of the U.S.S.R. The former British, French and Dutch colonies had gained their independence. A new order began emerging. Those who won the Second World War wanted to create a world free from war and man-made calamities in the future. The United Nations was formed and compared to the League of Nations it is a much larger body with greater concern for mankind. Again Germany became unified. The USSR dismantled. The entire Europe is marching ahead to European Union with common currency 'Euro' and common citizenship. And communism eclipsed.

The role of the state in providing welfare to its citizens has been a subject of prolonged controversy. A social scientist like Herbert Spencer carried individualistic views to the extreme. In his *Social States* he argued that public education, poor relief, factory legislation, state controlled monetary and postal systems were all wrong. In the nineteenth century he had his supporters but much water has flowed under the bridge since he wrote it, and almost all states consider such matters as an integral part of their activities. In most parts of the world charitable work has been associated with religious institutions. The Hindu temples, Buddhist and Christain monasteries, and Muslim mosques have been helping the poor in various ways. In England the poor laws were administered by the parishes. The starting of educational institutions and hospitals was mainly done by religious institution operated by priests, monks or nuns. Devoted workers absorbed in charitable work have surpassed similar services by the government. The drastic changes in the socio-economic structure brought about by the Industrial Revolution had their effects on society. Like Karl Marx there were others who gave serious thought to the changes, and egalitarian ideas were in the air. In England an Oxford don named Thomas Hill Green (1836-1842) spoke eloquently of the need for governmental participation in promoting the welfare of the people. Green argued that material prosperity led to moral degradation which rendered the underprivileged incapabale of fulfilling 'any social function or contributing anything to the common good.' He said that contrary to Spencerian idea of negative freedom, it is necessary to have a meaningful positive freedom which he defined as 'a positive power or capacity of doing or enjoying something worth doing or enjoying.' He favoured collective responsibility and well-being of society through democratically controlled agents of government. Green's teachings had attracted the attention of many and some of the great men like Bernard Shaw, H.G. Wells, Sydney Webb, Graham Wallace and Ramsay Macdonald founded the Fabian Society which advocated social transformation. They were of the opinion that the competitive system assured the happiness and comfort of the few at the expense of the many and that society must be reconstituted in such a manner as to secure general welfare and happiness. Socialistic ideas were brought forward by them and this had a tremendous effect on those in Britain and in the overseas possessions like India. In 1906 the Labour Party was formed in Britain which advocated democratic socialism instead of class warfare and proletarian dictatorship. It believed in the nationalisation of basic industries, redistribution of income, social and economic planning and other measures of a revolutionary nature. 'Socialism and Communism are terms connected with, and flowing from the term society and community. But while we may identify the words 'society and community' , it would be incorrect to identify the words socialism and communism.' There were some who were dissatisfied with the point of view of the Fabians regarding the centralisation of power. The Guild Socialists, for example, argued that various functional groups like the church, industry, and educational organisations should have direct control over their own affairs and that the state should only make the minimum interference in the form of resolving disputes and making ultimate decisions. According to Edward Eermstein 'the aim of all socialist measures, even of those which appear outwardly as coercive measures, is the development and the securing of a free personality. The more exact examination always shows that the coercion included will raise the sum total of liberty in society, and will give more freedom over a more extended area than it takes away.'

Citizens and Political Participation

Universal adult franchise is a modern concept, and history shows that political power has always been vested in the hands of a few. It may be the king or his immediate relatives, a particular caste or religious leaders. In ancient days when slavery prevailed the slaves had no political authority and neither did not landless labourers. In most countries women were excluded from political participation. In modern democratic states each citizen has his voting right, and some of them democratic practices like accepting the verdict of the electorate, the decision of the court of law and so on are taken for granted. In a society people have different goals and this makes co-ordination necessary. 'Politics is about how a group of people with different goals manages to arrive at a common plan of action.' In politics there is both adjustability and hostility. Sometimes defeat in an election or strong differences of opinion may result in strife. The saying that 'war is simply a continuation of politics by other means.' illustrates this point. Military coup and take-over of government by force has become a common feature in Africa, South America and elsewhere. These are places where such customs as accepting cheerfully the opposition as is done in Britain and India is not established by practice. For the proper functioning of a government it is necessary to have an awareness among citizens about their social duties and responsibilities. Civic sense is a plant of slow growth, and its rate of growth differs from country to country.

Group consensus is achieved in various ways. In a tribal community, usually the advice of the tribal chief is accepted without hesitation. In some communities the elders sit together and work out solutions to problems. Major family differences are settled by appealing to subtle feelings like sentiments, traditions and prestige. There are some religious groups like the quakers who settle their differences after prayer and meditation. Blind obedience to a leader whether religious or political is on the decline in modern societies. It is in the primary groups that informal measures and adopted to settle subtle issues.

On the other hand, in modern complex societies unanimous decisions are rarely possible as differences between individuals always exist and hence such decisions are taken by voting where majority decisions are accepted by the minority also. For very important decisions like amending a constitution a higher percentage than a simple majority is required and rules regarding such amedments are prescribed in the constitution. Modern political elections have their flaws. All the voters may not be well informed about the problems involved and half truths and propaganda may influence their decisions. Such circumstances may pave the way for the emergence of a dictatorship. Many dictators have adopted democratic means to achieve political power. When there are numerous rival groups, an appeal to national pride and cultural tradition by a dictator may kindle the emotional feelings of the electorate. The Nazis under Hitler in Germany and the Fascists under Mussolini in Italy came to power in this manner, and eventually they were able to suppress all opposition and change democracies into totalitarian states. When a nation faces a crisis, normally people rally round the person who could turn out to be a saviour.

Winston Churchill, who led the British during the World War II, was one such charismatic leader, but he lost his leadership when the war was over. Examples of such leaders are numerous. In the Indian general election of 1984, the emotional feelings of the people following the assassination of Indira Gandhi, and the fear of the centrifugal tendencies prevailing in the country caused anxiety to millions who desired a strong government, and Rajiv Gandhi won a landslide victory. Polling in some regions was as high as eighty per cent and invariably they expressed their confidence in Rajiv Gandhi.

In some of the countries where the traditional one party system prevails election takes place, but there is no opposition worth mentioning as ruthless suppression of enemies is a characteristic feature of totalitarian states. However, they conduct elections to impress on the rest of the world that the people are behind them and their actions are right. Robert Faris has mentioned six assumptions underlying the democratic process: (1) reasonably clear issues will arise and become known to the people; (2) candidates, taking a stand on these issues, will become known to the electorate; (3) discussion on these issues and on the candidates will occur, so that they are evaluated and judged properly; (4) rational choices, largely based on enlightened self-interest will be expressed through ballot; (5) through such a process of selection will be chosen the candidates most satisfactory to the general interest; (6) these elected officials will subject to continuous and critical scrutiny by citizens, thereby being motivated to provide honest and efficient government. These appear to be ideal propositions which in practice are not. Observers of public participation in politics find that very often in normal situations many people feel that their votes do not carry any weight in governmental decisions. Social scientists point out that there will be higher voting rate if group interest is stirred on important matters, and that social pressure in favour of voting shall be high. It has also been pointed out that voting is not very rational and that people on the whole vote for the group of which they are members. The illiterates are advised by their leaders to remember the election symbol of their candidate and to put the appropriate mark on it. Election is associated with propaganda and lavish spending of money.

PLURALISM, ELITISM AND MARXISM

Pluralism

Pluralism, elitism and Marxism are theories of society, an understanding of which will help one know its functioning. Pluralists hold the view that the best way to preserve freedom in a society is to have a number of powerful groups with various interests functioning. These groups may have differences in interests, yet a harmonious blending of opposing interests is possible. Pluralism tries to answer the question, 'What makes it possible for a society to hold together? Such a question may not seem to have much significance when a society functions smoothly, but it is important when a society undergoes rapid and revolutionary changes. Such rapid and drastic changes occurred in the nineteenth century Europe which caused social scientists to undertake serious studies about them. The Industrial Revolution which brought about socio-economic changes in Western Europe and America, and political revolutions like the French Revolution and the American War of Independence had their impact on the lives of people and their thinking. The old patterns of village life centred around one's home, church and the little community to which one belonged. Each man had his place in the village and was known to others. The Industrial Revolution brought about changes in this pattern. The new industrial cities had no such personal touches and provided to emotional bonds. The serf of the village who found work in a factory was no more under the patron-client relationship. Instead the city life was impersonal, and people worked for their wages. All these brought about a change in the attitude of the people. The experiences of the city were supposed to have made the labourers rational and efficient.

Close knit societies with primary relationship were displaced by those having secondary relationship. Though France was shaken by revolutions, England had been comparatively safe. The Glorious Revolution of 1688 was followed by a number of parliamentary reforms which brought about many changes in voting rights. Towards the end of the nineteenth century the government was no longer an agency purely controlled by aristocrats, and more and more people were getting involved in it.

Writers like Tocqueville and Durkheim were fascinated by the theme of social integration. Alexis de Tocqueville, a French aristocrat, wrote a book called *Democracy in America* after visiting that country in 1831. He thought that even though American democracy was not highly appreciable, Europe would eventually borrow heavily from Americans. He thought that democracy would pave the way for cultural mediocrity and also that the tyranny of the majority would be more oppressive than the tyranny of the aristocracy. He also feared that democracy may pave the way for dictatorship. He had different ideas of protecting a democratic society from tyranny. He realised the importance of a free press and lawyers in safeguarding the liberty of the people, and voluntary organisations were to play a major role in the preservation of liberty. A single person cannot exert much pressure on the government while an organisation with many members can influential.

Like Tocqueville, Durkheim believed in Pluralism and was of the opinion that a plurality of competing, countervailing centres of power was necessary for the preservation of freedom in a modern society. The rise of national states in Europe resulted in the freedom of people from traditional ties like families and feudal obligations. Matters which once were the concern of the church, guild or the family now fell within purview of the state. The social controls were weakened and gave rise to deviance and political crisis. Durkheim thought that the organisation of like-minded people into groups would form a force which could preserve social integration. 'Pluralism refers to specific institutional arrangements for distributing and sharing governmental power, to the doctrinal defence of these arrangements, and to an approach for gaining understanding of political behaviour.' It has been pointed out that small, close knit, face to face groups constituted man's true communities and that to guarantee the right of individuals it was essential to strengthen the rights of associations.

Elitism

In the late nineteenth and early twentieth century there arose a few social scientists who argued that the state is always ruled and must be ruled by a small governing class called elite. Mosca, Pareto, and Michels were the main exponents of this theory. According to Mosca, 'It makes no difference, that the constitution may provide for universal suffrage, equality before the law, and individual rights. The masses never can govern, never can be organised so that they can govern. Minorities can be so organised, and are.'

The German sociologist Robert Michels studies the relationship between democracy and bureaucracy in politics and in 1911 wrote a book on political parties. In this study he brought out the theory of 'the iron law of oligarchy'. He pointed out that the German Social Democratic Party was an oligarchy. Elitism believes that an elite always gets the upper hand and governs the people. They scorn the pluralist theory and consider their belief in democracy as an illusion. Pareto's theory of the circulation of elite has captured the imagination of many. In order to analyse the condition of equilibrium of a total society Pareto made a division of its entire population into two: the small elite group and the large non-elite group. These are two significantly different classes in society. Among the elite themselves there are the governing elites and the non-governing elite. Elites are those who are noted for their high performances in their field of activities. Pareto said that the elites of the two types, the governing and the non-governing, rotate in positions of political power. The ruling elites are called foxes as they are clever and corrupt, while the counter-elites who aspire for power and who are idealistic are labelled lions. This process continues and as Pareto points out 'history is a graveyard of aristocracies' He had no appreciation of parliamentary democracy and in his book *The Mind and Society* he remarked, 'We need not linger on the fiction of popular representation--poppycock grinds no flour.' He prophesied the downfall of the soft-hearted, and of the pacifist parliamentary governments of the democratic countries, and prophesied also the emergence of rough militaristic aristocracies. There has been a Pluralist-Elitist synthesis and two of the well-known exponents of this theory are Karl Mannheim and Suzanne Keller.

Pluralist-Elitists agree that every society has leaders and that leaders are necessary. Mannheim mentions two types of powers; functional power and arbitrary power. Personal power is undesirable, but elites usually have functional, institutional power. Replacement of personal power with functional power is one of the characteristics of the modern age. According to Suzanne Keller 'an elite is a minority of individuals who serve a collectivity in a socially useful way.' In a society there may be many subgroups with their own elites. In modern complex societies such sub-groups with their elites are numerous. In the field of art, science, literature, engineering, medicine, education, religion, cinema, politics and the like there are elites. When elites are admired in a society social integration becomes easy, but if they are envied social conflicts become easy. If the elites in a society are snobbish and are indifferent to the common people, social integration becomes difficult. Keller is of the opinion that along with political leadership the elites must provide moral leadership also.

Keller mentions 'Strategic Elites' who make sure that people in each section of society are committed to the basic goals of the whole society. There is very little chance for one strategic elite group to dominate over others. The elites of the different groups compete among themselves and form no threat to democracy. Mannheim and Keller point out that elitism and pluralism are not opposites, but the term elite has a different meaning to them from the conventional meaning. Elites are moral pace setters and influential experts.

Marxism

Karl Marx, like the elitists, believed that every society, past or present, is dominated by a ruling class. However, he argued that a proletarian revolution would put an end to all social classes, and the domination of one class by another. Marx has little to say about the form of society which will replace capitalism. 'But he does conclude that between the defeat of capitalism and the realisation of true communism, a transitional stage will be necessary. This stage is necessary in order to secure the victory, to destroy the last vestiges of the old order, and to eliminate any remaining traces of class distinction.'

About liberty Marx thought differently from the pluralists. Freedom will appear only after the revolution, and freedom is not possible in capitalistic setup. He stressed on economic equality which alone was what really matters.

Some of the prophesies have not been fulfilled. Communist revolutions have occurred in unexpected places. The condition of the working class has not been deteriorating. Capitalism itself has undergone tremendous changes. Large corporations have emerged with millions of shareholders with the management carried on by salaried executives. This is different from the capitalism envisaged by Marx.

In modern times the Neo-Marxists point out that modern capitalism is corporate capitalism. Revolution is not considered as a struggle of workers against local capitalists, but instead it is a struggle of developing nations against capitalist nations. This new interpretation shows that most communist revolutions of modern times are struggles against foreign economic domination.

The constant occurrence of wars and the consequent miseries to millions of people had given rise to anxiety and after the First World War (1914-18) world leaders had formed the League of Nations which eventually failed. The Second World War which broke out in 1939 and the subsequent defeat of the Nazis and the Japanese was followed by negotiations for peace. The fear of a nuclear war was looming large in the minds of the top leaders who wanted to end all wars. The United Nations was founded in 1945 to maintain international peace and security and to develop international co-operation in economic, social and cultural and humanitarian fields.

REFERENCES

Aiyer, C.P. Ramaswamy, *Education,* Vol. I, Asia Book Co., Madras, 1970.

Anderson, W.A. and F.B. Parker, *Society,* Van Nostrand, Princeton, 1966.

Appadorai, A., *The Substance of Politics,* Oxford University Press, Madras, 1954.

Arblaster, Anthony and Steven Lukes (ed.) *The Good Society,* Methuen and Co., London, 1971.

Avinashilingam, T.S. *Educational Philosophy of Swami Vivekananda*, Ramakrishna Mission, Coimbatore, 1964.

Baldridge, J. Victor, *Sociology*, John Wiley and Sons, New York, 1975.

Barker, Ernest, *Reflections on Government*, Oxford University Press, 1948.

Barnes, Ernest William, *Scientific Theory and Religion*, Cambridge University Press, 1933.

Bartley, W.W., 'Karl Barth,' *Encounter*, March 1970.

Beals, R.H. and H. Hoijer, *An Introduction to Anthropology*, Macmillan, New York, 1969.

Benns, F. Lee, *European History Since* 1870, F. S. Crofts and Co, New York, 1947.

Bogart, E.L. and C.E. Landon, *Modern Industry*, Longman, Green & Co., New York, 1939.

Broudy, Harry S., *Building a Philosophy of Education*, Prentice-Hall, New Delhi, 1965.

Burgen, Ernest W. and Harvey J. Locke, *Family*, American Book Co., New York, 1945.

Burns, Tom (Editor), *Industrial Man*, Penguin, 1969.

Chapman, J. Crosby and George S. Counts, *Principles of Education*, Houghton Miffin Co., New York, 1924.

Chen, Theodore, Hsi-en, *Comparative Education*, Edited by Moehlman, A.H. and Joseph S., Roucek, Henry Holt and Company, Inc., New York, 1951.

Clark, T.T., *Encylopaedia of Religion and Ethics*, Vol. XI, Edinburgh, 1962.

Colby, C.C. and A. Foster, *Economic Geography*, Ginn and Co., Boston, 1944.

Cole, G.D. H., *Social Theory*, Methuen and Co., London, 1930.

Corry, J.A., *Elements of Democratic Government*, Oxford University Press, New York, 1947.

Cunningham, W. and E.A. McArthur, *Outlines of English Industrial History*, Cambridge University Press, 1910.

Davis, Kingsley, *Human Society*, Macmillan, 1949.

Dawson, Christopher, *The Age of Gods*, Sheed and Ward, London, 1933.

Dawson, J. W., *The Origin of the World*, Hodder and Stoughton, 1888.

Drucker, P.K., *The New Society*, William Heinemann, London, 1951.

Drucker, Peter F., *The Changing World of the Executive*, Times Books, New York, 1982.

Durant, Will, *Our Oriental Heritage,* Vol. I, Simon and Schuster, 1954.

Durkheim, Emile (translated by J. W. Swain), *The Elementary Forms of Religious Life,* Chapter 9, Free Press, Glencoe, Ill., 1947.

Eliot, T.S., *Murder in the Chathedral,* Faber and Faber, London, 1969.

Farber, Bernard, 'Theories of Le Play'. in *Kinship and Family Organisations,* John Wiley, New York, 1966.

Faris, R.E. L., as quoted in C.C. Schrag, O.N. Larsen, and W.R. Catton, *Sociology,* Harper and Row, New York, 1968.

Fichter, Joseph H., *Sociology,* University of Chicago Press, 1957.

Firth, Raymond, *Elements of Social Organisation,* Travistock Publications, London, 1969.

Flather, Paul, 'Gandhi honours poll pledge,' *The Times Higher Education Supplement,* London, 18 January, 1985.

Fletcher, Ronald, *The Making of Sociology,* Vol. 2, Michael Joseph, 1971.

Frankfurter, Felix, *The Public and Its Government,* Beacon Press, Boston, 1964.

Frazer, James, *The Golden Bough,* Part IV, Macmillan, London, 1963.

Gadgil, D.R., *Industrial Evolution of India in Recent Times,* Oxford University Press, Bombay, 1945.

Galbraith, John Kenneth, *The New Industrial State,* Houghton Mifflin, Boston, 1967.

Gettell, R. G., *Political Science,* Ginn and Co., Boston, 1949.

Ghose, G. *Socialism and Communism in India,* Allied Publishers, Bombay, 1971.

Giri, V. V., *Labour Problems in Indian Industry,* Asia Publishing House, 1972.

Gisbert, P., *Fundamentals of Sociology,* Orient Longman, Bombay, 1960.

Gisbert, P., *Preliterate Man,* Manaktalas, Bombay, 1967.

Glock, Charles Y. and Rodney Stark, *Religion and Society in Tension?,* Rand McNally, 1965.

Goode, William J., *Religion Among the Primitives,* The Free Press of Glencoe, 1951.

Goode, William J., *The Family,* Prentice-Hall, New Delhi, 1965.

Green, Arnold W, *Sociology,* McGraw-Hill, Tokyo, 1964.

Harris, Seymour E., *The New Economics,* Dennis·Dobson, London, 1968.

Harrison, Frederick and Charles A. Meyers, *Education, Manpower and Economic Growth,* McGraw-Hill, New Delhi, 1970.

Herskovitz, Melville J., *Man and His Works*, Alfred Knopf, New York, 1956.

Hobhouse, L.T., G.C. Wheeler and M. Ginsberg, *Material Culture and Social Institutions of the Simpler Peoples*, Chapman and Hall, London, Chapter III, 1930.

Hoebel, E.A. and E.L. Frost, *Cultural and Social Anthropology*, Tata McGraw Hill, New Delhi, 1979.

Homer, *The Odyssey*, (translated by E.V. Rieu), Penguin Books, Middlesex, 1961.

Horton, Paul B. and Chester L. Hunt, *Sociology*, McGraw-Hill, New York, 1968.

Kapadia, K.M., *Marriage and Family in India*, Oxford University Press, 1954.

Karnick, V.K., *Indian Trade Unions*, Manaktalas, 1966.

Keynes, J. M., 'A General Theory of Employment, Interest and Money,' as quoted in *The Good Society* (edited by Anthony Arblaster and Steven Lukes), Methuen and Co., London, 1971.

King, David C, and M.R. Koller, *Foundations of Sociology*, Rinehart Press, 1975.

Kroeber, *Anthropology*, Harcourt, Brace and Co., New York, 1948.

Lindsay (Editor), *The New Cambridge Modern History*, Cambridge University Press, Cambridge, 1957.

Linton, Ralph, *The Study of Man*, Appleton-Century, 1936.

Lundberg, G.A., C.C. Schrag, O.N. Larsen and W.R. Catton, *Sociology*, Harper and Row, 1968.

MacIver, R.M. and C.H. Page, *Society*, Macmillan, London, 1964.

MacIver, R.M., *The Modern State*, Oxford University Press, 1950.

Malinowaski, B., *Argonauts of Western Pacific*, Routledge and Kegan Paul, London, 1964.

Marcuse, Herbert, *One Dimensional Man*, Beacon Press, Boston, 1964.

Marriott, J.A.R., *A History of England*, Vol. VII, Methuen & Co, London, 1950.

Marshall, Alfred, *Principles of Economics*, Macmillan & Co., London, 1910.

Mauger, Peter, 'Integrating the intelligentsia,' *The Times Higher Education Supplement*, London, 6 May, 1983.

Maxey, Chester C., *Political Philosophies*, The Macmillan Co., New York, 1949.

Mead, Margaret, as quoted in Arnold, Green *Sociology*, McGraw-Hill, New York,1964.

Merrill, Francis C., *Society and Culture*, Prentice Hall, 1969.

Merton, Robert, K., *Social Theory and Social Sturcture*, Amerind, New Delhi, 1968.

Micklem, Nathaniel, *Religion*, London, Oxford University Press, 1948.

Mill, John Stuart, *Representative Government*, Forum Books, New York, 1958.

Miller, D.C. and W.H. Form, *Industrial Sociology*, Harper International, New York, 1964.

Morrall, John B., *Aristotle*, George Allen and Unwin, London, 1977.

Mosca, Gaetano, *The Ruling Class*, McGraw-Hill, New York, 1939.

Mudaliar, A. Lakshmanaswamy, Chairman, *Report of the Secondary Education Commission.*

Munroe, W.E., *The Governments of Europe*, The Macmillan Co., New York, 1938.

Murdock, George P., *Social Structure*, Macmillan, 1949.

O'Leary, John, 'Mobility on the agenda,' *The Times Higher Education Supplement*, London, 25 November, 1983.

Ogburn, W.F. and M.F. Nimkoff, *A Handbook of Sociology*, Eurasia Publishing House, New Delhi, 1964.

Parsons, Talcott, *Essays in Sociological Theory*, The Free Press, Glencoe, Ill, 1954.

Pavitt, K.L.R., 'Harnessing development to specific objectives,' *The Times Higher Education Supplement*, London, 12 August, 1983.

Piddington, Ralph, *Social Anthropology*, Oliver and Boyd, London, 1957.

Popenoe, David, *Sociology*, Appleton Century, New York, 1971.

Pound, Roscoe, *Law and Morals*, The University of North Carolina Press, 1924.

Pritchard, E.E. Evans, *Social Anthropology*, Routledge and Kegan Paul, 1972.

Pritchard, E.E. Evans, *The Institutions of Primitive Society*, Blackwell, Oxford, 1954.

Queen, S.A., R.W. Habenstein and J.B. Adams. *The Family in Various Cultures, Lippincott*, 1961.

Radcliffe-Brown, A.R., *Structure and Function in Primitive Society*, Routledge and Kegan Paul, London, 1976.

Robinson, John A.T., *Honest to God*, S.C. M. Press, London, 1969.

Rogers, E, M., *Social Change in Rural Society*, Appleton Century, New Yrok, 1960.

Ross, Arnold, *Sociology*, Alfred Knopf, New York, 1957.

Rostow, W.W., *Politics and Stages of Growth*, Cambridge University Press, 1971.

Samuelson, Paul A, *Economics*, McGraw-Hill, Tokyo, 1980.

Schrag, C.C., O. N. Larsen and W.R. Catton, *Sociology*, Harper and Row, New York.

Seligman, C.G., *Races of Africa*, Oxford University Press, London, 1961.

Smith, E.C. and A.J. Zurcher, (Editors), *New Dictionary of American Politics*, Barnes and Noble, New York, 1949.

Smith, Marion B., *Survey of Social Science*, Houghton Miffin Co., New York, 1945.

Spencer, Metta, *Sociology*, Prentice Hall, New Jersey, 1979.

Spencer, Metta, *Sociology*, Prentice-Hall, New Jersey, 1979.

Sterling, John (Editor), *The Bible* (Authorised Version), Micah, Chapter 6, Verse 8, The British and Foreign Bible Society, Oxford University Press, London, 1966.

Stevenson, Jim, 'In the privacy of their own homes,' *The Times Higher Education Supplement*, P. VII, London, 9 November, 1984 (Information Technology).

Stewart, E.W. and J.A. Glynn, *Introduction to Sociology*, Tata McGraw-Hill, New Delhi, 1976.

Strong C.G., *Modern Political Constitutions*, Sidgwick and Jackson, London, 1975.

Thomson, J. Arthur, *Science and Religion*, Methuen & Co., London, 1925.

Timasheff, N.S., *Sociological Theory*, Random House, 1967.

Toynbee, A J. (abridged by D.C. Somervell) *A Study of History*, Oxford University Press, 1947.

Toynbee, Arnold, *Industrial Revolution of the 18th Century England*, Longmans, Green and Co., London, 1912.

Trevelyan, G.M., *English Social History*, Orient Longmans, Bombay, 1970.

Von Borch, H., The *Unfinished Society*, Hawthorn Books, 1962.

Voskuyl, Roger V. and others, *Modern Science and Christian Faith*, Van Kampen Press, Illinois, 1950.

Walker, J., *The British Economic and Social History,* Macdonald and Evans, 1979.

Wanlass, L.C., *Gettell's History of Political Thought,* George Allen and Unwin, London, 1956.

Webb, Sidney and Beatrice, *The History of Trade Unionism,* Longmans, Green and Co., London, 1935.

Weber, Max, *The Sociology of Religion,* (Translated by Fischoffs), Beacon Press, 1964.

Westermarck, Edward, *A Short History of Marriage,* Macmillan, New York, 1926.

White, Merry I., as quoted in Boyer, Earnest, 'What the country wants from Dr. Bell's Successor,' *The Times Higher Education Supplement,* London, 18, January, 1985.

Wilds, Elmer H. and Kenneth V. Lottich, *The Foundations of Modern Education,* Holt, Rhinehart and Winston, Inc, New York, 1961.

Williams, Burce, 'Technology's Social Consequences,' *The Times Higher Education Supplement,* 12 August, 1983.

5

Sociology of Economic Institutions

"Economy is going without something you do want, in case you should some day want something which you probably won't want"

—*Anthony Slope*

Since economic pursuits are fundamental, it is not surprising that they should also be pervasive in their effects on social life. Economic needs and activities are fundamental in society. Modern men spend most of their waking hours making a living. The getting and spending of wealth is the subject of a vast literature, which traditionally treated these phenomena as if they were a closed system. Modern economists concern themselves mainly with economic phenomena *per se,* but recognise the interrelations of economic and other societal factors. Sociology studies the economy solely as a sub-system of the wider society, stressing the community inter-relations of economic behaviour.

Economic institutions are closely interwoven with the other institutions of primitive peoples. Among the Hopi Indians, planting corn is accompanied by much religious and recreational ritual. Since food, clothing, houses, and tools are essential, their acquisition and use influence other phenomena, such as family life and the kind and size of community. The family was a more important institution for economic production before the development of trade and manufacture created factories and enlarged villages into cities. Recent research has shown that the type of family is related to the type of subsistence. The small nuclear family with which we are familiar in the industrial West is also associated with hunting culture, whereas the extended family is more common in agricultural societies. The changes in the various social institutions will be incompletely understood unless stock is taken of changes in the economic institutions.

Especially, in modern times, economic activities are so numerous and extensive that, aside from self-sufficing farming, they cannot be controlled or aided by the family, which has been replaced as an economic institution by a number of other organisations such as corporation- owned plants. Since the local community is too inadequate to exercise much control, there is an increasing amount of national legislation affecting industry. The main problem concerning present-day economic institutions is how in all their variety and magnitude they can be best integrated with the other parts of society--a condition well-fulfilled among stationary primitive peoples. We are interested in how economic institutions can be controlled when they use ruthless power, how they may be made to evolve towards greater efficiency and production, and at the same time how they may be aided, particularly in times of disturbance.

ORIGIN AND DEVELOPMENT

The anatomical analysis of man's foot and hand suggests that he once may have been a tree dweller, in which case his earliest economic activities consisted largely in searching for fruits, nuts, and green shoots. We find him first, as man, living in the food-gathering cultures. Here the general picture is one where the procuring of roots, fruits, berries, greens, grains and seeds is supplemented by some hunting and trapping of land and water animals. The proportion of food from animals and plants varies, but in general the proportion of plant food is large. In some of these cultures, however, the reliance on meat is preponderant; for instance, the Plains

Indians depend mainly on the buffalo. Indeed, where animals are abundant, the technique of hunting highly developed so that it may be desirable to separate the hunting cultures from the other food-gathering cultures which rely largely on plant food.

The Family and the Community as Economic Institutions: The family is an important institution in both the production and consumption of goods. The wife ordinarily prepares the food, which the men, or the men and women of the family, bring in. However, the family is not the only producing and consuming organisation. Some hunting, for instance that for the buffalo or caribou, is undertaken by parties of men larger than the number of men in a single family. The walrus and other big game are best hunted by groups of men also. The hunting parties may be away for weeks or months. The consuming organisation is generally the family group, but even so on many occasions there are groups of eaters much larger than the family unit, especially at festivals and ceremonies. Accordingly it may be seen that the community as well as the family, at times, becomes the producing and consuming unit.

Sex Division of Labour: An early organisation in the procuring of food and its preparation is the division of labour between men and women. Men, and not women, are generally the hunters where hunting is an important source of food. Women are more often the gatherers of roots, berries, nuts and grains. Sometimes there are exceptions and variations from one people to another. The division of labour between the two sexes.There are not many places where men and women share the same jobs; the occupational cleavage is fairly sharp.

The Origin of Trade: The early primitive communities are self-sufficient economically, and hence do not depend upon trade. Moreover, the distance between settlements is often great and the means of transportation rudimentary. Those who have boats or who drive dogs hitched to sleds may travel considerable distances. But since in general the hunters do not have domesticated horses, the means of transportation do not favour much intertribal trade. Another obstacle to trade is the absence of a standard medium of exchanges. Durable objects of an ornamental nature, such as jade or shells, seem to have a wide acceptance and occasionally assume the nature of money. Generally, however, trade is between neighbouring tribes and the procedure is barter. The earliest trade results from differences in natural resources in particular areas, which occasion abundance or scarcity of desired commodities, such as fish, nuts, or skins. But, as has been suggested, trade plays a relatively small part in the total economy of the hunter.

Apparently, some hunting peoples do not seem to know how to trade. Early white traders sometimes found well-mannered primitive hunters who depreciated their goods and insisted they were not worth enough to trade. They professed surprise that anyone would want their material possessions. In other places there is the custom of silent trade. One group leaves on a designated spot the objects it has to offer. Later, upon return, they find that the objects have disappeared and other goods have been put in their place. Trading does not appear to be instinctive or even natural.

The Gift as a Medium of Exchange: For many early cultures the mechanism of exchange seems to have been effected by hospitality or by gifts. A gift is a social substitute for money among moneyless cultures. Thus, if a wedding occurs, gifts are brought, which sometime later are reciprocated. The system is much like our Christmas giving, which effects a rudimentary exchange of goods. As among us, the people of the hunting cultures remember with great precision the value of the gift. If a task is to be done which calls for co-operative service, such as building a dwelling, and if one co-operation works vigorously and another lazily, this fact will be remembered with exactness for a long time and the reciprocation made with the proper vigour or laziness.

Hospitality as an Economic Service: We have seen that before the invention of money and credit, gifts rendered a function like that which money renders with us. In the absence of banks and before the inventions of rent and interest, these service functions were rendered by the practice of hospitality. Hospitality, which is sometimes mistaken for communism, is the rule everywhere in hunting communities. This system of extending hospitality works out reciprocally in the long run and is not wholly one-sided. Any traveller is entitled to food and rest without payment. Indeed, no person in the community is allowed to starve if anyone else possesses food.

The practice of hospitality is at times quite extreme. It even permits the borrowing of a great variety of material objects that are not in use. The custom of lending for money, or of renting, had not been invented among hunters. The ever-present custom of hospitality was extended to cover borrowing, which again is reciprocal. The objects used in the hunt, such as the hunting boat and the harpoon, are not allowed to be lent to others, for they must always be at hand. But other objects may be taken, sometimes even without the owner's knowledge. Moreover, if in use another person's property becomes damaged, it is not always obligatory for the user to make restitution.

To a modern observer such practices suggest common ownership. This generosity is especially notable in cases where everyone on a hunt gets a share of a big catch or kill whether he gives the death stroke or not. Also the common for hunting is very widespread.

We have seen how the economic functions of wages; rent, interest, trade, and money are largely absent from early organisation. However, the functions which they render are achieved in early economic life by two widespread practices, the giving and receiving of gifts and of hospitality. Marketless economies, characterised by the lack of institutions of exchange, operate through the mechanisms of reciprocity and redistribution. As an example of the former, the coastal villages of the Trobriand Islands supply the inland villages with fish and the inland villages reciprocate with yams. Redistribution occurs when the produce of the group is brought together, either physically or by appropriation, and then distributed among the members.

Early Attitudes towards Property. These habits of gift-giving, hospitality, free borrowing, and lending, and the common use of land have led to the idea that communism existed among the primitive hunters. Did communism exist among primitive peoples, or was there individualism and private ownership of property? The point is considered by many to be of value because it appears to throw some light on the nature of man. In the private capatalism of to-day the pursuit of money and private possessions seem to be a part of our nature. Many individuals feel that a common sharing of goods would be unnatural. There are others who argue that primitive hunters were communists throughout the hundreds of thousands of years that man was in this stage of culture, and that communism mirrors man's nature. Private property, it is claimed, was a late development, and man's original nature has been twisted abnormally into selfish patterns by the rise of the institution of property.

With reference, however, to the economic life of primitive hunters, it is apparent from the preceding paragraphs that there are both common usage and private ownership. Clothing, ornaments, weapons, tools, utensils, lamps, and usually houses were individually owned, much as with us. Primitive hunting lands, on the contrary, would be called by a modern the property of the clan or band. Indeed the idea of property among many primitive peoples was not applied to land any more than we apply it to air. In general what we call public property consisted of the basic means of production. Certain essentials of life, such as land and the food supply, were generally identified with the group, whether it was the family, the clan, or the whole tribe, rather than with the individual. The communal practices appear to have been the outgrowth of the conditions of life. The mobility of animals hunted and the distance to be covered would seem to make individual ownership of hunting lands difficult.

The absence of money was naturally accompanied by a system of gifts. The relative scarcity of material inventions and of property seems to mean that property was much more subdued as an elements in the social life of primitive peoples than it is with us, where it is plentiful. The prestige of wealth and property is very great with us. Among primitive peoples the prestige of prowess, or reputation in lines other than wealth, was great, as evidenced by the fact that often among primitive hunters slander or malicious gossip was severely condemned and might lead to serious punishment or even to death.

Economic Incentives: Property vs. Reputation: The modern economic system with all its elaborate structure moves, it is said, because of man's desire to make money. The socialists call this driving force which puts all the capitalistic machinery in motion, the profit motive. If there were not this lure for private gain, why would a man work long and hard? Such is the capitalistic view of economic incentives. It is argued that communism will not work because it removes the great incentive to effort, namely, the lure of gain. On this interesting point, the primitive economic system should throw some light, since it was a system where there was very little private property, where wealth was poorly developed, and where much of what we call property, like land, was communal.

The food gather who works the hardest has the most

food to eat and can give the biggest feast. But observation shows that the best hunter not only has the most food; he also has the biggest reputation. The lazy hunter receive the scorn of the community. If the incentive for property is slight, certainly the incentive of reputation is very great among peoples with little property. It spurs men to action. A very interesting illustration is the potlatch competition of the American Indians of the North-west Pacific Coast.

These Indians meet in a great celebration and certain goods are distributed by the wealthy. These are usually blankets, which are highly prized. The person who takes them expected to return them with interest, that is, more blankets. The individual who returns the blankets with the most additional blankets receive the greatest honour. One borrows them it the highest rate of interest possible means of as one owes rate as with us. Glory goes with the payment of high interest. As Barnett puts it, "Virtue rests in publicly disposing of wealth, not in its mere acquisition and accumulation. Accumulation in any quantity by borrowing or otherwise is, in fact, unthinkable unless it be for the purpose of immediate redistribution." Thus the goals men work for are determined by their culture.

Economic Life and Culture: These examples illustrate a general aspect of economic processes in primitive society: they are woven into close relations with other institutions. The potlatch is related to celebration and festival. The exchange of goods is facilitated by gifts at weddings or ceremonies. The custom of hospitality prevents the complete control of personal property. Also, hunting is sometimes closely tied in with religion and magic. Some animals become the totem for a clan and may not be killed. Again, as was seen, the beginning of trade among hunters is often governed by what we would call good manners. There is thus a close connection between economics and group standards. The economic processes concerning exchange, trade, production, and distribution are very much in accord with the values of the community. Primitive economic life is closely interrelated with family, religion, and community folkways and mores.

THE DEVELOPMENT OF ECONOMIC INSTITUTIONS

Economic Life and Material Culture

Economic life is not only related to community standards; it is also decidedly a function of tools and inventions. Two great discoveries eventually were made which gradually replaced the hunting life with new superior economic forms and greatly speeded the development of some of the economic processes familiar to us. These discoveries were, first, the domestication of animals, particularly the big animals such as cattle; and second, agriculture. Most of the hunting peoples had already domesticated the dog, which aided in the hunt and helped somewhat in transportation. With planting and domestication came other discoveries and mechanical inventions. The course of economic organisation is closely dependent upon the new inventions in material culture.

Early Agriculture

Agriculture tended to emphasise the private onwership of land, though there are many agricultural peoples whose land is owned by the clan as in the hunting cultures, and is assigned in plots for use to different families. The crops, however, are the property of the individuals working them. In some cases planting or harvesting may be done co-operatively, so that the food belongs to a number of families collectively.

Farming without a plough, and where the main implement is a digging stick, is called hoe culture. Hoe culture, like hunting, is not as simple as it may seem, but becomes quite an art. For instance, when the Hopi of the south-western American desert plant corn, the days of planting are announced by the town crier. The land is then allotted. The Hopi methods are so expert that modern students of scientific agriculture have not been able to offer any improvements, if the same tools and seed are used. Even so, the Hopi must keep one year's supply of corn ahead as insurance against drought, for despite all their careful methods of agriculture some crops are lost.

With the stable life of agriculture there seem to have been associated other inventions. Pottery-making is partially correlated with agriculture and seldom found among hunters. The weaving of hair, or wool, or cotton is more often found among agricultural groups, for whom it replaces somewhat the hunters' use of skins as clothing. With agriculture, housing is more highly developed, since habitation is more settled and invention has made some progress.

With cloth, pottery, baskets, and crops, property begins to accumulate and to become of considerable significance. Moreover, the advanced skills required in these pursuits lead to further sepecialisation. Out of one hundred individuals, some will do a job better than others. These are the ones likely to specialise. The foundations of exchange are thus laid. Under agriculture there is greater chance of trade.

Domestication of Animals

Domestication means the continued presence of food, in contrast both to the uncertain supply in the wild state, and to the capricious situation in the case. Also, if the herds increase there is more wealth for exchange and trade. The domestication of cattle is clearly a man's work and frequently the male assumes a more dominant position among pastoral peoples than he does in the hoe cultures.

In so far as pastoral peoples wander with their herds, their life is more like that of hunters than that of settle agriculturists. They are not so likely to carry pottery with them, for instance. Shelters that can be quickly constructed are most suitable. The wandering type of life of some herders seems to fit them for marauding expeditions, the stealing of cattle, or raids on agricultural granaries. Such is the case especially where the horse has been domesticated. The horse is a great aid in war, comparable relatively to the gun or the airplane in later times. The horse is swift and can be ridden; sudden attacks and departures are readily possible, and one may fight from horseback. Cavalry are a great advantage in a fight against people who do not possess horse.

The Growth of the Handicrafts

With the development of the domestication and breeding of animals, pastoral life and farming eventually became fused in many land so that farmers possessed some sheep, cattle and horses. Such was particularly the case where the plough pulled by an animal had been invented. At this stage of plough culture, property had become quite highly developed. There was individual ownership of farm land, equipment and products. By planting in rows dug by a plough and by using the power of domesticated animals, a much larger and more certain food supply was possible, and the population became still more dense. In favourable locations the agricultural produce was sufficiently plentiful to exchange. Where the boat and horse were practicable, travel occurred over great distances and the means for carrying on trade were thus established. Meanwhile progress was made in many of the arts. The potter's wheel made better pottery, and glazing was developed. Spinning, which was done earlier by twirling a stick across the knee, was improved with the spinning wheel. There were also improvements in weaving.

The economic significance of the development of the handicrafts is varied. In the first place, it meant a growth of property. In the competition between man's quest for possessions and his desire for intangible values such as reputation or affection, the former was gaining ground. Second, the greater the variety and number of such objects of hand manufacture, the greater the requirement of labour, and hence there was an impetus to an extension of the division of labour beyond the principles of sex and age.

Social Instituions that Came with the Plough and Cattle

Land and Property: When the plough and domesticated animals were added to the hoe in agriculture, land became very important. The yield of land was increased by improvement in methods, as the decades and centuries passed. Individual ownership became the rule, though some pasture and woodland may have been held in common. By individual ownership is meant individual family ownership; and the family, including kin, was sometimes a very large one. Since land was the basis of wealth, and men desire wealth, large land holdings resulted by purchase, by marriage, or by force, where enough labour could be had to do the work. This labour was in some places kin, in others slaves or serfs, and in still others sharecroppers. There thus arose social classes, peasantry and landed aristocracy. The large landholders fought among themselves. Wealthy families became very powerful and assumed governmental functions, including the judicial and the military. They sometimes sponsored art, architecture, and religious undertakings. Gradually and sometimes by revolution, family control was wrested away from a single family; and states were born. And villages, sometimes owned or dominated by rich landlords, worked their way to freedom and grew into independent towns and cities.

Feudal Organisation: Preceding the emergence of our modern order, the necessity for protection against marauding groups in Europe led to the feudal type of organisation, especially where a central government did not exist or was breaking up. Owners of property and large holders of land found they could exact payments of money or goods from weaker farmers. With this money soldiers could be maintained. A big farmer, called a lord, with little farmers grouped round him, could do the same. These lords lived in large houses called manors, or castles, near villages or farms. They secured control over surrounding neighbours, exacting material tribute and giving them protection from robbers, pirates, and marauding groups in general. There was thus built up a type of economic organisation much larger than the family. It led to greater division of labour and to an increase in the variety of goods, because of the potentialities which exist when wealth is accumulated in the hands of a few. The manor and feudal systems were very widespread, being found even among many preliterate peoples, sometimes in incipient forms and sometimes well-developed.

In feudalism, government was closely tied to the economic system. The most powerful family that extended control over smaller and weaker families and that controlled--often by brute force--a large amount of land, exercised the sort of control over the smaller farmers, serfs, and slaves that the head of the family had exercised over the family and labour on the family farm. The lord was a head family man and an autocratic ruler.

As feudal states grew and became integrated into larger national states, out of the nobility evolved the autocratic monarch, who, of course, endeavoured to control and derive unusual benefits from economic production, then largely agricultural.

The Growth of the Division of Labour: Specialisation was furthered by the discoveries of the use of copper, tin, gold, bronze and iron. Such metals were very valuable as tools, weapons, and ornaments, and were put to uses formerly served by clay, wood, stone, grass and beads. The distribution in nature of metals was less widespread than the substances they displaced, and on this account it was not easy for each household or each male in a household to become adept in the working of metals. Thus specialists such as the tinsmith arose. When the water wheel replaced the mortar and pestle, the miller appeared. And with the use of the wheel, invented in only one place in the world, there came the wheelwright. The development of specialists outside each family meant that there had to be a further exchange of goods.

The exchange of goods over distances means transportation as well as trade. The boat possessed by all peoples living near water was a great agency for transportation even after the domestication of the horse. A horse can be ridden over plains, but it cannot be driven well through the woods without roads. Road-making is a fairly late development of man. Roads that would carry a wagon were, until quite recently, very poor. All during the Middle Ages the mileage covered by a loaded wagon over the rough roads was around a dozen or a score a day.

The Origin of the Commercial and Industrial City: With specialisation in the handicrafts and improvements in transportation, the volume of trade increased. One evidence of this was the city, which may be thought of as a place where the inhabitants do not grow enough food to feed themselves. They therefore must important it from outside, which means transportation and trade. They cannot get food gratis, so they must make cloth, leather, metal goods or something else to exchange for it. Within these early cities, located on water routes, there developed certain places for trade. The goods were assembled at certain places on certain days to be inspected, bought and sold. Such an impromptu market-place was the origin of the store. Although trade was predominantly by barter, there were some goods in frequent demand which were exchanged most often. When such goods were light and durable, as was the case with gold and silver ornaments, money developed. The volume of trade coincident with a city's life was a stimulant for the use of money. Special stores dealing in money alone, that is, banks, did not flourish until modern times, though there were pawnbrokers in the Middle Ages and money-changers in Biblical times.

The economic life of cities soon became linked with the institutions of war. Cities on or near the coast were able with their wealth, power, and population to conquer territories near and far with the aid of their ships. The cities became city states, and some expanded into empires, as, for instance, Rome.

The student who has followed the development of technologies in the preceding paragraphs must be cautioned against reading into the argument any notion of unilinear evolution, namely, the idea that all societies in their development go through the same set of sequential stages, which is an outmoded theory. It is only when cultural evolution is examined as a whole, that is, of the world as a whole and over the whole range of time, that some stages of technological and economic development are seen as preliminary to others, making it possible to reconstruct a general set of stages of increasing complexity and productivity.

The Modern Economic Order

Capitalism is the designation for the system that makes use of capital, usually expressed in terms of money but really consisting of capital goods, namely, the instruments of production. The capital goods of a state may be owned by individuals or by the government. In the former case the economic system is spoken of as *private capitalism* or simply *capitalism*. It is the system under which most of the readers of this book live. When the capital goods are owned by the government we call it state capitalism or *socialism*, a system under which many millions of people in Asia and Europe live.

To understand private capitalism we must designate its essence, which is the drive to sell for more than costs, the difference going to the private sellers. When exchange is by barter, instead of by the use of money, it is more difficult to measure the gain in a trade. The idea of profit may not exist.

But to-day under the system of private capitalism, if business men did not sell for more than costs they would either go bankrupt or get no money reward for their work and risk.

The development of the notion of profit and interest was not easy. For the ideology of the Christian church of the Middle Ages was one of service and production for need, in opposition to usury, the charge of a monetary return for a loan, as Max Weber and Richard Tawney have reminded us. They also argue that the ethics of the Protestants of Northern Europe were based upon such conceptions as thrift, individualism, the virtues of hard work, and proper rewards for personal industry. The Protestants denied that the Scriptures were in opposition to an interest rate. Thus the ideology of the Protestants was less hostile to capitalism than was that of the Catholics; and the institution of religion was related to the adoption of the new economic system. It should also be observed that coal and iron, a fundamental part of the structure of modern capitalism, are found more extensively in Protestant Northern Europe than in Catholic Southern Europe. This moral approach of the medieval Church to capitalism is found in arguments of socialists who would have the government take over the production, and produce according to needs or for social objectives; if sales are more than costs, the difference would accrue to the government, which under socialism is supposed to belong to the people.

The Industrial Revolution: The second outstanding characteristic of modern economic life is the application of mechanical power to production, a development which has paralleled the rise of capitalism.

In 1850, in the U.S.A., of all the energy used, only 25 per cent was from mechanical sources, whereas in 1950, the figure had risen to 98.6 per cent. In 1850, before the Industrial Revolution had developed very far, a worker produced 34 cents (1950 prices) worth of goods per hour, but in 1944 he produced $1.94 worth, or about six times as much. Another way of showing how increased efficiency of production has raised our income is the following. In 1950 the labour force of the United States produced 204 thousand million dollars of income to spend. But if this same labour force had worked at the same rate of productivity as in 1900--that is, with the same tools and machines and for the same number of hours--they would have produced only 79 thousand million.

Mechanical power actually brought two revolutions. One was the extensive and rapid change in the making of material goods and services, and was evidenced in the flowering of many economic institutions. The other was the revolution in the many social institutions that were closely linked to the economic activities.

The Economic Revolution: In the economic revolution, factories replaced the households as centres of production, except on farms. In factories the work was divided up into little pieces, each worker doing a single piece, as, for instance, in a clothing factory where one worker may only mark the cloth for a slit to be cut for a pocket. Machines also do work without human workers; thus music is now supplied by machines. The process still goes on. The machines that watch and control other machines usher in the age of automation.

Machines duplicate easily and rapidly. The result is that they turn out their products in great quantities. Mass-production raises the plane of living by making available at cheap prices consumer goods that cover the land like the dew. Thus pins and cloth and lamps are much more plentiful and cheap than if produced by hand. Even such expensive goods as automobiles are mass-produced.

With mechanical power came large plants, and particularly large corporations owning many plants. Sometimes these corporations own all the plants in a particular industry, thus becoming monopolies. Production processes become highly interrelated, which is not the case with self-sufficient farming or primitive hunting.

These developments of mass-production, specialisation, exchange, division of labour, and interrelationships of industries are accompanied by different systems, notably socialism and private capitalism.

Finally, with the Industrial Revolution there was a proliferation of economic organisations such as banks, stock markets, brokerage houses, insurance companies, industrial corporations, advertising companies, trade associations, chambers of commerce, merchants' associations and lobbyists.

Social Relations in Industry: In the household economy, when the family was the prevailing organisation, the labour force commonly consisted of members of the family and kin. When it was made up of slaves, serfs, or peasants, the numbers were small on an estate, and the head of the family knew them as persons and by name. Face-to-face contact was a common occurrence.

With the coming of the Industrial Revolution, factories or company-owned industries began to employ thousands of workers whom the owner or manager did not know. These workers were engaged in repetitive monotonous tasks and were so mechanically viewed that they began to be called factory "hands." A factory was seen as a mechanistic arrangement and not as a society of human beings. From the beginning of the Industrial Revolution, social workers legislators, religious leaders, and some socially minded employers protested against this lack of the human touch in employer-relations. Labour unions argued that labour was not "a commodity" like pig iron and insisted upon the dignity of man. Laws were passed to safeguard the life and health of workers, to prevent employment of children and to provide a measure of security in case of accidents, unemployment, sickness and old age.

During the World Wars when the supply of labour was short, when immigration had stopped, and when production had to be continuous, sociologists and other social scientists were drawn into industry in the United States to improve the relations between employees and management, with the goals of preventing work stoppages, reducing labour turnover, and increasing efficiency.

Industrial Sociology: Sociologists had developed a science of the interaction of individuals, as has been described in earlier chapters. They showed that a factory employee was not merely a factory "hand" but a social being sensitive to status and rank, who had ideas of what his role should be, which were often different from those of the management. Sociologists proved that consultation on work problems was often more efficienct than dictatorial decisions. The sociometry of group positions reduced friction and intrigues and led to increased output and decreased labour turnover, as well as increasing the satisfaction of the workers. For instance, in one experiment work partners were reassigned on the basis of preferences. As a result, there was a 5 cent saving in total costs and a reduction in labour turnover. Sociologists introduced the concept of the factory as a social system.

Analysis of the interaction of the members of this social system in their place of employment was not the sole contribution to the sociology of modern industrial life. Outside the plant, the lives of workers are lived in communities. The factory is located in a town or city. The community situation also affects the life and production in workplaces. Ethnic and race relations are important for successful employment outside the factory as inside. Social mobility, status and role in the community are not without significance to modern industry.

In this manner management of mass factory production in large units has learned the importance of social and community relations, a systematic knowledge of which was less urgently needed for production in the times of the household economy.

Agriculture: In agriculture, manpower had been supplemented many centuries ago by the power of animals as pullers and carriers. Not until petrol was used in the light internal-combustion engines in the first quarter of the twentieth century did farming begin to be mechanised. Tractors are rapidly replacing horses and mules on farms. Machines now exist for most of the agricultural crops. Cotton, for instance, is now planted by the use of the tractor, cultivated by a mechanical chopper and weed-killers, and dusted by an airplane, and harvested by a mechanical cotton-picker. Concurrently science has brought to farms better seeds, superior fertilisers, more thorough pest control, and finer breeds of animals. Science and technology have increased the production per man hour and production per acre.

The Accompanying Changes in Social Institutions

The revolution in industry did not occur in a vacuum. It produced another revolution in the related social institutions, as is shown in many different chapters of this book.

For instance, a revolution was produced in the family, which was formerly the chief economic institution of society. The homestead was the "factory" of the agricultural economy, which is sometimes called the household economy in comparison with the factory system of to-day.

The Industrial Revolution brought cities. In the United States in 1790, 97 per cent of the population lived in the open country or in places of 8,000 population or less. Even in China in 1940, only about 10 per cent of the population were non-farmers living in cities. Cities not only became more numerous but the existing ones became larger. Rome had a population of 150,000 in 1800. In 1960 it was fourteen times as large. With cities came radical changes in other institutions and ideologies, as, for instance, in government, in the Church, in recreation, and in attitudes towards morals.

Under the modern economy, the material plane of living has been greatly raised for the masses of the people. The average unskilled worker in the United States to-day has many more conveniences than did royalty in the days before the Industrial Revolution, when kings and queens were without radios, electric refrigerators and automobiles. Even bathtubs with running water were not common among the aristocracy of the agricultural era. The application of inanimate power to metal tools and machines brought changes in social classes and a different type of distribution of wealth. In the household economy there had been slaves, serfs, peasants, and rich large landowners. But with factories the wage earners of the cities were a new low-income class, called in European writings, the proletariat. The rich were designated capitalists.

However, there are, some who see such an unequal distribution of income as just, for they argue that the higher incomes are the result of superior ability and that those with little ability, rightly, should not receive so high an income. Variation in wealth is seen as caused by variation in ability. It is true that some are more able than others by nature. The distribution of such inherited ability is thought to be shaped like the contour of a bell, with few of great ability and few of little ability and many of ordinary abilities. Such is the shape of curves of nearly all biological traits, such as stature and weight. The curve of mental ability of students entering colleges, as shown by psychological tests, is bell-shaped like that of the normal probability curve.

Observers of social classes since the Industrial Revolution often note that the "proletarians" of the cities do not own the tools with which they work and have no income-bearing property, facts which no doubt colour their political views. However, income from property does not go exclusively to the rich. In the United States of all those males with incomes between $2,000 and $3,500 in 1953, 12 per cent received some income other than from their earnings. Income from dividends, interest, and rent probably affects the political and economic views of the recipients. Under private capitalism in the United States, the average family income, in money of constant purchasing power, doubled during the first fifty years of the twentieth century, and urban poverty has been reduced about 85 per cent during that time. The greatest amount of poverty at the mid-century in the United States is in rural areas, and especially among non-white populations, though there is some urban poverty, too.

The Stages of Economic Growth: At the present time, there is a special, practical interest in this evolution which is being shown by the underdeveloped nations, interested in policies and programmes designed to help them industrialise and raise their standard of living. These nations are mainly agricultural or peasant economies. As a recent study indicates, these traditional societies, governed by a set of pre-Newtonian attitudes towards the physical world, are limited by a ceiling by a ceiling which exists on the level of attainable output per capita. The preconditions for take-off (stage 2) in quest of a modern society, are an effective centralised national state and a shift to a predominance of industry, trade and services rather than agriculture. Political instability is an obstacle to economic development. The take-off (stage 3) occurs when resistances to steady growth are overcome, when the rate of investment and saving rises from, say, 5 per cent to 10 per cent or more. The proximate stimulus for take-off in Britain was mainly technological, leading to the rapid expansion of new industries and the diffusion of new techniques in agriculture also. Stage 4 is the drive to maturity, activated when 10 to 20 per cent of the national income is invested. At this stage of economic development, the nation can produce anything it chooses to produce, although generally it does not produce everything. Historically, sixty years have normally been required from take-off to maturity. Stage 5 is the age of high mass-consumption, exemplified by modern America. In 1948, 54 per cent of American families owned cars and in 1958, 73 per cent. Rostow expresses the hope that "the end of all this is not compound interest forever"; rather that it may be "the adventure of seeing what man can and will do when the pressure of scarcity is substantially lifted from him." Meantime, Kuznets has warned of the danger of "over-consumption,' indicating that the rate of economic growth in the United States in recent years has been checked by the limited availability of savings.

Adjustment Problems

With our modern economic institutions, are we better adjusted or less so? With the speed of turning wheels and moving machinery there are more accidents than in the age of handicrafts, though probably not so many as in the hunting cultures where big game was pursued. In the United States there are some 10,000,000 disabling accidents per year--of which 100,000 are deaths--an accident a year for every sixteen persons, and a death by accident for 1,600 persons. But the total death rate has been lowered to 9 or 10 per thousand from perhaps 35 or 40 per thousand.

Conditions of Work: In the early factories in England, children worked twelve to fourteen hours a day, much of the year starting work while it was still dark and leaving after dark. Hours of labour were around sixty a week one hundred years ago. Some factories were not sanitary, and in others workers were stricken by industrial diseases. But by the middle of the twentieth century, working conditions have been greatly improved. The above description of the early factory system, while true, exaggerates the evils because it does not present the alternation. It pictures the little factory hands engaged in monotonous routine and compares them with children frolicking carefree in the country-side, unmindful of children succumbing to hunger in the rural hovel or in the ditch by the wayside. The reality of the situation in the early nineteenth century was that the poverty of the agricultural labourers surpassed that of the factory workers, and for certain segments of the labour force at least, the factory system meant an improved standard of living.

Work in factories is repetitive, speedy; and, with minute division of labour, it is not highly varied. Therefore, the modern factory worker does not feel the joy of creation. But he has more leisure time apart from the job in which to be creative or to play or relax than the worker of the past. Even as machine power and mass-production upgraded unskilled labourers into semi-skilled operatives, so the promise of automation is in part that it will up-grade semi-skilled operative into highly-skilled technicians. Some see in automation the prospect of increased unemployment for the worker, whereas others like Norbert Wiener anticipate the greater "human use of human beings" owing to greater stress on the use of the mind. One competent observer sees the research scientists, the mathematicians, the economists and the managers of the new computer technology as the new leaders of the modern economy, replacing the businessmen and the executives. He believes that the answers to the crucial questions regarding the growth and balancing of the economy will come from research on new products and processes, including "simulation techniques" to test alternative consequences of economic decisions. The leadership, according to this view, will in the future rest less with traditional corporations and more with research corporations, industrial laboratories, experimental stations and universities. Working conditions are now greatly improved. Social legislation was partly responsible, as were shrewd and farsighted employers who saw that improvement was good for the quality and quantity of output.

Business Depressions: In the agricultural era there were crop failure which brought hunger and sometimes death by famine. In the industrial era there are business depressions that bring business failures and unemployment. These hard times come because production increases faster than does the demand for the products at the prices charged. The idea that business fluctuations are a necessary concomitant of economic growth is supported by many scholars, although more confirmation is needed. Hard times alternate with good times. In the bad years business fail and workers lose their jobs. The number of unemployed per 1,000 workers is much greater than the number of business failures per 1,000 business. The averages per year are 98 unemployed and 5 failures per 1,000. In the long stretch of years of good business since 1940, the unemployment has been around 3 per cent and business failures about 0.3 per cent. But during the great depression of the 1930's, failures were approximately 1 per cent and unemployment 20 per cent. In the early 1960's the unemployment rate was over 5 per cent.

It has been said that business depressions eliminate the weaker businesses and thus encourage efficiency. The same idea was once expressed regarding the unemployed. But the loss of a job in a depression is not the fault of the worker in the sense that the failure of a business is the failure of the owner. When masses of unemployed exist, there is no selection on the basis of ability. The workers lose their jobs because great numbers are laid off or because the factory shuts down.

Business conditions alternate from good to hard times. When the latter are very severe, great tragedy and suffering are caused to business and all of society. These violent swings are one of the problems of the capitalistic system. (From the Cleverland Trust Company, Cleveland, Ohio.)

Unemployment is a terror to the wage earner and a tragedy to his family. A business depression is a great loss to the country. The unemployment of 1930-38 amounted to a loss of 43 million man-years of employment in the United States. Also in this decade of business depression, 165 billion dollars of income, as measured in 1940 purchasing power, were lost.

There were idle factories, idle skills, idle mines, idle money. All the ingredients existed for production, but they could not get together in an operating whole. The bad adjustment of production to purchasing power leads to bad individual adjustments. During the good times of the 1940's and 1950's there was optimism over the prospect of reducing the intensity and duration of depressions. But in the 1920's prior to the depression of the 1930's there was optimism, too, for it was said then that depressions had been banished. Difficulties lie in our lack of knowledge of causes and also in the difficulties of administration and policy-making. Perhaps the fluctuations of business will be lessened in time, though hardly eliminated.

Big Business: Bigness is frequently said to be a characteristic of modern economic institutions. General Motors had assets of 8 thousand million dollars, in 1962. Standard Oil of New Jersey, with assets of 10 thousand million dollars, has wells, refineries, and sales outlets scattered over the world. The American Telephone and Telegraph Company in 1962 had more than 2 million stockholders.

In 1962, there were 4.5 million business enterprises in the United States, most of which were small. Of these businesses, 13 per cent were corporations, of which only a relatively few were big. But, of 263,000 firms in manufacturing, 361 employed 40 per cent of all the employees in manufacturing. Firms having research and development staffs totalled 15,500 but 44 firms employed 45 per cent of the scientists. The significance of the later statement lies in the fact that scientists provide the new products and processes which are important bases for the further growth of the firms in the future.

The problem of the big size of economic institutions lies in their power, particularly the power to control prices. If a single company manufactures all the corn-binders made, it has power over the prices of corn-binders; though, if the prices are high, few will be sold. The fewer firms the greater is the opportunity for reducing the range of competition. Thus four companies produce 90 per cent of the output of cigarettes. By contrast, it is difficult for several hundred thousand cotton farmers to control the price of cotton.

These few big companies, even though they control a large proportion of the output, are nevertheless competitive, generally, and some quite keenly so. The competition may be more on terms of advertising and product differentiation than in terms of price. They may compete often with companies in other industries which offer substitutes. Thus a purchaser may buy rayon clothing instead of cotton, or synthetic rubber instead of natural rubber. These big industries compete for the consumer's dollar. A television set may be bought instead of a "deep freeze" box.

However, these large companies show power in other areas than prices. They possess, because of their size, certain advantages over little business, as in advertising or purchasing. Their power may be co-ordinated, as, for instance, in regard to lobbying for legislation to control labour unions. This co-ordination is helped by the fact that the president of one company may be on the board of directors of several other companies. Big business acts somewhat in concert on some political issues and on *national policy*.

Wealth has always had power, in the agricultural era as well as in the industrial. The maladjustment appears in the lack of protection of the weak or the small. This need of correcting and preventing the abuse of power does not invalidate the obvious excellent achievements of great productive units.

Divorce between Ownership and Control: The problem of economic power has been made more complex by the development of new forms of property under capitalism. The joint stock company was a device to mobilise the large quantities of capital required by expanding industry, and to limit risk.

But the rights of the shareholder are limited mainly to a share in the distributed profits, plus (usually) voting at the meetings of the company. The property of the company is vested in a legal personality, the corporation, whose powers are exercised by the officers of the company, elected by the shareholders at the annual general meeting. The precise location of power, therefore becomes problematic. Berle and Means have documented the devices such as pyramiding and holding companies by which relatively small amounts of capital can control vast industrial empires. J.H. Burnham has argued that effective control is passing to the new managerial class of experts on whom the efficient working of the increasingly complex organisation of private capitalism is *more and* more dependent. P. Sargant Florence has shown that control by the majority of shareholders is difficult or impossible, partly because the numbers involved are frequently very large indeed, but primarily because in the larger companies a few shareholders usually hold about one-third of the voting shares.

Big Unions: A phenomenon of our times in the United States is big unions, a far cry from the situation in the 1930's when the unions fought just to survive. In earlier decades of the century, the power of the private employer was monistic and the bargaining power of workers with grievances was generally very weak, although permanent associations of wage-earners have existed since about 1700 in the British Isles and since-1792 in the United States when the shoemakers of Philadelphia organised. The central problem of the 1930's for the workers was "unions of their own choosing." Only the federal government, responding to the crisis of the deep depression, could through legislation help to redress the balance of power through government-sponsored security for workers. In doing so, government added to its own powers, leading to the present pluralistic, tripartite system, with the distribution of power divided among big business, big government, and big unions.

Unions negotiate contracts covering income, leisure, job security, retirement, pace of work, job opportunities, and discipline, but their influence now extends beyond industry into the political process, affecting the selection and election of candidates for office. The number of union members in the United States in 1962 totalled more than 17 million. Big unions are powerful and sometimes corrupt, and in terms of social responsibility, some of them in their evolution are now at a stage which may be roughly where big corporations were in the 1930's. The main current issue respecting the unions, it is said, is the freedom of the worker. Some loss of freedom is inevitable as an industrial society gains in efficiency through organisation, but the issue is how much? Unions are now firmly established and it is clear that they have contributed to industrial peace, and not--as had been feared by some--to industrial turmoil.

National unions are less subject than local unions to democratic pressures. A study of the relationship of size of locals and union democracy reports that the smaller locals generally contribute less to the democratic process at the national levels and also tend in some respects to be less democratic internally than the larger locals. Smaller 'locals are less likely to send a delegate to the national convention. Smaller locals have better attendance at meetings, a higher proportion of the membership voting in elections and more frequent turnover in leadership but also a higher proportion of uncontested elections. Lipset has argued for two-party government in the interests of union democracy but others argue that it is not realistic because the idea of one union in one jurisdiction is firmly established in American policy. Other methods of achieving democracy which have been proposed as more feasible include increased membership interest, professional labour leaders, local autonomy, union decertification, and the dismissal of leaders through rebellion of the members. Studies of American trade unions have reported that the objective conditions conducive to union activity are those which encourage personal contact with work colleagues, those which stimulate job satisfaction, and those which promote acceptance of the work group as a salient reference group.

To big business and big unions in contemporary America we must add big government. The people accept government as a balancer of the conflicting interests of business and labour. Greatly affecting the economy are government policies regarding purchases, credit regulation via the Federal Reserve Board, taxes, defence expenditure, tariffs, and outlays for research, to mention only some of the more important areas. With reference to research and development, a key to economic growth, government expenditures for fiscal 1963 came to $12.3 billion, twice the amount spent by private industry, universities, foundations, and other nonprofit organisations combined. The growth of independent administrative and regulatory agencies is a further evidence of federal governmental power. Of the 30 most influential agencies in 1962, only two were in existence in 1900, only seven by 1920 and nine by 1930. The critical problems of the economy during the great depression led to the establishment from 1930 to 1940 of *ten additional regulatory* agencies that still exist, and eleven were added from 1940 to 1960. As big government has in the relatively recent past developed regulatory policies with respect to big business, so in the future it may, in the public interest, move further in the direction of regulating big unions.

The rapid development of economic institutions in size and in power since the coming of steam and steel has led to an imbalance in the social system, as shown in the labour struggle, in the protests of little businesses, in governmental regulations and legislation. The attempt to adjust to these great centres of power in the economic institutions and to control or regulate them led to such close connection with government that the subject of economics was called political economy. But economic institutions are not only to be balanced with the governmental institutions but with all the other institutions of the social system. Economics may yet become social economics.

Summing Up

In fact, economic activities are a proper concern of the sociologist because economic and other aspects of social life are closely interrelated. In the hunting cultures where our present elaborate economic organisation had its humble origins, there is no separate economic organisation such as we have today. There is a division of labour between men and women, and the family carries on important economic activities, which are supplemented by those of the community. Since the early hunters are self-sufficient, they do not depend on trade. Within the community, the chief mechanism of exchange are hospitability and gifts. Services, are rendered or goods given without payment but with the expectation of a later return in kind. Land and food are shared but there is also private ownership of personal property such as clothing, weapons and songs. Because material goods are scarce, primitive people generally strive not so much for private gain as for status and reputation.

The development of agriculture and of the parallel pastoral economy meant a more certain and substantial food supply, a larger population, and further development of the handicrafts which led in turn to trade, exchange, payment, and specialisation. Eventually the pastoral and agricultural economics were combined in the farm as it appears in historical times. Another great step forward was taken with the development of power beyond that supplied by human beings and domesticated animals--especially the development of steam in making steel tools, later augmented by electrical power and industrial chemistry--which contributed largely to the enrichment of our material life.

The older family and feudal economic organisations were not adequate to finance the new abundance. The extensive use of money ushered in capitalism; the application of steam power to tools brought the Industrial Revolution. There were actually two revolutions, one in goods and services, and the other in the many social institutions closely linked to the economic activities. As such the Industrial Revolution brought drastic changes to the family, to cities, to social classes; changes sometimes resulting in serious maladjustments. Human relations in industry are affected by social factors like the large size and impersonal nature of the modern factory which may result in low morale among the workers, and in friction, between workers and management. Also our complex economic system depends for smooth functioning on the synchronisation of many parts which are easily thrown out of gear, with resulting depressions and unemployment.

With declining business, production is cut but not necessarily prices, because of the growth of monopolies fostered by the large-scale capital requirements in certain lines of business. As a protection, government undertakes to prevent large monopolistic enterprises, to regulate them, or to absorb them. The regulation of economic activities by the group is not a new phenomenon but is as old as society itself. Only the form of the control, which changes with changing conditions, is new.

The above discussion presents an historical account of economic institutions. As now in 21st century, the scenario is changed tremendously. And in a new economic world order, the shape, size and regulatory process of economic institutions have changed.

REFERENCES

Allen, V.L., *Power in Trade Unions* (London, 1954).

Berle, A. A., Jr., and Means, G.C.: The Modern *Corporation and Private Property (New York, 1933).*

Burnham J.: The Managerial *Revolution (London, 1943).*

Clark Kerr, *Unions and Union Leaders of their Own Choosing* (New York: The Fund for the Republic, 1957).

Daniel Bell, "The Post-Industrial Society,' Background Paper, Liberty Mutu*al Forum on the Impact* of Technological and Social Change (Boston, Mass., June 14, 1962).

Druker, Peter: *The New Society (Ne*w York: Harper and Brothers, 1950).

Eblen, T.: Absentee Ownership and Business Enterprise (1924).

Flanders, A.D.*, and Clegg, H.A.:* The System of Indust*rial Relations in B*ritain (London, 1956).

Flor*ence, P.S.: The Logic of British a*nd American Industry (London, 1953).

Galbraith, *J.K.: The Affluent S*ociety (London, 1958).

Gerald F. Winfield, *China: The Land and the People* (New York: William Sloane Associates, Inc., 1948), p. 34.

Gerth and M*ills: From Max Weber--Essays in Sociology (London:* Routledge and Kegan Paul, 1947).

H.G. Bernett, "The Nature of the Potlatch,' *American Anthropologist* (new serie*s), vol. 40, p. 353, July-S*eptember, 1938.

J. Frederic Dewhurst and Associates, *America's Needs and Resources* (New York: The Twentieth Century Fund, 1955).

John B. Knox, *op. cit.;* W.E. Moore, Industrial Relatio*ns and the Social O*rder (New York: The Macmillan Company, 1946); F.J. Roethlisberger and W.I. Dickson, M*anagemen*t and *the Worker* (Cambridge, Mass.: Harvard University Press, 1939).

L.L. Thurstone, "Primary Mental Abilities,' Psychometric Monograph, No. 1 (Chicago: The University of Chicago Press, 1938), p. 21.

Lowe, *A.: Economics and Sociology (*London, 1935).

Lowie, R.H.: Prim*itive Society (London, 1929).*

M.F. Nimkoff and Russel Middleton, "Types of Family and Types of Economy,' *American Journal of Sociology,* Vol. 66, pp. 215-25, November, 1960.

Max Weber, The Protestant Ethic and the Spirit of Capitalism, tr. by Talcott Parsons (New York: Charles Scribner's Sons, 1950); Richard Tawney, *Religion and the Rise of Capitalism* (New York: Harcourt, Brace & Co., Inc., 1952).

Moore, W.E.: *Industrial Relation an*d Social Order (New York, 1951).

Moses Abramovitz, "Economics of Grow*th,' in Bernard F. H*aley (ed.), A Survey *of Contemporary* Economics, Vol. II, pp. 132-78.

Nosow, S., and Form, W.F.: *Man, Work and Soci*ety (New York, 1962).

R.H. Van Zelst, "Sociometrically Selected Work Teams," in John B. Knox, *The Sociology of Industrial Relations* (New York: Random House, Inc., 1956).

Ralph Linton, *The Study of Man* (New York, 1930).

Robert J. Myers and John H. Chandler, "Toward explaining International Unemployment Rates,' *Monthly Labour Review, September, 1962, pp. 969-74.*

Robert Dublin, '' Prospects of Industrial Conflict--A Prediction,'*in Arther* Kornhauser. Robert Dubin, Arther M. Rose (ed.), Ind*ustrial* Conflict (New York: McGraw-Hill, 1954).

Rostow, W.W.: The Process of Economic Growth (New York, 1952).

S.M. Lipset, M. Trow and J. Coleman, *Union Democracy* (Glencoe, Illinois: Free Press, 1956).

Selig Perlman, *A History of Trade Unionism in the United States* (New York: The Macmillan Company, 1923), p. 4.

Sidney and Beatrice Webb, *The History of Trade Unionism* (London: Longmans, Green and Co., 1911).

Simon Kuznets, Capital in the American Economy: Its Formation and Financing (New York: National Bureau of Economic Research, 1961).

Talcott Parsons and Neil J. Smelser, *Economy and Society* (Glencoe, Illinois: The Free Press, 1956).

Tawney, R.H.: Religion and the Ris*e of Capitalism (London, 1927).*

U.S. Bureau of the Census, *Current Population Reports: Income of* Persons in the United *States. 1953,* Series p. 60, No. 16, Table 7, p. 20. See Chapter VII for references to the relation be*tween* income and voting behaviour.

W. Lloyd Warner, *The Corporation in* the Emergent American Society (New York: Harper and Brothers, *1962).*

W.F. Ogburn, "Technology and the Standard of Living in the United States,' *American Journal of Sociology*, Vol. 60, pp. 380-6, January, 1955.

W.H. Hutt, "The Factory System of the Early Nineteenth Century,' in Capitalism and the Historians, edited by F.A. Hayek (Chicago: University of Chicago Press, 1954).

W.L. Warner and J.O. Low, *The Social System of the Modern Factory* (New Haven, Conn: Yale University Press, 1947); W.F. Whyte (ed.), *Industry and Society* (New York: McGraw-Hill Book Company, Inc., 1946).

W.W. Rostow, The Stag*es of Economic Growth (A Non-*Communist Manifesto), (Cambridge: University Press, 1960).

Walter C. Neale, "Reciprocity and Redistribution in the Indian Village,' in Karl Polanyi et al. (ed.), *Trade and Market in the Early Empires* (Glencoe, Illinois: The Free Press and The Falcon's Wing Press, 1957).

Warren Thompson, *Population Problems* (3rd ed. New York: McGraw-Hill Book Company, Inc., 1942), p. 312.

William A. Faunce, "Size of *Locals and Union Democracy*,' American Journal of Sociology, vol. 68, pp. 291-8, November, 1962.

William Spinard,"Correlates of Trade Union Participation: *A Summary of the Literature*,' American Sociological

6

Social Conflict and Change

"All progress and growth is a matter of change, but change must be growth within our social and government concepts if it should not destroy them.

-- *Herbert Hoover*

As a phenomenal development many writers indeed have pointed to a marked decline of interest in the subject from the beginning of 20th century until the last decade or so. Lewis Coser, observes that while the early American sociologists (particularly Small and Cooley) recognised the importance of social conflict, and even assigned a positive value to it, the sociologists of the 1950s showed little concern with the subject, and when they treated it at all it was to dismiss it briefly as a purely disruptive phenomenon. This was in like with the prevailing functionalist conception of the nature of human societies. Alastair Buchan, has remarked, with reference to international conflicts, that '. . . until very recently...the study of war and peace attracted nothing like the degree of intellectual attention that has been devoted for three or four generations to economic analysis...and, whatever the reasons, there is no generally acknowledged corpus of theory...'

Of course, there was no interest at all in the phenomena of social conflict after the period in which the founders of sociology and the classical nineteenth-century writers made their studies. Marxism, which has been the pre-eminent social theory of the last hundred years, treats conflict, especially class conflict, as a fundamental characteristic of society. Even in this case, however, it is true to say that the underlying interest in social conflict did not produce much in the way of new reflection upon, or empirical investigation of, the class struggles and the international wars of the twentieth century. It is chiefly since the mid-1950s that social scientists have rediscovered the significance of conflict--a belated awakening to the character of this century, with its two world wars, its ideological confrontations, its dictatorships, its revolutionary movements and wars of national liberation, and finally its possession of the means of mass destruction through nuclear war.

From a somewhat unreal view of societies as harmoniously integrated wholes, disturbed only by minor and transitory 'deviations,' we seem now to have moved toward a conception of the co-existence of integrating and disruptive forces in the actual historical life of particular societies and the system of relations between societies, a conception close to that which was set forth long back by Simmel: '...there probably exists no social unit in which convergent and divergent currents among its members are not inseparably interwoven. An absolutely centripetal and harmonious group, a pure "unification',' not only is unreal, it could show no real life process...Society, too, in order to attain a determinate shape, needs some quantitative ratio of harmony and disharmony, of association and competition, of favourable and unfavourable tendencies."

As yet this recognition of the social significance of conflict is hardly even the beginning of wisdom. Any man, let alone a social scientist, living in the world of the 2004, must be remarkably insensitive if the daily experience--either direct or through the mass media--of armed struggles in Asia, Africa, and Latin America, of Negro revolts in American cities, of student rebellions in many countries, does not awaken in his mind some notion of the ubiquity of conflict and its importance in shaping human affairs. From the social scientist, however, we expect more than this simple acknowledgement of a fact. What is it that the sociologist, in particular, may be expected to provide? The list is long, and encompasses the main problems of a sociological theory of conflict. The diverse forms of conflict should be enumerated; the incidence and extent of conflict more precisely stated and their fluctuations noted; the varying balance between division and conflict on one side, integration and harmony on the other, more carefully described; the causes of conflict investigated the effects of conflict examined.

Types of Conflict

Let us see, first of all, what the earlier writers contributed toward a body of useable theory. Not all of them attempted to distinguish in a formal way between types of conflict; nevertheless, a simple distinction was made implicitly between international conflict (wars between nations, or empires, or tribal groups), and internal conflict (revolutionary struggles, civil war). The relative importance of these two types of conflict was variously estimated. Comte and Spencer were chiefly concerned with international conflict (and with a historical contrast between militant and industrial types of society); so, later on, were Gumplowicz and Oppenheimer. Marx, on the other hand, regarded internal conflict (the struggle between classes) as the most significant form, and his social theory has little to say about international conflict. Later, there were attempts to develop, within Marxism, a theory of imperialism and war (by Lenin, Hilferding and Rosa Luxemburg among others) but this still assumed as its starting point the fundamental conflict between classes. This simple distinction between internal and international conflict, though important, is clearly not adequate.

There are variations in the intensity of conflict, and in the extent to which the use or threat of force is involved; there may also be qualitative distinctions to be made. Simmel, for instance, distinguished between conflict and competition, treating the latter as an indirect form of conflict; 'linguistic usage reserves the term only for conflicts which consist in parallel efforts by both parties concerning the same prize. He went on to examine some specific features of competition, namely, that its outcome itself does not constitute the goal, that each competitor aims at the goal without using his strength on the adversary, and that it does not begin from hostility. Within the forms of direct conflict, both internal and international, there is a range of means employed, from intellectual persuasion, the influence of prestige or propaganda, economic or political pressure, up to the use of overt violence. One of the characteristic forms of conflict in modern societies, industrial conflict, displays several of these features. In the early stages of industrialisation in the Western countries, industrial conflict was sporadic and often violent (notably so in the United States); in the advanced industrial societies today such conflict is continuous, regulated, and generally nonviolent. Yet it is still not confined entirely or permanently to purely industrial issues or to the sole use of argument, influence, and economic pressure in disputes. Marx's theory envisaged an extension of industrial conflict into the political sphere and the eventual formation of a revolutionary working class; and although the actual course of events has not conformed in detail with these predictions (particularly in respect to the growth of a revolutionary movement), it has been close enough to leave open the question as to the scope and character which industrial conflict may assume.

It is evident, in any case, that even in the most peaceful times the threat of force is never far distant from any major industrial dispute. Such attempts to classify the forms of social conflict have been intended to make the problem more amenable to investigations. They do not presuppose the absence of more general characteristics which are perhaps to be found in all diverse forms of conflict, or which link these forms together. Conflict may have its source in some universal element of human nature, as Simmel suggested when he wrote that 'it seems impossible to deny an *a priori* fighting instinct, and as a number of recent writers, whose work we shall review later, have indicated. Or it may be that there are universal features of social structure which necessarily generate conflict.

Measurement

It is worth noting that the rudimentary classification at least makes it easier to move on to a further stage of theoretical construction, namely, the search for regularities in the emergence, extent, and duration of social conflicts. This requires an accumulation of quantitative historical information concerning different types of conflict; and the work in this field, which in any case presents great difficulty, has so far been fragmentary. The two kinds of conflict which have been most fully examined from this point of view are war and industrial conflict.

Among the early sociologists, Comte and Spencer both discussed the prevalence of warfare, but their conclusions on the tendency of warfare to diminish in and industrial state of society were not based upon any quantitative comparisons. Similar objections may be raised against most of the sociological discussions of war until quite recently. The earliest attempt to deal comprehensively with the incidence and scale of warfare in different periods was probably that of Pitirim Sorokin in the third volume of *Social and Cultural Dynamics,* but the measures which he used were fairly crude and some of the inferences drawn from the material are invalid.

A few years later an exhaustive historical examination of warfare was published by Quincy Wright under the title *A Study of War,* and this too assembled much quantitative information. The most thorough and reliable quantitative inquiry to date is that of L.F. Richardson in his *Statistics of Deadly Quarrels,* which brings together a large volume of data--though covering a relatively short period (roughly from 1820 to 1949)--and attempts to discover the correlates of war, that is, other social events which are associated with the occurrence of war. Richardson's study did not yield any very significant positive correlations, but it did dispose of some facile generalisations about the causes of war and the conditions of peace, while at the same time suggesting that there had been a tendency for the incidence of warfare to decline in relation to population size in the twentieth century. There remains the possibility that an extension of such investigations to other historical periods would reveal long-term fluctuations in warlike activity.

Further, the studies of industrial conflict have also been somewhat disappointing from the point of view of rigorous quantitative comparisons, even though many countries now publish statistics of some kind on the incidence, extent, and duration of industrial disputes. The most thorough statistical study is K.G.J.C. Knowles's Strikes: *A Study in Industrial Conflict* which deals with the United Kingdom in the period 1911--1945 and attempts to correlate strike activity with other social phenomena. There is no work of similar scope on other industrial countries, and there have been few attempts to make comparisons between countries or between historical periods. Two short studies in this field--Clark Kerr and Abraham Siegel, *'The Interindustry Propensity to Strike: An International Comparison,'* and Arthur M. Ross and Paul T. Hartman, *Changing Patterns of Industrial Conflict*--do bring together data for international comparisons. The first suggests reasons for a greater strike-proneness in certain industries, which Knowles also discussed, while the second distinguishes varying patterns of strike activity as between different groups of countries, and also examines long-term trends. The authors discern a decline in strike activity--a 'withering away' of the strike, as they call it--and also a change in the character of strikes, from major instruments of bargaining to sporadic protests; but it is possible that these are actually short-term fluctuations.

While pondering over the difficulties which arise in measuring with any precision such phenomena as wars and strikes, and note how little work has yet been devoted to these problems, it is not surprising that other types of social conflict should have presented seemingly unmanageable difficulties for sociological analysis. How are we to measure that extent of class conflict in a society?

How are we to determine the degree of competition, or its fluctuations over time? How then can we determine the balance between the forces of harmony and conflict, integration and division, within given societies; how can we make comparisons between societies in this respect; and how can we relate the phenomena to other social events?

There is no obvious answer to these questions, except to say that in many cases it will be necessary to use a variety of indirect measures, and to employ such imprecise numerical terms as 'more' and 'less.' For example, in the study of class conflict it is relevant to consider the formation of trade unions and employers' associations, the occurrence of conflict in various forms and especially the incidence of violence, the expression of attitudes in manifestoes, journals, and other media, the emergence of political movements, and the elaboration of conflicting social doctrines. Some of these phenomena can be measured fairly precisely, while in other cases the magnitude has to be estimated very roughly in a mainly descriptive account. Notwithstanding these difficulties, which are additional to the conceptual difficulties encountered in dealing with such social entities as class or ideology, some tentative historical and intersocietal comparisons could be formulated, when all the relevant criteria are brought together. If not, we should be obliged to conclude that conflict theories are as untestable as are functionalist theories.

Roots of Conflict

So far the inability to demonstrate any significant patterns in the occurrence of major forms of social conflict has not prevented the appearance of theories which claim to provide casual explanations of conflict, and especially of war, by correlating it with other phenomena; in the case of war, for example, with imperialism, with overpopulation, or with national characteristics. These claims must be regarded, for the present, as vain. This does not mean that any kind of casual explanation is ruled out. Leaving aside, for the moment, a more systematic inquiry into possible regularities and fluctuations in conflict, there are two other approaches, which may be considered.

One of these is to look for the causes of conflict in human nature, and to posit, as did Simmel, a 'fighting instinct.' In an exchange of letters with Einstein on the prevention of war, Freud asserted the existence of a destructive or aggressive instinct in human beings which cannot be suppressed, though it is always countered by another instinct, of sympathy or love. Recent biological and anthropological studies have generally supported the notion that there is an aggressive instinct, resulting from natural selection, which is widely distributed among the vertebrates and is to be found among the primates, including man. Washburn suggests that men 'inherit the biology of aggression that was adaptive in the past,' and that it is nurtured by many customs, although it is no longer adaptive: 'for the modern, crowded, scientific world, the human actor, particularly the male, is too dominance-seeking and too aggressive.' Similarly, Konrad Lorenz examines aggression as 'the fighting instinct in beast and man which is directed *against* members of the same species,' and which has as its chief positive functions the apportionment of territory, sexual selection, defence of the young, and the establishment of social ranking.

Obviously an explanation of actual conflicts along these lines cannot be complete. Neither individuals nor groups are perpetually engaged in conflict, and a theory which depends upon a permanent and constant aggressive instinct cannot explain the cycle of conflict and absence of conflict. What it does is to draw attention to an underlying propensity to engage in aggressive behaviour, and to show the biological basis of such a propensity. In order to explain actual conflicts we have to determine, in addition to this general condition, more specific causes. This may be done by adopting a theory of *interests.* Conflict occurs when territory is invaded, when young are threatened, when social ranking is disturbed or challenged. In human societies, biologically determined interests become culturally elaborated, and Lorenz recognises this by the use of the term 'militant enthusiasm' to describe the human version of biological aggressiveness in relation to interests. These considerations lead back to the sociological aspects of the problem. Assuming the existence of an aggressive propensity, can we explain actual conflicts by means of a theory of interests and of the clash of interests, broadly along Marxist lines?

Marx's theory is, in a formal sense, genuinely explanatory. His conception of the universality of class conflict provides only a general model; the important part of the theory is that which deals with classes in capitalist society, and which asserts that the increasing divergence of interests between bourgeoisie and proletariat (together with a growing awareness of the divergence) will result in increasing conflict.

Let us suppose that Marx's assertions have been falsified, that class conflict has in fact diminished in the advanced industrial societies--a view which many sociologists appear to hold strongly, even in the absence of rigorous measures of the extent of class conflict. If this is so, then we have now to explain the diminution of class conflict by arguing that divergence of interests is not so closely correlated with conflict, or that the divergence of interests between the classes has decreased, or that some other factor has affected the degree of conflict. For example, we may refer, as I myself have done in a descriptive way, to the influence of nationalism in moderating internal conflict. Another argument against the Marxist theory has been presented by Ralf Dahrendorf, who suggests that the intensity of class conflict in the nineteenth-century capitalist societies was due to the super-imposition of political conflict upon industrial conflict: 'The opponents of industry--capital and labour--met again, as *bourgeoisie* and proletariat, in the political arena...' Dahrendorf argues that industrial and political conflicts have been dissociated in what he calls 'postcapitalist societies'; there are now criss-crossing lines of conflict in place of a fundamental cleavage in society. From this criticism of Marx, Dahrendorf proceeds to outline a more general theory of conflict, which is, very briefly summarised, that conflict is a necessary element in all imperatively co-ordinated associations. If then it can be shown that imperatively co-ordinated associations are a universally necessary feature of human society, it follows that conflict is also universally necessary.

This theoretical model, which does not of course encompass intersocietal conflict, resembles the biological theory of aggression in accounting for the occurrence of internal conflict in general, while not explaining the periodicity, scale, or intensity of conflict. To deal with the latter questions we need not only the kind of sociographic and statistical studies but also an investigation of possible variations in the structure of social groups which favour or discourage conflict.

Simmel observed that conflict might become particularly bitter in groups based upon very intimate relations (such as kin groups or sects), or between groups which represented causes rather than interests (for example, classes since the time of Marx); but his remarks provide clues rather than conclusions. Coser sets out in a more formal way the propositions implicit in Simmel's essay, but his treatment is analytical, and does not attempt to establish generalisations about the actual occurrence of conflict under varying conditions of group structure and goals. Similarly van Doorn, following Simmel, distinguishes between a coalition type of organisation and a sect type of organisation, and he suggests that tensions in the latter tend to produce extremely radical and ruthless internal conflict. The empirical evidence to support such assertions is admittedly slight. Do we know, in fact, that the intensity of conflict varies significantly with the structural difference between coalition and sect, between groups based upon intimate or impersonal bonds, between interest groups and ideological groups? Is it possible to establish that variations in conflict are correlated with the degree to which organisations are imperatively co-ordinated? These questions can hardly be resolved, perhaps not even properly formulated, without a much more satisfactory natural history of conflict.

Effects of Conflict

Lewis Coser's summary of his work on the functions of social conflict probably represents well the main direction of sociological interest: '...we have examined a series of propositions which call attention to various conditions under which social conflict may contribute to the maintenance, adjustment or adaptation of social relationships and social structures.' These 'positive' functions of conflict, which were initially set out by Simmel, may be described as follows: intragroup conflict, if it is kept within limits, may help to maintain the unity of the group by providing a safety valve, or it may serve to re-establish unity; intergroup conflict sets the boundaries of groups, it may maintain a whole social system by upholding a balance of power between various groups, and it may enhance the internal unity of groups which are engaged in conflict.

Simmel refers particularly to the way in which the modern centralised states were formed as a result of warfare, and he notes that estates and classes were also created by conflict. Marx had earlier expressed the same idea: classes engage in conflict, but they are also its product, as fully constituted and conscious groups. In these examples Simmel suggests the influence which conflict may have in promoting social change, and he argues more generally that without conflict a social group can show no 'real life process.' The recent studies of conflict have not emphasised to the same extent the connection between conflict and social change, in part perhaps because such an association is a prominent feature of Marxist theory. The point becomes clear if we consider how little attention sociologists have devoted to the study of revolutionary movements in the twentieth century, except occasionally as advisers on counterinsurgency.

Revolution, like war, and perhaps even more than war, brings to the forefront those moral considerations which are interwoven with any kind of reflection upon the social meaning of conflict, the implications and influence of which are not always candidly avowed. However, the impact which revolutionary movements are beginning to have upon social thought may be seen in the recent appearance of new reflections upon the phenomenon of revolution, and in the attention now given to the theoretical writings of revolutionaries, from Mao Tse-tung to Che Guevara, Frantz Fanon and Regis Debray.

Before turning to this theme, there are some other aspects of the connection between conflict and the maintenance or transformation of a form of social life which need to be elaborated. Simmel, and most of the later writers, have been concerned with clarifying concepts and indicating possible relationships, rather than with asserting correlations. For example, Simmel observed that intergroup conflict would be likely to increase the internal cohesion of the groups involved in it, but he also observed that it did not always do so. To take a current example: the American war in Iraq is quite obviously not increasing the unity of American society; in fact, it is dividing the society in an extremely bitter conflict. A more general case is that in which defeat, or the likelihood of defeat, in an external conflict produces serious divisions within the group concerned.

In the twentieth century, revolutions have often followed military defeat. Yet the association is not constant; there have been defeats without any accompanying revolutionary struggles, and there have been revolutions without defeat in an external conflict. The Chinese revolution took place after victory.

Thus it is far from sufficient to indicate possible connections between the existence and outcome of external conflict and the degree of internal cohesion. Some more elaborate theoretical model has to be constructed which would allow us to make precise empirical statements about the effect of various types of external conflict upon various types of social groups. The general relationship between conflict and social change also needs to be investigated much more closely. Conflict between groups and within groups may evidently bring about change, or create a propensity to change by unsettling established ways of life. Simmel observed that '...in the early stages of culture, was is almost the only form in which contact with alien groups is brought about at all,' and many sociologists have attributed to warfare the extension of the scale of early societies, and in more recent times, the creation of nation states.

Warfare has been held by some writers to have a major influence upon the development of technology, and thus to contribute to more profound changes in society; while modern war, which affects the whole population of a society and which may be taken to date from World War I, has been credited with important political consequences, from the enfranchisement of women to the extension of social welfare legislation. Equally, internal conflict may bring about important social changes.

Marx adopted, as he said, the view of bourgeois historians that modern Europe was the product of class struggles, and he expected new class struggles to result in still more fundamental changes in society; in fact, Marxist political movements in many countries have radically transformed the structure of their societies. Less dramatically, it may be argued that the conflict between organised political parties in the industrial countries, and in some developing nations, has been a major influence in establishing the rights of the individual, and notably the rights of dissent, criticism and opposition. One form of conflict which Simmel examined, but which has received little attention subsequently, is competition. Simmel disagreed with the view of the socialist, and of such liberals as J.S. Mill, that the effects of competition were generally harmful, and he emphasised what he termed the 'socialising and civilising function of competition.' 'Modern competition,' he wrote, 'is described as the fight of all against all, but at the same time it is the fight *for* all'; this in the sense that economic competition is directed toward maximum output at minimum cost. Furthermore, 'given the breadth and individualism of society, many kinds of interest, which eventually hold the group together throughout its members, seem to come alive and stay alive only when the urgency and requirements of the competitive struggle force them upon the individual.'

Competition, and the whole *laissez-faire* economy of nineteenth-century capitalism, may have been important in promoting economic growth; moreover, the exceptionally rapid development of the American economy may be attributable to the greater scope of competition in the United States. But still we can produce no exact correlations between the extent of competition, or the intensity of the competitive spirit, and the rate of economic growth in different societies. And on the other hand, there are ground for supposing that competition has other less welcome effects; its civilising influence, which Simmel sees in the manner of Durkheim as the creation of a network of mutual obligations and dependencies, may be counteracted by its effect upon the rate of mental illness and of crime.

Again, however, the demonstration of an exact correspondence is wanting. Simmel, and following him Coser and others, have devoted much of their attention to the positive functions (meaning the *beneficial effect*) of conflict. One of these positive aspects is, as we have seen, that conflict engenders changes which are themselves judged to be on the whole beneficial. But aside from the fact that conflict may also produce changes which are judged to be harmful (a possibility of which we are uncomfortably aware in the nuclear age), there are other aspects of the relation between conflict and change to be considered. It cannot be demonstrated that all change results from conflict, although Hegel's philosophy of history and (with some qualifications) Marx's social theory, and the many theoretical schemes derived from them, assert or insinuate that it does.

There may be changes which occur without conflict--thc accumulation of scientific knowledge, for example--and which themselves them provoked conflict, as did modern science in the 'battle of the books,' in the conflict between science and religion, and more remotely in the struggles among interest groups and classes which were incited by the rise of a new technology. On the other side, there is no warrant for asserting that all conflict produces change. Some kinds of conflict, as Simmel suggested, help to maintain or strengthen an established form of social life; in tribal societies ritualised conflicts seem intended to enhance social solidarity and to reinforce existing institutions.

Toward Future

The revamped interest in the study of conflict has been determined very largely by practical concerns, and in particular by the desire to find some means of avoiding, or at the least controlling and limiting, war in the nuclear age. This has given rise to a whole new field of inquiry, under the name of 'strategic studies,' which is concerned on one side with those conditions and situations which seem likely to result in war, and on the other side with the outcome or consequences of war. A work which reflects better than any other these new interests, and which is illuminating also in the variety of methods which it employs, is Raymond Aron's *Peace and War: A Theory of International Relations.*

After discussing those concepts and classifications which are needed in any study of war and peace--power, force, the international systems of states, types of war, and types of peace--and considering the determinants of war, Aron turns, in the third and fourth parts of his book, to a historical examination of the global system of states in the nuclear age, and to a consideration of some moral evaluations of war and their political and strategic implications. Several of the subjects treated in the latter part of the book have been widely discussed.

One of these is the question of the influence of the level of armaments (or more generally, military preparedness) and especially of an arms race, upon the probability of war. Richardson also constructed mathematical models of arms races, one of which (the runaway arms race) he applied to the periods preceding the two world wars; at the time of his death he was studying the third arms race, which began in 1948, but he had not yet reached any conclusions about the outcome. It may not be possible to make any strict inferences from such work as to the probability of an arms race ending in war; but it is reasonable to argue that a stabilisation or reduction of armaments is likely to diminish the chances of war, first because it represents already a measure of agreement between the conflicting nations, and secondly, because it will probably affect the mood of the nations involved.

Further, another question discussed by Aron is that of an alternative to war as a means of regulating the relations between states, each of which is pursuing its own national interest. He examines two possibilities: peace through law, and peace through empire. Either course would involved a greater or lesser sacrifice of national sovereignty. Peace through law may be conceived, up to a point, as an extension of present international agreements, but its full realisation would seem to require the creation in some form of a supranational legislature, executive body, and administration. Peace through empire would quite plainly involve the loss of independence of the nations incorporated in it; it is also quite unrealisable at the present time, since neither the United States nor the Soviet Union is capable of establishing a universal empire. There is also a third possibility: peace through the balance of power, as it now exists. Here the question is whether, and under what conditions, as stable and enduring balance of power is achievable.

Is war any longer a rational instrument of policy, in Clausewitz's sense? Here we are obliged to distinguish between different kinds of wars. Wars of national liberation, counter-revolutionary wars, and some others, fought on a limited scale with what are now called 'conventional weapons,' may be rational in the sense that the gains may clearly outweigh the losses for one side, and that the common ruin of the contenders, though possible, is not necessary. But what of thermo-nuclear war between major powers? Majority opinion throughout the world would probably now consider that such a war would not be rational, that it would entail a common ruin, and even perhaps the extinction of mankind. There are, however, dissenters from this view, one of the best known being Herman Kahn, who has argued, that the cost of such a war in casualties and destruction would not be prohibitive. One new element in these studies is the use of game-theory models as an aid to determining strategy; a use which, in the extraordinary fascination which it has for some social scientists and policy makers, has attracted much criticism. Aron concludes his study of peace and war with a criticism of the spurious realism of these models, and he advocates paying more attention to 'reasonable policy' than to 'rational strategy.' While acknowledging that game theory offers a conceptual framework in which strategic analogues of conflict situations can be clearly formulated, points to the limitations of the theory, especially in non-zero-sum games in which a rational choice cannot be prescribed.

Apparently, one circumstance which accounts for the rapid growth of strategic studies is the widespread desire to control war in the nuclear age, both on rational and on moral ground. The same degree of concern, and of moral agreement, does not exist in respect of other forms of social conflict. Hence the reluctance to see revolutions, industrial conflict, and until fairly recently, ethnic conflict, as subjects which might engage the attention of any substantial number of sociologists, or figure prominently in the theoretical models or descriptive accounts of a social system. Hence, too, the uneasiness which becomes apparent when the attempt to investigate such conflicts is made.

Revolutions do not fit very comfortably into a conceptual scheme which regards the positive functions of conflict as being to maintain, with minor adaptations, a given social system. Only if a revolution is defeated is the social order maintained; if it succeeds, society transformed. And whereas sociologists, like other men, are generally *against* war and can without any qualms see their studies of war as having the practical objective of limiting or avoiding it, they may be either for or against revolution (and other kinds of internal conflict) and suddenly become aware of the intrusion of moral attitudes and commitments into their inquiry.

They may, and do, approach the study of revolutions with sympathy or aversion; they may become advisers to revolutionary leaders, or more frequently to counterinsurgency agencies. This should not deter them form such delicate inquiries, nor should it prevent them from expressing as clearly as possible the point of view which guides their research and writing, and which makes their studies humanly significant. We see little to criticise in the expression 'positive functions of conflict,' if it can be taken to cover revolutionary transformations, as well as more gradual changes, or the maintenance of an existing order; and if the contrasting negative functions are defined and given their due importance. What is open to criticism is the view which seems often to prevail that a sympathy with movements of rebellion is somehow more ideological, and a greater threat to sociological objectivity, than is an attachment to the status quo; or more generally, that a preoccupation with social conflict is less scientifically pure than is a concern with social order.

Under democratic pattern of governance, which is popular these days dissension also causes social conflict. Moreso, if society is multicultural, multiracial or divided under different castes and creeds, the corrupt politicians play different cards to manoeuvre the public opinion. In the race of seizing vote bank they play various tactics. Taking the case of India, the reservation policy is such a card of triumph, which the current UPA government at the centre is playing subtly. And there is severe social conflict. Similarly Nepal is burning because of conflict opting for democracy and ousting monarchy.

It is pertinent here to note that the recent studies of conflict have made an important contribution, not least to sociological theory in a broader sense. The studies of war, at present the most advanced, have begun to amass the kind of historical and statistical knowledge which is essential for any causal analysis, and they have been fruitful in developing models of conflict situations which, for all their shortcomings, are a powerful aid to investigation. If these studies have not yet produced any general theory of war, they have at least made clearer the complexity of the phenomenon, they have identified some of the proximate causes, and they hold out the prospect of an eventual rational control of this form of conflict.

The same degree of intellectual effort has still to be applied in the study of other types of conflict--class conflict and revolutionary movements, industrial conflict and ethnic conflict--and these phenomena present in some respects greater difficulties because both the practical end in view and the extent to which rational control of them is desired are more ambiguous. Nevertheless, it seems likely that the methods which have been used in studying conflict in an international system could be applied with profit in studying the relations among groups within a society or within segments of a society, so long as we keep in mind the difficulties of judging what is positive and what is negative in different forms of social conflict.

Apparently, the clearest gain from recent studies of conflict is the change which they have initiated in our general conceptions of the nature of a social system. It is no longer possible to place such great emphasis upon social harmony, integration, and equilibrium, or to adopt such a static view of social structure, as has been done in the last sixty years under the influence of structural functionalism. *Deviance* no longer seems an adequate category to embrace the varieties of dissent, conflict, rebellion, and repression which occur in all societies and which have assumed such vast dimensions in the rapidly changing societies of the 20th or 21st century.

Conflict is an intrinsic part of social life, sustaining, modifying, or destroying the groups in which it takes place. It cannot be treated satisfactorily as a minor and exceptional form of social relationship, in a brief apologetic appendix to a theory of social solidarity, as has so often been done. Whether we like it or not, we shall have to pay increasing attention to conflicts of interest and doctrine, and to the role of violence in upholding or overthrowing a social system, if we are to explain events and provide the means by which men can make reasonable choices between alternative courses of social action.

REFERENCES

Arthur Kornhauser, Robert Dubin, and Arthur M. Ross, *Industrial Conflict* (New York, 1954), pp. 189-212.

Coser, *op. cit.;* J. A. A. van Doorn, 'Conflict in Formal Organisations' in *Conflict in Society,* op. cit., pp. 111-32.

Freud's letter was originally published in 1933 by the League of Nations International Institute of Intellectual Co-operation. It is reprinted in Sigmund Freud, *Collected Papers,* Vol. 5 (New York, 1959), and also in *War: Studies from Psychology, Sociology, Anthropology,* Leon Bramson and George W. Goethals (eds) (New York, 1964). This latter book very usefully assembles some of the major writings on war by Tocqueville, William James, Sumner, Park, Spencer, Malinowski, Freud, and Raymond Aron, among others.

John C. McKinney and Edward A. Tiryakian (eds), *Theoretical Sociology* (New York, 1970).

Max Gluckman, *Custom and Conflict in Africa* (Oxford, 1955; New York, 1964).

Ralf Dahrendorf, 'Uber einige Problems der soziologischen Theorie der Revolution,' *European Journal of Sociology,* Vol. 2 (1961); Hannah Arendt, *On Revolution* (New York, 1963); Carl J. Friedrich (ed.), 'Revolution,' *NOMOS*, Vol. 8 (1967).

S.L. Washburn, 'Conflict in Primate Society,' in Anthony de Reuck and Julie Knight (eds), *Conflict in Society* (London, 1966), pp. 11-12.

7
The Family

If you would have a happy family life, remember two things: in matters of principle, stand like a rock; in matters of taste, swim with the current.

THE ROOTS OF THE FAMILY

The fact that man is a member of a biological species implies that there are certain deterministic conditions imposed upon his life. Human nature has been defined as the inevitability of having to breathe, eat and drink, sleep, procreate and eliminate waste matter from inside the human body. Whereas some of these functions, the first and (to some extent) the last, can be performed individually, the others cannot be so performed, but only when men organize themselves into a cooperative group. Speaking from the point of view of physical endowments, man is not well-equiped with the same. However, he has the gift of a highly developed brain which enables him to engage in organized behaviour to exploit and harness nature. The groupings that come thus into existence may have for their immediate cause and binding force several principles of integration; the simplest and most obvious of these is the principle of kinship, that is, relationship between different members of a family based on marriage and on descent. The relationship is of a three-fold nature: that between husband and wife; that between parents and children; and that between siblings (children of the same parents). The second and the third relationship need not necessarily be blood-ties as children are often adopted. The implication is that family is not to be defined solely with reference to man's biological nature.

The Family as a Functional Unit

From the composition of and the principles of integration underlying the family, it is obvious that it is a functional unit. It grows out of biological needs, particularly those of the expectant mother and the infant child, who cannot support and live by themselves. Another contributory cause is the need for the exploitation of environment which is essential to permit the satisfaction of the more intimate biological needs; and this cannot take place without organized co-activity. For a healthy and satisfactory living man seeks a secure satisfaction of his biological drives. By cooperating with other members of his family, and dividing work with them, he is able to satisfy his own basic need for food, and also make some contribution to the similar satisfaction of those other members who are cooperating with him. Thus, when a member of the Kadar tribe, of Cochin, joins his family members in the search for edible fruits and roots, he helps in the satisfaction of the hunger of the group as a whole of which he is a member. The same cooperation obtains, and for the same reasons, when he joins in other economic activities. Thus, we find that the family as an economic unit has a personal and a collective aspect. It provides for the personal satisfaction of the individual. Collectively it does the same for the family, and besides, provides the unit for the total economic pattern of the tribe or the nation.

When we look upon the family as the means of regular and channelized sex-satisfaction, the two-fold aspect is again visible. By providing for mating, the family as an institution (that is, as a mode of rendering service) makes it possible for the individual's sex urge to be satisfied. But this primary satisfaction often leads to a fuller, though slightly impersonal satisfaction; cohabitation leads to conception and children are born, not only satisfying the psychic instincts of parental love and solicitude but also leading to the socially very significant fact of the perpetuation of the group and the species.

Every great association of people, it may be a state, a nation or a tribe, has its own distinctive culture, its modes of living and thought, which are developed as a response to the peculiar circumstanced of the environment, natural and, alongside of it, ideological.

The family is the agency through which the impressionable rising generation is made familiar with such traditions. The purpose is, once again, two-fold. By teaching the individual what situations to anticipate, how to behave and what behaviour to expect, by giving him the gifts of language and dress which integrate him within his cultural ethos, the family provides a personal satisfaction; it facilitates adjustment to people and groups outside the family circle.

Even if a society does not impart the lessons mentioned above in any organized manner, still the pattern which its family life exhibits inculcates certain kinds of behaviour responses and thinking and feeling-patterns typical of the society and its culture. Thus, transmission of the cultural traditions proceeds from generation to generation, and thereby takes place the preservation of the individual by his being spared various stresses and strains of adjustment, and also of the culture by its transmission to the next generation being ensured and its extinction precluded. The family thus acts simultaneously as an educative unit and a socio-cultural agency. The importance of this aspect of the family lies in the fact that whereas all children everywhere get their earliest instruction in the family, instruction in such elementary, but supremely important, things as language for instance; in the case of most of the world's children, the rest of the education also takes place within the family, and not in any other institutional setting. Thus, all over tribal India, barring tribes like the Naga and certain Middle Indian tribes like the Munda, the Oraon, and the majority of the Gond, who have the dormitary institution, which might be regarded as an institution for imparting education, no deliberately initiated institution for such purposes is found to exist under tribal ways of living.

The Family as an Association

There are two ways of looking at the family. It can be regarded and studied as one of the universal and permanent institutions of mankind, that is, as a functional unit, and it is as such that it has been examined above. There is yet another way of studying the family, that of regarding it as a group, or a deliberately formed association. Such an approach would study the form and the content of the family, i.e., its character and composition, as also its variations from time to time and place to place.

As has been pointed out that the family has a biological matrix; it is the expectant mother and the infant who require familiar protection most. However, it is never the mother and the infants alone who constitute a family: there are always the mother's mate and their children, who complete the initial membership. This basic grouping of the mates and their children, has been called by such various names as the *nuclear*, the *immediate* or the *primary family.* The implication of all these terms is, however, the same, viz. that the nucleus of all types of families consists of those individuals who are bound together by a procreative urge and grouped with their children into a protective-cum-productive association. If this nucleus is extended, as it very often is, by the addition of other closely related kin, then it is called an *extended family.* Extended families are of various types. Firstly, there are those which grow mainly round the nucleus, and secondly there are those which are extended still further, by extending the principle of kinship, like in the Hindu *joint family.*

If a nucleus of blood relatives is surrounded by a fringe

of spouses, the resultant grouping is called a *consanguineous family*. It consists of members related by birth, and individual choice does not operate. Consequently, it is more stable. Maturation of children or break up of the marriage bond does not destroy the consanguineous family. Owing to marriage between close relatives being universally ruled out, the consanguineous family can meet any demand of its members except that for sexual gratification; and it is this fact that necessitates the fringe of spouses. Thus, we find that the emphasis is on the blood relationship and not the marriage bond. The Nayar of Malabar are said to have had a family of this type till the earlier years of this century. They did not grant any social recognition at all to the husband, nor even to the father for that matter. The type of family that we are more familiar with in our own society, viz. that in which there is a nucleus of spouses and their offspring surrounded by a fringe of relatives is called a *conjugal family*, and is found among many tribes like, e.g., the Kharia. The emphasis here is on the conjugal bond, and, therefore, this type of family is not stable among such people who do not hold this bond as indissoluble. Such a type of family also posits a dynamics in family membership in so far as everybody changes his/her allegiance to the family in which he/ she was born when he/ she gets married. There may be, however, an immense difference in the degree of this change. Thus, under conditions of patrilocal existence, the in-coming wife would almost completely break away from her family of birth, whereas the husband would not.

The family in which one is born is called *the family of origin* or *orientation*, and the family which one helps to set up after one's marriage is called the *family of procreation*.

There can also be other types of extension to permit the inclusion of all those people whom it may not be possible to include in the primary family. Thus, we have *polygynous families* where a man marries more than one wife, a condition of marital arrangements common all over tribal India. Or, there are *polyandrous families* in which the husbands are more than one, as for instance among the Khasa of Jaunsar Bawar, U.P., where several brothers marry one wife without any exclusive right of cohabitation for any one spouse. An interesting case would be the combination of the above two principles of organization; and the Toda have recently developed such a family, based on group marriage.

Next, there is the *joint family,* so very prevalent in India, hedged in and sanctioned by tradition, history, pseudo-history, myths and religion. It is a collection of more than one primary family, on the basis of close blood ties and common residence. Consequently, there can be two types, the *matrilocal joint family* like that of the Nayar and the *patrilocal joint family* like that of the tribes in Central India and all Hindus. In both these types of family, the offspring (female in case of the matrilocal type and male in case of the patrilocal type) do not, as a general rule, leave their families of origin on their marriage. So we find that joint families are an amalgam of what might have otherwise been several families of. origin and procreation. Such members of a joint family as do have to leave their family of origin on marriage (the daughters in a patrilocal joint family, and the sons in a matrilocal joint family) may not lose completely the membership of their original families, thus bringing about the dual membership. The nuclear and the extended families may be diagramatically represented thus:

When primary families link up with each other only on the basis of kinship, and not residence, we will naturally have a much wider and bigger grouping which has been called *clan,* or *sib.* Whereas the family is a *bilateral* grouping in spite of frequent one-sided emphasis, the sib is *unilateral.* Thus there can-be either *mother sibs* or *father sibs.* In the former, descent is reckoned through the female line, and in the latter through the male line. There being no restrictions of a common residence, or even territory in some cases, the sib group is much wider than the family, alongside of which it is often found. Sibs are generally exogamous; and, therefore, a family contains members of several sibs.

Sibs being as wide and extended as they are, actual recording is not possible, and often mythical ancestors are invented.

When several sibs or clans combine to constitute a stilt wider grouping, it is called a *phratry.* If sibs are, however, subdivided into groups with known historical ancestors, they are called *lineages.* The Toda have their social life structured on the basis of sibs. The tribe as a whole is divided into two phratries, Teivaliol and Tartharol, Each of these two phratries is further sub-divided into father sibs. The family as a bilateral grouping is, however, present in both the Toda as well as the Khasi social structures, the latter being based on mother sibs. Thus the primary and the extended families are not mutually exclusive.

Similar to the sib is the *gotra* kin group as it is found among the Hindus all over India, and in a modified form, as a result of culture contact, among tribal people, like the Baiga for instance who call it *got.* In practice, a *gotra* consists of a large number of cognates supposed to be descended from the same *rishi*-ancestor, who lived in the ancient past. In course of time the number of descendants of each *rishi*-ancestor has increased so that not only have all ties of common residence and even territorial proximity been snapped, but a large number of new derivative *gotra* kin groups has sprung up named after new *rishis.* It is not merely the cognatic relationship that determines the association into a *gotra,* but there are cases when the disciples of a *rishi* have adopted the *gotra* of their preceptor. *Gotra* comes to have its social significance in so far as the members of the same *gotra,* even if they have never known or heard of each other nor are related by blood, cannot intermarry. So long as the *gotra* was regarded as a group of Consanguineous kin, the question of marriage within the *gotra* did not arise. But today we find that each *gotra* consists of a large number of culturally heterogeneous people, among whom there are no traces of historical links. It has, therefore, become imperative to advocate a relaxing of *gotra* restrictions on marriage.

In the foregoing pages, the family has been viewed from the functional and the compositional points of view, leading up to a classification mainly from the compositional or structural point of view. However, the form and structure of a family is not determined only by she type and number of people who are its members, but also by how the spouses are, in the beginning, recruited. Thus, families have been classified as *monogamous, polygynous, polyandrous,* and as based on group marriage, besides, of course, as primary (or, single) and extended (or joint) from these various points of view. From the point of view of authority, a family may be classified either as *patripotestal,* or *matripotestal,* or *avuncupotestal.* The mode of inheritance of family name and property, of reckoning of descent and succession to rank and office may lead to a two-fold, classification of *patrilineal* and *matrilineal* families. Finally, a residential classification into *patrilocal, matrilocal* and *avunculocal* is also possible.

Salient Features of the Family

The family is, in the first instance, characterised by some form of institutionalized mating, i.e., some type of marriage. Secondly, there is some mode of reckoning descent by having a nomenclature. Thirdly, a family is an economic unit, particularly so far as the mother and the infant are concerned. Finally, a family is always associated with a common habitation for all its members.

The family, a grouping as outlined above, has the following distinctive features, as listed, and elaborated, by MacIver.

1. *Universality.* In view of the fact that all the aspects of an individual's life, ranging from deterministic biological to deterministic cultural, are considerably influenced and made possible by the family grouping, family is found all over the world and at all levels of culture. Besides, there is no conclusive or convincing evidence that there ever was a time when the family did not exist. Modern civilization has not so far succeeded in providing a complete and fully satisfying substitute for this grouping. The scope for compositional variation has in the past often clouded the presence of the family in various so-called primitive societies, but its absence has never been proved.

2. *Emotional basis.* The integrative bonds in a family are mutual affection and blood ties. The cords that tie together the members of a family are the outcome of such an emotional factor as love, and not an intellectual factor like reason. This emotional basis of the family makes it ideally suited to perform the all-important role of early education, which makes it an institution of considerable importance as a transmitter of culture.

3. *Educative role.* The most plastic years of every individual's life, that is, his childhood, are spent in his family. It is here that he gets the earliest and the most fundamental lessons in socialization. He is mentally formed according to the norms of society, which get ingrained in him to re-appear in his adult life as conscience or super-ego. The cultural traditions that are imbibed by an individual are imbibed by him in the familial setting, making the formative influence of the family supreme. Speaking from a limited point of view, his family also exerts a formative influence on the biological growth of the individual by making available particular and defined types of basic satisfactions to meet the basic needs in such matters as metabolism, safety, growth and so on.

4. *Nuclear position.* With regard to all the different types

of groupings, the family plays an important role in so far as it prepares the individual for participation in all these secondary groups, for their demands and situations. It serves as the nucleus for the growth of other types of groupings which never deal with the cultureless creatures that a newly-born child is.

5. *Limited size.* The family, throughout the world, is characterized by its precision as compared to other types of groupings, like the sib or clan for instance.

6. *Sense of responsibility among members.* Even though emotions and feelings are the main basis of family life, it is not completely devoid of reason. A sense of responsibility among its members in relation to each other is an aspect which is more rational and reasoned than emotional and instinctive. This feeling of personal responsibility towards each other is very important to ensure the smooth working of the familial grouping, and, consequently, of society as a whole; and, therefore, we find society stepping in to ensure it through customs and mores.

7. *Social regulation.* Society, that is the collectivity, keeping the collective and wider view in mind, has to ensure, by evolving mores and folkways, that the individual members in a family do perform all those functions towards each other on the basis of which the wider network of social relationships is dependent for its success. Thus, for example, there are social restrictions on divorce varying in intensity, in almost every society.

8. *Persistence and change.* Whereas the family as an institution is the most permanent and universal one in human societies, as an association it is subject to constant change in composition and structure, even within the same society. Time runs parallel to the family considered as an institution, but gets intimately involved in it when it is looked at as an association.

Family as a Process

The family has been viewed, not only as a permanent functional institution and an ever-active affective association, but also as a process. The process called the family can be divided into three or four well-defined stages on the basis of data available to us in India. In the first instance, we have the *formative* stage, when the individual as a growing child is prepared for his adulthood roles as a responsible member of society. Then follows the *nuptial* stage among most of the rural and urban groups, particularly in the former, child marriage having been a very distinctive feature of the Indian rural social structure. Tribal societies in India correspond to modern Western society in having a *pre-nuptial* stage after the formative and before the nuptial stages. This pre-nuptial stage among the Middle-Indian and some Naga tribes is spent in mono- or bi-sexual dormitories and in taking training in all the activities of adulthood, including those pertaining to sex. Among the rural and urban sections of the people, where marriages are parent-arranged and no courtship takes, place, no such pre-nuptial stage evists.

After marriage come the children, i.e., the *post-nuptial* stage. Speaking from the point of view of society at large, this stage is the most significant. As the growing generation of children come of age, they set the same process going again. Thus, the family is an ever-continuing process, on the smooth continuity of which depends the continuity of society itself.

ORIGINS OF THE FAMILY

Much sociological/anthropological research and speculation has gone into examining the historical origins of the family. It seems that the student of social sciences these days is not much interested in the question of origins, but the earlier stage of the modern phase of anthropological studies was highly historical-minded, being dominated by the evolutionary doctrines of Darwin and Spencer. Evolution was conceived of as a simple process of unilinear development, and the beginnings of social institutions were often presumed to be the reverse of the contemporary West European forms of these institutions, even though there was no sanction of a fully established biological analogy for such an attitude.

Basing himself on such evidence as licence on festive occasions, exchange of wives, lending of wives, and the use of the same kinship term, like father, for several individuals, Lewis Morgan came to the conclusion that the family was unknown among the simplest and the rudest of peoples. His picture of primitive society was one of atomistic existence, the only form of groupings existent being sibs. He further held that due to free sex relations and ignorance of the role of paternity, fathers were unimportant, and mother-sibs were the earliest groupings. Morgan's evolutionary scheme has no more than an historical interest now. It has already been indicated above that the family, as an association, permits for so much variation of form that the unwary or a biased student may fail to see it. Morgan's premises were correct, but by no means universal. Besides, his deductions are more logical and academic than actual and historical. Morgan has postulated a sequential growth of the institution of the family. Since his time it has been stressed often that in view of the accepted fact of diffusion, such rigidly sequential and unilinear evolution of institutions is not an acceptable proposition.

Morgan listed five different and successive forms of family, each being associated with a corresponding and distinctive type of marriage. They were, in succession, as follows:

1. The *consanguine* family, consisted of a group which was founded upon the intermarriage, in a group, of siblings, own and collateral, i.e., of brothers and sisters and of cousins.
2. The *Punaluan* family was founded upon the

intermarriage of several sisters, own and collateral, with each other's husbands in a group. The joint husbands were not necessarily related to each other. Such a family was also founded upon the intermarriage of several brothers, own and collateral, with each other's wives, in a group, these wives not being necessarily related to each other. However, in actual practice, the husbands as a group, and the wives as a group, must have been kin of each other. In each case, one group was conjointly married to another such group of members of the opposite sex.

3. The *Syndyasmian* or pairing family was founded upon marriage between single pairs, without giving the right of exclusive cohabitation to any person over another. Consequently such a marriage continued during the pleasure of the parties.
4. The *patriarchal* family was founded upon the marriage of one man with several wives, each wife being secluded from every other.
5. The *monogamian* family was founded upon marriage between single pairs, with the married couple having exclusive cohabitation with one another.

The first significant denial of Morgan's scheme, and its basis-particularly, came from Westermarck. He, on the basis of a detailed study of the institution of marriage, concluded that the family was the outcome of male possessiveness and jealousy, and a growth in property and of the sense of property. So, man, and not woman, becomes the central figure in the scheme of development here. However, it is also true that Morgan also dated the origin of the family only after man's role in begetting children became known, and the right of passing property to his own, rather than to his sister's or mother's children, had been recognized and accepted.

Westermarck's scheme was also characterized by the

evolutionary attitude to the growth of institutions; and he carried it to extreme limits. He traced monogamy back to mammals and birds, and opined that man bad inherited it from the earlier stages of the ladder of evolution. Any further evolution which had taken place was essentially in the moral ideas evolved by man with regard to marriage and not in the institution itself. The rigidity of these views strikes at their own roots. Briffault went back to Morganian inspiration and rejected Westermarck's views as unacceptable. He roots the institution of the family in yet another institution, viz. the *mother-right,* that is, the supreme authority of the mothers. The patriarchal and monogamian families are regarded by him as later in point of time and development.

Modern students of the subject have not concerned themselves with this tricky problem of origins, not because the failures of the earlier writers discouraged them, nor because the historical approach has been completely displaced, but because of what has been regarded by some as its relative futility and uselessness. Data collected by conscientious investigators from all parts of the globe, and at all levels of culture, have borne evidence to the existence of the family. Prehistoric reconstructions have not yielded any positive evidence of importance to the contrary as yet. The classical anthropologists made much of the primitiveness of the Australian aborigines, but it is fully accepted now that the Andaman Islanders are even more primitive, and these as well as the Australian aborigines do have the family as a vital and socially significant grouping. Within the subcontinent of India, the most backward, materially and socially, of tribes like the Kadar, the Paniyan, the Malapantaram, the Chenchu, the Birhor and so on do have the familial organization. Sibs, which were assigned by Morgan to the crudest level, have been found to have developed among tribes which live on some kind of agriculture.

Mainly the family is based on simple and obvious facts.

It involves the recognition of just those who are closely related to one's self through constant physical contiguity, physical cooperation, emotional bonds, and blood ties. It does not involve complicated differentiation or selection as, for instance, the sib does. In view of the basic deterministic drives, the satisfaction of which only a grouping like the family makes possible and must have in the past made possible, the conclusion is apparent, viz. that the family must have been always existent, coeval with human-culture. It is, however, quite understandable that it must have developed in varying contexts and, therefore, acquired varied forms.

The sex and hunger urges, the economic compulsives, and the cultural traditions have everywhere provided the theoretical justification for the recognition of the existence of the family. As soon as there is some permanency in sex relations and cooperative economic endeavour, a family comes automatically into existence. The birth of offspring cements and integrates family life. It can, however, never be overemphasized that although the family is our response to the challenges of our bio-psychical, natural and environmental setting, yet it is universally conditioned by the local cultural traditions. And it is this fact of varying cultural conditioning that seems to have deceived the earlier students of this institution. What is more, even if there may be a single pattern of familial organisation in a society, in practice several variant forms may emerge.

Residence and Descent

The family, we have said, is a bilateral grouping. But it has been observed that there has always been, of necessity, some stressing of one side to the partial neglect of the other. Thus, for instance, the married couple and their offspring cannot live simultaneously in the houses (families) of origin of both the husband as well as the wife. Similarly, though not for similarly obvious and compelling reasons, we find that property inheritance, descent and succession are often traced through only one of the lines. When the married couple and their offspring put up with the husband's family, or in a new household which he sets up on his own, the situation is described as a *patrilocal* residence. The reverse of this would be *matrilocal* residence. When property inheritance and reckoning of descent takes place along the male or female line it is called *patrilineal* or *matri-lineal* inheritance respectively. If the offspring inherit the father's name, they will be described as *patronymic*, and if the mother's then *matronymic*.

THE FAMILY IN THE EAST AND THE WEST

Contemporary Western Society is heavily characterized, among other things, by the declining importance of all primary groups, including the family, and their supersession by secondary groups. Most of those functions which the family used to satisfy are now fulfilled by various commercial and state-operated institutions like creches, kindergartens, schools, trade unions, clubs, hotels, and restaurants. The disintegration of the family has been hastened by freer sex relations made possible by changing notions about morals and by birth control techniques. With the decline of religion, the religious sanctions behind family and marriage have also vanished, making dissolution easier to obtain. The changed notions about the status and role of women have also aided this break up. Individualism is the basis of all contemporary Western culture. Individual happiness is often possible only at the cost of the family as a whole. Divorce, looked at from the individual's viewpoint, is a safety valve which prevents strains and saves an individual's happiness.

Many contemporary sociologists attribute most of the social and personal neuroses of Western Society to this fact of the disintegration of the family. The emotional basis of the family, where love, sharing and solidarity are the main drives behind the adult's role as the teacher and the preceptor, spares the learning child all unnecessary strains and anxieties, thereby laying solid foundations for fully integrated and secure personality structures. The secure, emotion-laden atmosphere of the home has no substitute whatever. The decline in the importance of the family has meant the growth of individualism and the decline of social responsibilities. Self-seeking is becoming dominant over social and collective interests. In totalitarian societies it is the state and not individualism which is threatening the family with the deprivation of its educative and other roles *vis-a-vis* the child. In no society except the Chinese, in which the teachings of Confucius and Lao Tse have reigned supreme over all these centuries, besides, but to a lesse extent, the Indian, has the family been held up as the ideal grouping. Recent tidings from China, however, indicate a drive against these teachings as they are becoming obstacles in the path of the sweeping changes that are under way in the socio economic structure.

There exists no single pattern among the tribal communities in India. The Naga in the east are monogamous or polygynous, patriarchal, and patrilineal--a pattern different from the neighbouring matriarchal Khasi tribe or the Nayar society. The Toda, the Kadar and the Khasa seem to belong to a combined maternal-paternal complex. The tribes of Middle India are mostly characterized by strong male influence. A uniform familial pattern is, however, exhibited by Hindu society. The family to a Hindu is a sacred institution, deriving sanction from religion and hoary social traditions and hedged in by all sorts of pseudo-history, myths and legends. Those, and they are millions, who are familiar with the tremendous popularity of the epic *Ramayana,* the story of Rama's filial love and obedience, of Sita's wifely love and devotion, and Lakshmana's loyalty to his brother, and even the unbounded love of the ape-man servant for his human master, cannot minimize the influence such myths and legends have had in shaping and preserving' the social organisation of Hindu society. The Hindu family is extended, and of the type described above as 'joint'. The father's authority reigns supreme. Residence is patrilocal. Property and name pass from father to son. Descent is reckoned along the male line. Whatever the heights of glorification to which the epics and the myths raise woman, in actual practice she often enjoys no comfort or status, being generally a drudge and an appendage of the husband, particularly so among the semi-urbanized lower middle classes. At the rural end, women enjoy a high degree of power and independence, although the males dominate, giving no share in property to females. At the urban end, there is to be witnessed both the gradual emancipation of women, leading to their being engaged in more kinds of satisfying and socially utilitarian pursuits, as also the sorry spectacle of the imitation of the manners of Western society. Marriage under Hindu Law is indissoluble, being in the nature of a permanent, sacramental bond.

Of late, it has been felt that the laws laid down by the *Dharmasastras* regarding the family life of the Hindu require to be modified in the light of the demands of contemporary social life and change. The need for relaxing (he rule of *gotra* exogamy has been already pointed out. After 1950, when the new Constitution became operative, India's legislators have been debating a Hindu Code Bill which has provoked much controversy, support and condemnation, making it imperative to split it up into piecemeal legislation. The main purposes of this Bill are to permit divorce and registration of marriage in harmony with ritual ceremonial, and also to provide for the inheritance of property by daughters. Various consequent issues like the religious and secular status of children born in inter-religious marriages, without the parents having to change their religious loyalties, have yet to be worked out. Widow remarriage is already accepted as a desired innovation by a majority of the Hindus of India. Widow marriage was legalized as far back as 1856 due to the pioneering efforts of social reformers like Ishwarchandra Vidyasagar.

REFERENCES

Linton, R. (1936), *The Study of Man*, New York.

Lowie, R. (1921), *Primitive Society*, London: Routledge & Kegan Paul Ltd.

MacIver, R.M., C.H. Page, (1953), *Society*, London: Macmillan

Morgan, L.H. (1977), *Ancient Society*, New York.

Murdock, G.P. (1949), *Social Structure*, New York: Macmillan.

8

Kinship: System and Usage

KINSHIP

According to the dictionary meaning, kinship has to do with relationships by blood or consanguinity, affinity with relationship brought about by marriage. Kinship and marriage are the basic facts of life. The study of kinship is the study of what man does with the basic facts of life--mating, gestation, parenthood, socialisation, siblingship etc. Kinship is social relationship based on consanguinity.

In its commonest definition, "kinship" is simply the relation between "kin", i.e. persons related by consanguinity. The bond of blood or marriage which binds people together in group is kinship. The central components of kinship studies are questions of social paternity for the purpose of inheritance, the nature of marriage, and the varying social forms and behaviours of three biological pairs, parent/child, husband/wife, and brother/sister.

All cultures distinguish various kins and affines, and these categories, with their associated patterns of rights and obligations, make-up what social anthropologists call the kinship system. Even in the simplest societies, kinship exists, which provides various categories for distinguishing between the people one is born among, and one's relations with them. Human beings consciously and explicitly use the categories of kinship to define social relationships. It provides a way of transmitting state and property from one generation to the next and in some societies, it serves to establish and maintain effective social groups.

Types of Kinship Bonds

In all societies people are bound together in groups by various kinds of bonds. The most universal and the most basic of these bonds is that which is based on reproduction, an inherent human drive, and is called *kinship.* The desire for reproduction gives rise to two kinds of bonds. Firstly, there is the bond between spouses and their relatives on either side; and secondly, there is the bond between parents and their children, and that between *siblings* i.e., children of the same parents. The first kind of bond, which arises out of a socially or legally defined marital relationship, is called *affinal kinship,* and the relatives so related are called *affinal kin.* The affinal kin are not connected to each other through blood, which is the case with relatives of the second kind enumerated above, who are called *consanguineous kin.* The relationship based on blood-ties is called *consanguineous* (same blood) *kinship.*

As such this context it is necessary to point out that in determining consanguineous kinship it is not the biological fact that is important but social recognition. Among many primitive societies the role of a father in the birth of a child is unknown, as among the Trobriand Islanders of Melanesia for instance. Among them it is the wife's husband who is conventionally accepted as father. Among the polyandrous Toda, until another brother makes the ceremonial presentation of a bow and arrow to the common wife, all children born to her of several brothers are regarded as the children of that brother who last performed the ceremony, even though he may have been away or dead for a long time. Here is an instance where ignorance of the biological role of fatherhood is not implied; only social recognition is shown to override biological fact. Among some African primitives, in case a husband dies, a woman assumes the role of father to the expected child of the wife of the deceased.

A universal example of the overriding nature of social recognition is the practice of adoption. An adopted child is everywhere treated as if it were one's own biologically produced offspring. So, in kinship social recognition overrides biological facts.

There are two types of kinship bonds:

(i) *Affinal:* It is a relationship by marriage. When a person marries, he establishes relationship not only with the girl whom he marries but also with a number of other people in girl's family. The affinal kins are not related to each other through blood.

(ii) *Consanguineous:* It is a relationship based on blood. The bond between parents and their children and that between their siblings is consanguineous.

It must be pointed out that in determining consanguineous kinship the biological factor is not important, but social recognition. A consanguine is someone who is defined by the society as a consanguine, and blood relationship in a genetic sense has not necessarily anything to do with it, although one the whole, these tend to coincide in most societies of the world.

Thus anthropologists tend to distinguish, for example, the *pater* or legal father from the *genitor,* or actual father. But as has been recently pointed out in many societies, the genitor is also a socially defined character. In the polyandrous tribes the actual father of a child is unknown. Moreover, an adopted child, even though he is not related by blood to this parents and siblings, assumes the role of a member of the family.

Degree of Kinship

If a person is related to ego directly, then he is ego's *primary kin;* e.g., one's father is one's primary consanguineous, and one's wife one's primary affinal kin.

Any kin related to ego through primary kin, themselves being primary kin of ego's primary kin, are our kin of the *secondary* degree; e.g., ego's father's brother, or ego's step-mother are ego's secondary consanguineous kin, and secondary affinal kin respectively.

Likewise, the secondary kin of our primary kin and the primary kin of our secondary kin will be our *tertiary kin.* The degree of kinship can thus be calculated, at least theoretically, to the nth degree.

On the basis of nearness or distance in relations three orders of relationship can be distinguished.

(i) Primary kin: According to Dr. Dubey there are eight primary kins. They are husband-wife, father-son, mother-daughter, father-daughter, mother-son, young-elder brothers, young-elder sisters and sister-brother.

(ii) Secondary kin: They are the primary kins of the primary kin. For example, father's brother, sister's husband.

(iii) Tertiary kin: They are the secondary kins of our primary kin and the primary kins of our secondary kins. For example, wife of brother-in-law's.

According to Murdock there are thirty three secondary and 151 tertiary kins of a person.

Descent

The modern family recognizes kinship with both the parents' families of origin and therefore, it has been called a *bilateral* grouping. Of course, this recognition may not be equally weighted on either side.. For example, a mother's maiden surname may not be perpetuated in the names of the offspring. In primitive society other kinds of descent are also recognized. Thus, there are sibs which completely ignore one of the two lines of descent and are, therefore, called *unilateral* groups. Opposed to such groups are *double-descent* and *bilinear* kin groups. The latter consist of only those persons who are related to ego through both patrilineal and matrilineal ties. Double descent involves the inclusion of some kin representing each line. If a common ancestor is the binder among a people, they are called *cognates.* In case their common ancestor is a male they are called *agnates* or *agnatic kin* or *patrilineal kin:* whereas the descendants of a common female ancestress are called *uterine kin* or *matrilineal kin.*

Those kin who are related to each other directly through descent are called *lineal kin* and those who branch out from the main group, like uncles and cousins, are called *collateral kin.*

In our own society, our consanguineal relatives are always related to us biologically; this is what we mean, of course, when we loosely call them "blood" relatives. Ego's recognised consanguinel relatives--the ones to whom he is bound by the kinship system-- are, in general, persons to whom he may normally look for emotional support and various kinds of help in case of need. Their importance depends upon the fact that they are few in number as compared with the whole population of the society. Hence every society limits the circle of ego's consanguineal relatives. The principle or set of principles by which ego's consanguineal relatives are determined is known technically as 'Rules of Descent'. There are three basic rules of descent.

(i) In *Patrilineal descent,* each individual automatically becomes a member of any consanguineal kin group to which his father belongs, but not of those to which his mother belongs. As a synonym, *agnatic* is sometimes used, and patrilineally related person is therefore an agnate.

(ii) In *Matrilineal descent*, an individual joins the consanguineal kin group of his mother, but not of his father. As a synonym *utrine* is sometimes used.

(iii) In *Bilateral descent*, an individual inherits some but not all of his father's consanguineal relatives and also the corresponding consanguineal relatives of his mother. In a general way, the significant relatives in this system are also the close biological relatives; how far in the everwidening circles of relationship the kin relation is recognised i.e. involves social obligations will vary somewhat from one bilateral society to another. We tend to become rather vague about our kinship with relatives beyond first cousins.

Unilinear and Bilinear Consanguineal Kin Groups

When the descent is traced from only one parent it is called unilineal descent.

The most important consanguineal kin group associated with unilineal rules of descent are lineage and sibs. A lineage is the simplest type of unilateral grouping which consists of all the probable blood relations of one line of descent exclusively. A lineage consists of descendants in one line, who know their exact genealogical relationships and who recognise obligations to one another. A lineage is thus smaller, more localised and more function-laden than the broad kinship grouping. The lineage is only one form of corporate kin group. But though there are many kinds of kinship organisation, most can be classified into four major types: Patrilineage, Matrilineage, Clans and Kindred. They differ by virtue of the mode of tracing descent. The two widespread modes are unilineal and bilineal.

Bilineal descent is also known as cognate descent or omnilinear descent. In this case, some difficulties may arise. The groups formed on this basis are bound to overlap for a start, according to this arrangement, I am a member of both my mother's and father's group. These could scarcely be groups of permanent territorial residence because I could not be permanently resident in two groups at once.

Thus, the unilineal descent has some obvious advantages. First, it assigns an individual to one group only and thus avoids the problem of overlapping groups. The unilineal principle restricts the number of man's heirs; it prevents the indefinite proliferation of inheritors that the bilateral principle demands.

Clan or Sib (lings)

Sib is a patrilineal or matrilineal kin group whose members have assumed to have a common ancestor but who do not know their exact genealogical relationship to one another. It is as if all persons named Smith at birth considered themselves bound by ties of kinship.

Generally, when the simplest type of unilateral group i.e. lineage is extended to include all those believed to be related through common descent, then we have a sib or clan. Thus, a sib or clan is often the combination of a few lineages and descent may be ultimately traced to a mythical ancestor who may be human, human-like, or even inanimate. The *gotra* of the IIindus is an example of clan. The term clan or sib describes larger, more geographically dispersed, near-functionless unilineal groups. Clans usually practice exogamy and frequently have religious, political, economic and other functions.

Murdock has suggested that sib be used to cover an unilineal groups, while clan is reserved for a localised descent group including the spouses of members.

Phratry

Any grouping of clans is phratry. It is an exogamous group of two or more clans which have a special bond between them and which associates with various activities. The various phratries within a tribe or society sometimes may be the result of the splitting of a large clan into several units or sometimes of the uniting of two distinct clans into a phratry. If all the clans of a tribe are constituted into just two phratries, then this type of social structure is called dual organisation and each phratry a moiety i.e. one half.

Range

A kinship group is called broad range or narrow range according to the number of persons it includes. The modern kinship system is a narrow range system, whereas the primitive clan or sib is a broad range system which includes people scattered over relatively large areas among whom it is not possible to trace relationship without binging in a mythical common ancestor.

Bilateral Consanguineal Kin Groups--Kindred

Bilateral is a term used to describe the transmission of descent or of property rights through male and female parents, without emphasising one or the other lines. The membership is loosely defined by the bilateral rules of descent. Seen in comparative perspective, the kindred has a peculiar feature in that its membership and duties are defined strictly in relation to a given ago. Unlike lineage and sibs therefore, kindred are not mutually exclusive in membership they overlap one another. The members have no group activities apart from their several connections with on specific person. The tenaciousness or weakness of the kindred as a cooperative group points to a more general fact; namely, that bilateral descent, unlike either kind of unilinear descent, may be best thought of in negative terms: it amounts to a lack of emphasis on either line of descent and hence on descent as such.

Importance of Rules of Descent

In every society, the rule of descent is important for at least two reasons:

(a) It automatically establishes for every individual a network of social positions in which he participates with obligations and rights. Aside from mutual aid of various kinds, the rights and obligations ascribed on the basis of descent always include some regulations of marriage and sexual relations.

(b) Descent always prescribes, to some extent, inheritance of property, and it often prescribes succession to titles or rank.

Probably the most important supplements to descent for the disposal of property rights at death are: rights established by marriage; rights established by creditors unpaid before the death of the deceased; inheritance taxes and the right of testamentary freedom.

Rules of Residence

Apart from rules of inheritance of property and status, kinship also provides for rules of residence. Rules of residence denote the pattern in accordance with which the couple decide their place of residence after marriage. These rules and practices are generally incidental to the forms of marriage and family patterns in a patriarchal society, generally bride takes the *gotra* of her husband and lives with husband's family.

The change of residence becomes essential because society forbids through incest taboos marriage between father and daughter, mother and son, brother and sister. The primary incest taboo limits the choice of marital partner except in some royal families. As a consequence of incest taboo, at least one of the partners of in marriage must leave the family of origin and take a new residence.

Generally, the following six kinds of variations in the pattern of residence are found:

(i) Patrilocal Residence: It is the pattern by which married couple come to stay with the groom's family or takes residence

near their residence. The groom has the privilege of living with his family and in the locality of his parents.

(ii) Matrilocal Residence: In matriarchal societies couple stay at the bride's residence.

(iii) Matri-Patrilocal Residence: A little variation of the above is this type where for sometime the couple stays in bride's family and then goes to stay with groom's parents. This is more or less common in those cultures where instead of dowry for the groom, the groom has to pay the bride price. The groom works and pays back the money and till then stays with bride's parents.

(iv) Bio-local Residence: Through this pattern of residence the couple express their choice of residence either near the groom or bride's family's residence.

(v) Neo-local Residence: This practice is generally followed in Western countries, where the couple neither stay with the groom's family nor with the bride's. They take up new residence and prefer to stay far from their families of origin.

(vi) Avanculocal Residence: In this pattern the couple goes to stay with the groom's brother. This practice is a common usage in matrilineal families but it is not totally absent in patriarchal families.

II

KINSHIP USAGES

Usage is a uniform or customary way of behaving within a social group, which each kin group, whether it is a particularist family or an extension thereof, like the joint family or the sib, there are certain types of coercive behaviour, verbal and non-verbal, which constitute kinship usages.

Kinship usages or the rules of kinship accomplish two major tasks:

(i) They create groups or special grouping of kin. Thus, the social invention of marriage assigns each mother a husband and makes her children his children, thereby creating a special group of father, mother and children which we call family. By use of additional rules and social conventions, larger kin groups are created, such as extended family, lineage, sibs or clans.

(ii) The second major function of kinship rules is to govern the role relationships among kin. Kinship provides a sort of social grid. It defines proper acceptable role relationships. It assigns guidelines for interactions among persons in these social grouping. Kinship usages thus act as a regulator of social life.

In practice, the importance of kinship as a regulator of social life depends on three things:

(a) The extent to which a person is surrounded by kinsmen. Kinship usage would have a limited role when the kinsmen are dispersed over a wider geographical area.

(b) The degree of development of alternative basis for assigning people to roles. In urban areas our own behaviour is not affected by kinship rules as much as we do not ordinarily interact with kinsmen.

(c) The degree of development of patterned kin behaviour. Certain kin relationships in certain societies are so highly patterned that little leeway is allowed for spontaneity. In some societies, kin relationships have little patterning which leaves much room for individualised behaviour.

Types of Kinship Usages

(i) Rules of Avoidance: These rules are designed to curtail intimacy and usually apply to cross sex relationships. There are three common avoidance relationships: brother and sister, a man and his mother-in-law, and a woman and her father-

in-law. These extreme avoidance relationships are focal because they appear to determine other and less common avoidance relationships. If a man must avoid his sister, he will often avoid various female cousins.

One of the earliest explanations of this practice was given by Tylor. He said that in early stages of human history, when son-in-law went to live with their wives, they were obliged to be on restricted relations with their mothers-in-law. Thus Tylor related son-in-law and mother-in-law avoidance usually to matri-local residence.

After Tylor, Frazer and Freud gave their own explanations of the kinship usage of avoidance. Both based themselves on the repugnance, among all societies, for tabooed sexual relations.

Frazer's explanation applies to brother-sister avoidance. No kind of intimacy or familiarity can ever develop between them. Freud's psycho-analytical explanation is also based on the prevention of sexual intimacy between various kinds of relatives. According to Freudian explanation avoidance represents a sort of institutionalised neurotic symptom. According to functionalist approach, avoidance rule serves to forestall further and more serious trouble.

So it can be said that avoidance rules are prescribed restrictions on behaviour and formalised patterns of behaviour that function to maintain social distance between persons. Avoidance rules limit the degree of individuals involvement in a social relationship and help to maintain a certain level of formality in the relationships.

As a mode of behaviour, avoidance always express respect. Although it involves two parties, and although the prohibitions are binding on both, it is usually the duty of one party specifically to avoid the other. The extent of avoidance varies from society to society.

(ii) Joking Relationship: It is a reverse of avoidance rule. Joking relationship is a socially approved and standardised pattern of interaction which allows certain relatives with specific social statuses to joke, tease or otherwise express privileged familiarity with one another without offense or impropriety.

Joking relationships may be indicative of equality and mutual reciprocity. They may also be indicative of potential sexual relationship, e.g. the joking relationship between wife's younger sister, or between wife and husband's younger brother. It may also between grandson and grand daughter and grand parents.

It is a formulation derived from Radcliffe-Brown's observations regarding the type of social interaction often seen between mother's brother and sister's son in a matrilineal society. The joking relationship is a social mechanism by which the tensions inherent in a relationship are not only socially recognised but also released through the symbolic use of particular joking formulae.

Radcliffe-Brown regards the joking relationships as having a symbolic meaning. He says that joking relations may be a kind of friendliness expressed by a show of hostility.

Some anthropologists refer to the possibility that joking relationship permit a sort of safety valve for giving expression to the pent up feelings and emotions.

(iii) Teknonymy: A word coined by the English anthropologist Sir Edward Burnett Tylor to denote of naming the parents of the child, the husband not being a member of the wife's family. Tylor regarded this kinship usage also a relic of the former supremacy of woman, who never accepted the son-in-law as one of them in their residence and recognised a secondary relationship with him through the children he helped to bring to life. Through extension, a mother may likewise be referred to as teknonymous.

(iv) Avanculate: This term from the latin word *avanculus* (mother's brother) is sometimes used to describe the authority of the mother's brother over his sister's children in a matrilineal society and sometimes to describe the indulgent relationships that exists between maternal uncle and nephew in many societies.

It is an institutionalised social relationship in which an especially close tie exists between a mother's brother and her son, with authority over the son falling on the maternal uncle rather than upon his father. The uncle often transmits his property to his nephew rather than to his son.

The maternal uncle's authority is called avuncupotestality. If nephew and nieces are brought up in their maternal uncle's family, the condition is referred to as avunculate residence. This is a common usage among matrilineal people.

(v) Amitate: Amitate is a special relationship between a child and his or her paternal aunt found in certain societies. This usage is more common among patrilineal people. It would seem that whereas avanculate in a matrilineal society and amitate in a patrilineal society may be the obvious outcome of one particular group of relative, such emphasis expressed through avanculate in patrilineal society and amitate in matrilineal society may be the social mechanics for preventing certain kinship bonds from falling into neglect.

(vi) Couvade: A custom found in some societies in which after the birth of a child the husband is expected to observe certain taboos and restrictions. Symbolically, he may imitat the female experience at childbirth and in extreme forms even act as though he was suffering all the pains of childbirth.

This is a queer usage which is found among many primitive tribes like the Khasi's and the Todas. This usage has been variously explained. Some authorities have seen in it a survival of the transitional stage of maternal paternal complex. At the paternal stage there is no excuse for treating the father so, for patrilocal residence leaves no room for doubt concerning the paternity of the child. It is only in the maternal paternal stage, where residence may be matrilocal but inheritance patrilineal, some conventional method of ascertaining paternity is needed.

Other writers have sought to give a psycho-analytical explanation. They have attributed this usage to the husband's desire to lighten the wife's discomforts by a process of participation through identification. Malinowski, considered couvade to be a cementing bond of married life and a social mechanism designed to secure paternal affection.

Kinship Theories

All types of kinship theory depends on the hypothesis that kinship and affinal relationship constitute coherent social institutions with related norms and behaviour. The parent child couple determines inheritance and inter-generational rules as well as politico-jural units and societal models. The husband/wife couple influences relationships between groups as well as various types of rights in women's labour, sexuality, reproductive powers. The sibling link can also be associated with these and is critical to the formulation of incest taboos.

Descent Theories: Particularly associated with Radcliffe-Brown and Fortes, suggest that kinship system function to ensure the inter-generational continuity of lineage groups by the maintenance of descent links through either or both parents. They stress inheritance and succession.

Alliance Theory: In Alliance theory of Levi Strauss the vital unit of kinship is a son's relationship to his maternal uncle (mother's brother) because it is latter who released his sister for formation of an alliance, through marriage exchange, with man from another group. Alliance theorists tend to study marriage and incest rules and regard kinship systems as existing not so much to allocate rights and duties as to generate marriage possibilities or impossibilities.

REFERENCES

Avinashilingam, T.S. *Educational Philosophy of Swami Vivekananda*, Ramakrishna Mission, Coimbatore, 1964.

Beals, R.H. and H. Hoijer, *An Introduction to Anthropology*, Macmillan, New York, 1969.

Benns, F. Lee, *European History Since* 1870, F. S. Crofts and Co, New York, 1947.

Bogart, E.L. and C.E. Landon, *Modern Industry*, Longman, Green & Co., New York, 1939.

Broudy, Harry S., *Building a Philosophy of Education*, Prentice-Hall, New Delhi, 1965.

Chen, Theodore, Hsi-en, *Comparative Education*, Edited by Moehlman, A.H. and Joseph S., Roucek, Henry Holt and Company, Inc., New York, 1951.

Clark, T.T., *Encylopaedia of Religion and Ethics*, Vol. XI, Edinburgh, 1962.

Colby, C.C. and A. Foster, *Economic Geography*, Ginn and Co., Boston, 1944.

Davis, Kingsley, *Human Society*, Macmillan, 1949.

Dawson, Christopher, *The Age of Gods*, Sheed and Ward, London, 1933.

Durant, Will, *Our Oriental Heritage*, Vol. I, Simon and Schuster, 1954.

Durkheim, Emile (translated by J. W. Swain), *The Elementary Forms of Religious Life*, Chapter 9, Free Press, Glencoe, Ill., 1947.

Eliot, T.S., *Murder in the Chathedral*, Faber and Faber, London, 1969.

Farber, Bernard, 'Theories of Le Play'. in *Kinship and Family Organisations*, John Wiley, New York, 1966.

Faris, R.E. L., as quoted in C.C. Schrag, O.N. Larsen, and W.R. Catton, *Sociology*, Harper and Row, New York, 1968.

Fichter, Joseph H., *Sociology*, University of Chicago Press, 1957.

Firth, Raymond, *Elements of Social Organisation*, Travistock Publications, London, 1969.

Flather, Paul, 'Gandhi honours poll pledge,' *The Times Higher Education Supplement*, London, 18 January, 1985.

Fletcher, Ronald, *The Making of Sociology*, Vol. 2, Michael Joseph, 1971.

Frankfurter, Felix, *The Public and Its Government*, Beacon Press, Boston, 1964.

Frazer, James, *The Golden Bough*, Part IV, Macmillan, London, 1963.

Gadgil, D.R., *Industrial Evolution of India in Recent Times*, Oxford University Press, Bombay, 1945.

Galbraith, John Kenneth, *The New Industrial State*, Houghton Mifflin, Boston, 1967.

Gettell, R. G., *Political Science*, Ginn and Co., Boston, 1949.

Ghose, G. *Socialism and Communism in India*, Allied Publishers, Bombay, 1971.

Giri, V. V., *Labour Problems in Indian Industry*, Asia Publishing House, 1972.

Gisbert, P., *Fundamentals of Sociology*, Orient Longman, Bombay, 1960.

Gisbert, P., *Preliterate Man*, Manaktalas, Bombay, 1967.

Glock, Charles Y. and Rodney Stark, *Religion and Society in Tension?*, Rand McNally, 1965.

Goode, William J., *Religion Among the Primitives*, The Free Press of Glencoe, 1951.

Goode, William J., *The Family*, Prentice-Hall, New Delhi, 1965.

Green, Arnold W, *Sociology*, McGraw-Hill, Tokyo, 1964.

Harris, Seymour E., *The New Economics*, Dennis Dobson, London, 1968.

Harrison, Frederick and Charles A. Meyers, *Education, Manpower and Economic Growth*, McGraw-Hill, New Delhi, 1970.

Herskovitz, Melville J., *Man and His Works*, Alfred Knopf, New York, 1956.

Hobhouse, L.T., G.C. Wheeler and M. Ginsberg, *Material Culture and Social Institutions of the Simpler Peoples*, Chapman and Hall, London, Chapter III, 1930.

Hoebel, E.A. and E.L. Frost, *Cultural and Social Anthropology*, Tata McGraw Hill, New Delhi, 1979.

Homer, *The Odyssey*, (translated by E.V. Rieu), Penguin Books, Middlesex, 1961.

Horton, Paul B. and Chester L. Hunt, *Sociology*, McGraw-Hill, New York, 1968.

Kapadia, K.M., *Marriage and Family in India*, Oxford University Press, 1954.

Karnick, V.K., *Indian Trade Unions*, Manaktalas, 1966.

Keynes, J. M., 'A General Theory of Employment, Interest and Money,' as quoted in *The Good Society* (edited by Anthony Arblaster and Steven Lukes), Methuen and Co., London, 1971.

King, David C, and M.R. Koller, *Foundations of Sociology*, Rinehart Press, 1975.

Kroeber, *Anthropology*, Harcourt, Brace and Co., New York, 1948.

Lindsay (Editor), *The New Cambridge Modern History*, Cambridge University Press, Cambridge, 1957.

Marriott, J.A.R., *A History of England*, Vol. VII, Methuen & Co, London, 1950.

Marshall, Alfred, *Principles of Economics*, Macmillan & Co., London, 1910.

Micklem, Nathaniel, *Religion*, London, Oxford University Press, 1948.

Mill, John Stuart, *Representative Government*, Forum Books, New York, 1958.

Queen, S.A., R.W. Habenstein and J.B. Adams. *The Family in Various Cultures, Lippincott*, 1961.

Smith, E.C. and A.J. Zurcher, (Editors), *New Dictionary of American Politics*, Barnes and Noble, New York, 1949.

Wanlass, L.C., *Gettell's History of Political Thought*, George Allen and Unwin, London, 1956.

Weber, Max, *The Sociology of Religion*, (Translated by Fischoffs), Beacon Press, 1964.

9

Religion

Generally, it is observed that in and for the conduct of his mundane life man has evolved certain mechanisms. Thus there are his economic organization and technology. These are his response to himself, i.e., to his own biological needs, and bring him into particular contact with his natural environment. His relations to other human beings, necessitated by the need to organize (without doing which no basic drive can be satisfied), are made possible by language, education and social organization, and are controlled by political organization.

Then there is religion; it is the human response to the apprehension of some thing, or power, which is supernatural and suprasensory. It is the expression of the manner, and type, of adjustment effected by a people with their conception of the supernatural.

Religion had been regarded as a product of civilization until Tylor gave convincing proof that primitive societies have their own versions of religious activity, not very different from that of civilized societies. Ever since Tylor's views were published no ethnographer has reported any primitive society without religious beliefs and practices. From the etymological point of view, Bouquet has shown, religion is derived from the Latin word *rel (I) igio,* which itself is derived from either the root *leg-*, which means 'to gather, count or observe', or from the root *lig-* which means 'to bind'. In the former sense the implication is belief in, and observation of, signs of Divine Communication. In the latter sense the implication is the performance of necessary actions which may bind together man and the supernatural powers that be. Both the implications are relevant in view of the fact that beliefs and rituals have been found to be the main component parts of religions.

Beliefs and Rituals

All religions consist of a mental, attitude-regarding the supernatural. The most widespread manifestation of this attitude is in the shape of *beliefs* and *rituals*, the former often wrongly called *myths*. What we call myths are believed in by the people to whom they belong, and are therefore better designated as religious belief or beliefs. All religions, primitive and modern, have this base of belief and ritual. Ritual consists in the observance, according to a prescribed manner, of certain actions designed to establish *liaison* between the performing individual and the supernatural power, or powers. Beliefs are a charter for the rituals, as also a rationalization of the same. These beliefs ensure that the rituals will be observed. What differentiates the so-called higher religions from the primitive variety is the relative absence of philosophical speculation in the latter. Primitive man has not been found to be given to philosophizing as much as modern man is. However, the presence of religion of one kind or another has been always reported by investigators; and today Jung has made it an essential feature of human life without which attainment of full integration of the human personality is not possible.

However, it may be kept in mind that the conception of the exact nature of the supernatural differs from society to society and people to people. For some the supernatural may be constituted of ghosts and spirits; for others it may be an impersonal power which pervades everything in this world; for still others it may be manifested through a pantheon of anthropomorphic gods and goddesses, or a single high God, and so on. Data collected from numerous primitive societies all over the world reveal that the primitive generally distinguish between two component elements in the supernatural field; there is a sacred part and a profane part. The sacred part, according to Durkheim, consists of, what has been termed, religion, and the profane part, of magic or primitive science. Malinowski, however, classified religion and magic as the sacred part and science as the profane part.

THEORIES OF RELIGION

Anthropological theories of religion have been concerned mainly with examining the content of various conceptions of the supernatural as prevalent in different societies at different times. The earlier sociologists also tried to trace the evolution of religion from cruder into developed forms. Recent theories concentrate on outlining the functions of religion.

Animism

The earliest anthropological theory about primitive religion, seeking to trace its origins and explain it, was given by Tylor. He said that although the origin appears to be multiple, yet there is only one idea underlying it, viz., belief in the soul *(anima);* hence the name *animism* for this theory.

Primitive man had certain experiences; in his dreams he engaged in various types of activities even while he was sleeping; he met his dead ancestors in dreams and had hallucinatory experiences about them, and other beings, while he was awake; he heard the echoes of his own voice; he saw his own reflection in ponds, pools and rivers; and he failed to disentangle himself from his shadow. Even while he was having these understandable experiences, something of a much deeper import must also have happened periodically and set the primitive man's mind thinking: people must have died. This catastrophe must have been a great intellectual challenge. What had really happened which had suddenly put an end to a person's actions, verbal and non-verbal? He looked the same, but was not the same. There must have been some unseen thing in him which must have escaped, unseen, making him dead. It was thus that the belief in such an unseen thing, or power, which kept people alive when it was in them, and made them dead when it left their bodies, emerged. Such a thing, or power, is called 'soul'. But how was it that sleep, so very like death, was not death, and how was it that people had all these various experiences in dreams, and while awake, heard echoes and saw shadows and reflections?

Certainly, Tylor says, primitive man must have thought there must be two souls in a human being; a free soul which could go out of him and have experiences, and a body soul which if it left the body resulted in its death. The former may have been associated with and represented by breath and shadow, the latter by blood and head. Primitive man must have come to the conclusion that when the body soul left the body permanently, the person concerned died; and his soul became a ghost or spirit.

The soul must have obviously appeared to be immortal because they could dream about people who had been long dead. The uncertainty whether the soul has left the body temporarily or permanently may be a reason for the practice of double funeral, a 'green' one and a 'dry' one, found among some contemporary primitive peoples of India and elsewhere. The first, green funeral, takes place immediately after death and the second, dry funeral, is observed after the lapse of some days when all hopes of the return of the soul are given up; and the second funeral is often the occasion for the more important ceremony, e.g., among the Toda and the Ho. The dry funeral symbolizes the complete severance of connexion between the dead and this world, and their entry into the other world.

So, Tylor believed that an attitude of awe and reverence

towards these intangible and non-material spiritual beings forms the core of the earliest form of primitive religion. These spiritual beings are not under our control, and have, therefore, to be propitiated lest they should do harm, and in order that they may render help.

Thus ancestor worship was the earliest form of worship and tombs the earliest temples. Animism consists of such a belief in the role of spiritual beings in human life; it is a kind of polytheism. Tylor believed that in course of time there was evolutionary development in religious beliefs and forms, and the progress was from polytheism towards monotheism. It has been complained that Tylor made a philosopher and a rationalist out of primitive man, which he certainly is not, and must never have been. Tylor had no field experience and did not know that primitive man lives an active life and is not given so much to thinking as his theory postulated. Instead, he observes life and nature and participates in it; he does not rationalize about it.

Consequently, other explanations were sought for. But it was not suggested that Tylor's theory was wholly wrong. It over-emphasized one aspect of primitive religion, viz., the belief in soul and spirits. Tylor's evolutionary sequence leading from polytheism to monotheism has, however, found no proof and therefore not many adherents.

Animalism and Manaism

Remarkably, Tylor's earliest critics said that animism is a later development in the history of religion. They postulated a pre-animistic stage when religious belief supposedly consisted mainly in the belief that everything has life and is animate. Prominent among these writers were Preuss and Max Muller. The latter's name is associated with the theory of *naturism*.

More recently, Marett evolved a special form of animalist theory which he called *manaism*. Marett said that the entire religious life of the primitive is born out of their belief in a certain ununderstandable, impersonal, non-material, and unindividualized supernatural power which takes abode in all the objects, animate and inanimate, that exist in the world. It lies more or less beyond the reach of the senses, but is manifested as physical force or such other excellences as man can think of in himself, others and also in objects around him. It may differ in intensity, the degree in which it is present in a person or an object, but in essence it is always the same. Such a set of beliefs Marett called *animatism* or *manaism* after the term *mana* used by Melanesians to designate this force. Majumdar's description and analysis of the conception of *bonga* among the Ho falls in line with Marett's theory of primitive religion. Some North American tribes call this power *orenda*. It is elsewhere known as *aren* and *wakita*.

But even this explanation is open, to some extent, to the main criticism levelled against Tylor, viz., that it invests the primitive with an aptitude for thinking and rationalization which he does not actually possess.

Naturism

Reference has been already made to the German theory of *naturism* associated with Max Muller. He said that the earliest form of religion must have been the worship of objects of nature; and evidence in support of such a view has come in from archaeological excavations conducted in Egypt and elsewhere. It is maintained that an attitude of awe or love and reverence towards objects of nature is born as a result of a 'diseased' mind which invests lifeless things with life and all the power that is associated with life. This error of mind is, according to this theory, born out of defective language. Such linguistic errors as the sun *rises*' and *sets*, or thunder *sends* rain, or that trees *bear* flowers and fruit, give rise to belief in some power inherent in the sun, thunder, trees, etc.

So far as it is maintained that objects of nature were worshipped, no difficulty arises; evidence in favour of such a practice is heavy.

But any claim to such worship being the earliest form of religion, or the explanation given, is not convincing. There is no proof to show that various conceptions follow linguistic expressions about the same. On the contrary, linguistic expressions may follow certain already existent ideas. The merit and usefulness of these various theories emerges when they are taken together, as each of them expresses some essential truth regarding primitive religion.

Functional Theories

Malinowski and Radcliffe-Brown have given functional explanations of primitive religion. Malinowski points out, with reference to the Trobriand Minders,, that religion is intimately connected with various emotional states, which are states of tension. For example, quite a few of their magical and religious practices centre round the fishing expeditions. These are the outcome of the state of fear which a possible disaster on the seas gives rise to. Similarly, hate, greed, anger, love, etc., may arise due to various situations, in a man's life. These situations create stresses and strains and, if permitted to exist over a long period of time, frustrate all action. A human being has to be an acting individual' and normal action is not possible in an emotionally upset state of existence, Religion is made use of in such a situation as a tool of adaptation its purpose is to purge the human mind of its stress and strain, i.e., it is cathartic in its action, a other words, religion has the function of bringing about a readjustment between man and the supernatural in upset states of existence. It is a device to secure mental and psychical stability in an individual's life. Radcliffe-Brown takes a different stand. The function of religion, he says, is not to purge fear and other emotional strains from the human mind, but to instil a sense of dependence in it. He says that, ultimately, the survival of the group is more important than that of the 'individual; and if the latter has to make some sacrifices it is in his own interest to do so, because without social survival individual survival is not possible. However, the individual does not seem to realize this always, and he seeks to chart out an individual course of action. If each individual were to do this there would be utter confusion and chaos and no organized activity would be possible.

Adherence to a norm of behaviour is essential in terms of social survival; and it is the fear of supernatural control and punishment, as also the anticipation of support in the case of socially approved conduct, that brings about this adherence. Therefore, the function of religion is to create a twofold feeling of dependence on society and thereby obtain the individual's concurrence with the social norms, the ultimate aim being social survival. The function of religion is the contribution it makes to that total activity which is designed to perpetuate society. Here again, we may say, that the truth lies in a conjunction of the views of Malinowski and Radcliffe-Brown. Their viewpoints might appear opposed, but they are not; they have to be taken as complementary. The individual is as important to society as society is to the individual.

Radcliffe-Brown's and Malinowski's sociological explanations are derived, in part, from Durkheim's theory of religion.

Durkheim says that religious notions are born and conceived of when we find the social group collecting together for festivals and other social gatherings. Social life on such occasions is at its intensest, and impresses the human mind which the transcendentalism and omnipotence of the group. It is conceived of as the source of all that man has and all that man is. Religion is the recognition of the superiority, moral and physical, of the collective over the individual. Durkheim defines religion with regard to the parts of which it is composed.

These parts are beliefs and rites; the former constitute the static part of religion and the latter the dynamic part. Mere beliefs constitute theology. In religion we have only sacred beliefs; beliefs which refer to gods and deities who are actually symbolic of society. These beliefs are put into practice by the performance of rites. Profane beliefs and practices are not sacred and do not form part of religion; they are magic.

RELIGION AND SCIENCE

Primitive man must have had to face the realities of life. He did so with his belief in some superior power, or powers, either by trying to coerce it into service, i.e., by magic, or by praying and offering worship to it, i.e., by the religious approach. Both magic and religion are tools of adaptation, the objective being to help man out of difficult situations and relieve his tensions. The two approaches seem to have always existed together and sometimes they come so near each other as almost to blend into each other. However, it is believed that the magical approach is the more primitive. Man must have resorted to supplication only after his ego driven magical approach failed to produce results invariably. On the basis of evidence collected from all parts of the world, Frazer found that magical formulae are based on two principles:

(i) Like produces like; and
(ii) Once in contact always in contact.

He has reduced these principles into laws. The first he calls the law of *similarity,* and the magic associated with it *homoeopathic, imitative or mimetic magic.* The second is called by him the *law of contact,* or *contagion,* and the magic associated with it *contagious magic.* On these two principles are based all the various magical rites found in primitive society. All types of magic are labelled *sympathetic* by Frazer, because he considers them to be based on the principle of sympathy between cause and effect. Magic, like modern science, is based on the observation of, and experimentation on, cause-effect phenomena.

Burning of effigies is yet another common form of imitative magic. It is believed that when the effigy is burnt, or nails driven into it, its original also will suffer likewise.

Contagious magic operates differently. Primitives have been found unwilling to use each other's clothing, not for reasons of hygiene, but because clothes are regarded a part of that person's body who wore them first. Similarly, nailcuttings and hair-trimmings and bodily excretions are also regarded as parts of the person to whom these belonged. The main implication of the law of contact is that a part is always associated with the whole to which it belongs or belonged; once a part always a part. This association is extended to clothing, nail and hair-trimmings, excreta, utensils, personal effects and so on. It is because of this that the personal effects of dead are not made use of by many primitive groups but are instead buried or cremated along with the dead body.

It is not necessary that the belief of the primitive in the supernatural follow their belief in the natural. For that matter, it is so very difficult for us to draw out a relation based on sequence between the two. The supernatural to the primitive must have been a projection of the *mana*, and ideas about it must have developed side by side with those about natural phenomena. The power that underlay these natural and supernatural forces needed to be controlled for social adjustment. Two dissimilar ways were evolved for doing so: coercion and submission.

This is a basic difference, one of approach, between religion and magic. There is yet another difference; an air of secrecy surrounds the magician and his disciples do not all know each other. Religion is public and communal; it has a congregational aspect. Both the magician and the priest mediate between this world and the other. The former is feared, the latter commands respect; the former is malevolent and the latter benevolent.

Science and magic both depend upon mechanistic procedures. The magician must follow the same type of process as is done by the scientist. But whereas the latter deals with the natural world, the former deals with the supernatural.

In magic there is assumed uniformity of cause and effect such as is postulated in natural laws. Frazer says that the two are essentially the same, the difference being that magic is based on wrong assumptions regarding causal relations. That is why he calls magic the 'bastard sister' of science. He holds that magic is false and, therefore, barren. Were it to become true and fruitful, it would no longer be magic but become science. The two attitudes, scientific and magical, differ; the former is matter of fact and the latter has in it an element of amazement, expectation, uncertainty, etc. Science assumes only natural causes and arrives at results after observation, experiment and verification. Magic assumes occult causes and works in an atmosphere of distinct unreality, excluding verification as part of its technique. The failures of science are due to inadequate knowledge and can be corrected by further research. The failures of magic are supposed to be due to some error in the performance of ritual, or else due to countermagic by more powerful magicians.

However, magic and religion are very close to each other in their role as tools of adaptation when common skills and capabilities are of no avail. Thus, Malinowski has shown that while making boats and canoes the Trobriand Islanders are perfect technicians and have a sound body of scientific knowledge. They know why a boat is made to have a certain shape, how it floats and how it may sink. But with the amount of science they know they cannot cope with the problem of why a storm comes at a particular moment and why particular canoes are sunk. So, magic and religion step in as post-scientific techniques. Malinowski has been criticized for postulating such a theory as 'double truth'.

Magic and religion are both imbued with the mystery of the world. But whereas one seeks an explanation in terms of spirits and gods, that is, religion, the other does so in terms of force, and that is magic. Nonetheless the roles of magician and priest are often combined in one person. The arts of the magician and many religious rituals are meant to create an atmosphere of suggestibility. In the case of religion the atmosphere is augmented by the character of architecture, dim lighting and incense burning, priestly robes and ancient and unknown languages in which prayers are uttered, often in a sing-song manner. The technique of both magic as well as religion is ritualistic. The entire performance is governed by a traditional order which must be strictly followed, otherwise the efficacy of the rite is lost. The veil between the two is very thin indeed. A slight change in the formulation of words may convert a magical formula into religious prayer.

Most often Magic is associated with *fetishism*. According to this belief certain objects are regarded to be possessed of powers to help man out of various difficulties, or in achieving his desires. Such objects are called *fetishes;* it may be a feather, a skull or an amulet.

Taboo

Taboo is used to designate all the restrictions, communicated through verbal 'Don't do's, and generally associated with ritualistic behaviour, which a member of a primitive society has to submit to. The question, therefore, arises as to why primitives show so much regard for a verbal injunction? In other words, what is the sanction behind taboo which instils in the mind of its would-be violator a cramping fear of punishment?

Taboo has been called the unwritten law of savage society, but society does not deal with cases of violation. The culprit himself becomes the chastizer and thus taboo avenges itself when violated. The culprit fears a calamity; therefore, taboo may be said to have a supernatural, or magical sanction behind it. It is also believed that the thing or action tabooed has a *mana* of its own. Wundt says that there must be some spiritual power inherent in taboo. The neo-Freudians explain that it is out of the objectified fear of demonic power thought to be concealed in the tabooed object that taboo arises.

The aim of taboo appears to be to limit an individual to the norms of his society. Therefore, it is society which is vitally affected by the observance or non-observance of taboo, yet the initiative always rests, to a certain extent, with the individual. The woof and warp of magical beliefs and practices is made up of positive and negative strands, and taboo is the latter.

Its purpose is threefold: productive, protective and prohibitive. Taboos associated with the process of cultivation are designed to be productive; those like 'keeping women, children and, in cases, men also away from certain places; actions and objects are protective; and those which seclude a person or limit contact with him or her, as is done in the case of a chief, a priest, a magician or a menstruating woman, are designed to be prohibitive in the sense that they prohibit the persons tabooed from doing harm to others.

Protective and prohibitive taboos are almost always the same. Various kinds of typical taboos have been found to be associated with totemism. These were explained by Freud by referring them to ambivalence, a pathological state of mind which includes mutually contradictory sub-psychical states. There is on the one hand the desire to do what should not be done, and on the other hand there is simultaneously the realization that such a thing should not be done. Accordingly to Freud conflict of this nature explains, the origin of all taboos.

Freud says that the Oedipus Complex (the desire to kill one's father, cohabit with one's own mother, followed by repentance) underlies the protection of the totemic animal and the practice of exogamy. The totemic animal or vegetable ancestor is like one's father, and therefore the danger of its being killed or eaten by the sons has to be precluded; also, the sons must not be allowed to marry their mothers, and hence the totemic taboos. These have been classified into two main categories: taboos which forbid the killing and eating of the totem and those which forbid certain forms of endogamous marriages.

Radcliffe-Brown, always seeks sociological explanations for social phenomena, has tried to place taboo among those various social mechanisms by which an orderly society is able to maintain itself in existence. This is said to be made possible by the fact that these social mechanisms like taboo (and totemism and kinship usages) help in establishing some of those fundamental social values which are vital to social survival. Radcliffe-Brown has emphasized the significance of the symbolism involved in rituals connected with both taboo as also totemism, the function of which symbolism is said to be the expression and maintenance of the solidarity of society.

REFERENFES

Boas, F. (ed.), *General Anthropology* (New York, 1938), Chapter on Religion by R. Benedict.

Bouquet, A.C., *Comparative Religion* (Pelican, A 89), Chapters I to V.

Ghurye, G.S., *The Aborigines--So-called--and Their Future* (Poona: Gokhale Institute of Politics & Economics, 1943), Chapter 1.

Herskovits, M.J., *Man and His Works,* Chapters XXI and XXII.

Hutton, J.H., *Caste in India* (Cumberledge, 1951), Appendix B.

Karsten. R., *The Origins of Religion* (London; Kegan Paul Trench, Trubner & Co., 1935).

Lowie, R.H., *Primitive Religion* (New York, 1924).

Malinowski, B., *Magic, Science* and *Religion* (Boston and Glencoe, III., 1948).

Marriet, R.R., *The Threshold of Religion* (New York, 1914). Radcliffe-Brown, A. R., *Function and Structure in Primitive Society* (London: Cohen & West, 1952), Chapter VIII.

Tylor, E.B., *Primitive Culture,* Vol. II.

Bibliography

Aiyer, C.P. Ramaswamy, *Education*, Vol. I, Asia Book Co., Madras, 1970.

Allport, G.W. and Leo Postman, *The Psychology of Rumour*, Holt, Rinehart & Winston, 1947.

Anderson, Walfred A. and Frederick B. Parker, *Society*, D. Van Nostrand Co. Inc., New York, 1966.

Appadorai, A., *The Substance of Politics*, Oxford University Press, Madras, 1954.

Arblaster, Anthony and Steven Lukes (ed.) *The Good Society*, Methuen and Co., London, 1971.

Arthur Kornhauser, Robert Dubin, and Arthur M. Ross, *Industrial Conflict* (New York, 1954), pp. 189-212.

Avinashilingam, T.S. *Educational Philosophy of Swami Vivekananda*, Ramakrishna Mission, Coimbatore, 1964.

Baldridge, J. Victor, *Sociology*, John Wiley and Sons, New York, 1975.

Barker, Ernest, *Reflections on Government*, Oxford University Press, 1948.

Barnes, Ernest William, *Scientific Theory and Religion*, Cambridge University Press, 1933.

Bartley, W.W., 'Karl Barth,' *Encounter*, March 1970.

Beals, R.H. and H. Hoijer, *An Introduction to Anthropology*, Macmillan, New York, 1969.

Benedict, R. (1946), *Patterns of Culture*, (Pelican Book).

Benns, F. Lee, *European History Since* 1870, F. S. Crofts and Co, New York, 1947.

Bentley, J.M., as quoted in W.A. Anderson and F.B. Parker, *Society*, Van Nostrand Co., Princeton, 1966.

Bidney. D. (1953), *Theoretical Anthropology*, (Columbia University Press.

Boas, F. (ed.), *General Anthropology* (New York, 1938), Chapter on Religion by R. Benedict.

Bogart, E.L. and C.E. Landon, *Modern Industry*, Longman, Green & Co., New York, 1939.

Bouquet, A.C., *Comparative Religion* (Pelican, A 89), Chapters I to V.

Broudy, Harry S., *Building a Philosophy of Education*, Prentice-Hall, New Delhi, 1965.

Burgen, Ernest W. and Harvey J. Locke, *Family*, American Book Co., New York, 1945.

Burns, Tom (Editor), *Industrial Man*, Penguin, 1969.

Chapman, J. Crosby and George S. Counts, *Principles of Education*, Houghton Miffin Co., New York, 1924.

Chen, Theodore, Hsi-en, *Comparative Education*, Edited by Moehlman, A.H. and Joseph S., Roucek, Henry Holt and Company, Inc., New York, 1951.

Clark, T.T., *Encylopaedia of Religion and Ethics*, Vol. XI, Edinburgh, 1962.

Colby, C.C. and A. Foster, *Economic Geography*, Ginn and Co., Boston, 1944.

Cole, G.D. H., *Social Theory*, Methuen and Co., London, 1930.

Cooley, Charles H., *Social Organisation*, Scribner, 1909.

Corry, J.A., *Elements of Democratic Government*, Oxford University Press, New York, 1947.

Cunningham, W. and E.A. McArthur, *Outlines of English Industrial History*, Cambridge University Press, 1910.

Davis, Kingsley, *Human Society*, Macmillan, New York, 1957.

Dawson, Christopher, *The Age of Gods*, Sheed and Ward, London, 1933.

Dawson, J. W., *The Origin of the World,* Hodder and Stoughton, 1888.

Drucker, P.K., *The New Society,* William Heinemann, London, 1951.

Drucker, Peter F., *The Changing World of the Executive,* Times Books, New York, 1982.

Durant, Will, *Our Oriental Heritage,* Vol. I, Simon and Schuster, 1954.

Durkheim, Emile, *The Elementary Forms of Religious Life,* Chapter 9, Free Press, Glencoe, Ill., 1947.

Eliot, T.S., *Murder in the Chathedral,* Faber and Faber, London, 1969.

Eros, J.S. and W.A.C. Stewart, *Systematic Sociology,* Routledge and Kegan Paul, London, 1957.

Farber, Bernard, 'Theories of Le Play'. in *Kinship and Family Organisations,* John Wiley, New York, 1966.

Faris, Ellsworth, as quoted by Francis E. Merrill, *Society and Culture--An Introduction to Sociology,* Prentice Hall, New Jersey, 1969.

Faris, R.E. L., as quoted in C.C. Schrag, O.N. Larsen, and W.R. Catton, *Sociology,* Harper and Row, New York, 1968.

Fichter, Joseph H., *Sociology,* University of Chicago Press, 1957.

Firth, Raymond, *Elements of Social Organisation,* Travistock Publications, London, 1969.

Flather, Paul, 'Gandhi honours poll pledge,' *The Times Higher Education Supplement*, London, 18 January, 1985.

Fletcher, Ronald, *The Making of Sociology,* Vol. 2, Michael Joseph, 1971.

Frankfurter, Felix, *The Public and Its Government*, Beacon Press, Boston, 1964.

Frazer, James, *The Golden Bough,* Part IV, Macmillan, London, 1963.

Gadgil, D.R., *Industrial Evolution of India in Recent Times,* Oxford University Press, Bombay, 1945.

Galbraith, John Kenneth, *The New Industrial State,* Houghton Mifflin, Boston, 1967.

Gettell, R. G., *Political Science,* Ginn and Co., Boston, 1949.

Ghose, G. *Socialism and Communism in India,* Allied Publishers, Bombay, 1971.

Ghurye, G.S., *The Aborigines--So-called--and Their Future* (Poona).

Ginsberg, M., *The Psychology of Society,* Methuen, London, 1949.

Giri, V. V., *Labour Problems in Indian Industry,* Asia Publishing House, 1972.

Gisbert, P., *Fundamentals of Sociology,* Orient Longman, Bombay, 1960.

Gisbert, P., *Preliterate Man,* Manaktalas, Bombay, 1967.

Gittler, J.B., *Social Dynamics,* McGraw Hill, New York, 1952.

Glock, Charles Y. and Rodney Stark, *Religion and Society in Tension?,* Rand McNally, 1965.

Goode, William J., *Religion Among the Primitives,* The Free Press of Glencoe, 1951.

Goode, William J., *The Family,* Prentice-Hall, New Delhi, 1965.

Green, Arnold W, *Sociology,* McGraw-Hill, Tokyo, 1964.

Harris, Seymour E., *The New Economics,* Dennis Dobson, London, 1968.

Harrison, Frederick and Charles A. Meyers, *Education, Manpower and Economic Growth,* McGraw-Hill, New Delhi, 1970.

Herskovitz, Melville J., *Man and His Works,* Alfred Knopf, New York, 1956.

Hobhouse, L.T., G.C. Wheeler and M. Ginsberg, *Material Culture and Social Institutions of the Simpler Peoples,* Chapman and Hall, London.

Hoebel, E.A. and E.L. Frost, *Cultural and Social Anthropology,* Tata McGraw Hill, New Delhi, 1979.

Homer, *The Odyssey*, (translated by E.V. Rieu), Penguin Books, Middlesex, 1961.

Horton, Paul B. and Chester L. Hunt, *Sociology*, McGraw-Hill, New York, 1968.

Hutton, J.H., *Caste in India*, Cumberledge, 1951.

John C. McKinney and Edward A. Tiryakian (eds), *Theoretical Sociology*, New York, 1970.

Kapadia, K.M., *Marriage and Family in India*, Oxford University Press, 1954.

Karnick, V.K., *Indian Trade Unions*, Manaktalas, 1966.

Karsten. R., *The Origins of Religion*, London; Kegan Paul Trench, Trubner & Co., 1935.

Keynes, J. M., 'A General Theory of Employment, Interest and Money,' as quoted in *The Good Society* (edited by Anthony Arblaster and Steven Lukes), Methuen and Co., London, 1971.

King. David, C. and Marvin R. Koller, *Foundations of Sociology*, Rinehart Press, San Francisco, 1975.

Krech, David and Richard Crutchfield, *Theory and Problems of Social Psychology*, McGraw Hill, New Delhi, 1976.

Kroeber, A.L., and C. Kluckhohn, *Culture: A Critical Review of Concepts and Definitions*, Harvard, 1952.

Kroeber, *Anthropology*, Harcourt, Brace and Co., New York, 1948.

Lang, Kurt and Gladys Lang, *Collective Dynamics*, Thomas Crowell, New York, 1961.

Lindsay (Editor), *The New Cambridge Modern History*, Cambridge University Press, Cambridge, 1957.

Linton, Ralph, *The Study of Man*, Appleton-Century, 1936.

Lowie, R., *Primitive Society*, London: Routledge & Kegan Paul Ltd., 1921.

Lowie, R., *The History of Ethnological Theory*, New York, 1937.

Lowie, R.H., *Primitive Society*, Chapter V.

Lundberg, G.A., C.C. Schrag, O.N. Larsen and W.R. Catton, *Sociology,* Harper and Row, 1968.

Lundberg, George A., A.C. Schrag, O.N. Larsen and W.R. Catton, *Sociology,* Harper and Row, New York, 1968.

MacIver, R.M. and C.H. Page, *Society,* Macmillan and Co., London, 1964.

MacIver, R.M., *The Modern State,* Oxford University Press, 1950.

Malinowaski, B., *Argonauts of Western Pacific,* Routledge and Kegan Paul, London, 1964.

Malinowski, B., *A Scientific Theory of Culture,* University of North Carolina Press, 1944.

Malinowski, B., *Magic, Science* and *Religion,* Boston and Glencoe, III., 1948.

Marcuse, Herbert, *One Dimensional Man,* Beacon Press, Boston, 1964.

Marriet, R.R., *The Threshold of Religion* New York, 1914.

Marriott, J.A.R., *A History of England,* Vol. VII, Methuen & Co, London, 1950.

Marshall, Alfred, *Principles of Economics,* Macmillan & Co., London, 1910.

Mauger, Peter, 'Integrating the intelligentsia,' *The Times Higher Education Supplement,* London, 6 May, 1983.

Max Gluckman, *Custom and Conflict in Africa* (Oxford, 1955; New York, 1964).

Maxey, Chester C., *Political Philosophies,* The Macmillan Co., New York, 1949.

Merrill, Francis C., *Society and Culture,* Prentice Hall, 1969.

Merrill, Francis E., *Society and Culture--An Introduction to Sociology,* Prentice Hall Inc., Englewood Cliffs, N.J. 1969.

Merton, Robert, K., *Social Theory and Social Sturcture,* Amerind, New Delhi, 1968.

Micklem, Nathaniel, *Religion,* London, Oxford University Press, 1948.

Mill, John Stuart, *Representative Government*, Forum Books, New York, 1958.

Miller, D.C. and W.H. Form, *Industrial Sociology*, Harper International, New York, 1964.

Morrall, John B., *Aristotle*, George Allen and Unwin, London, 1977.

Mosca, Gaetano, *The Ruling Class*, McGraw-Hill, New York, 1939.

Mudaliar, A. Lakshmanaswamy, Chairman, *Report of the Secondary Education Commission.*

Munroe, W.E., *The Governments of Europe*, The Macmillan Co., New York, 1938.

O'Leary, John, 'Mobility on the agenda,' *The Times Higher Education Supplement*, London, 25 November, 1983.

Ogburn, W.F. and M.F. Nimkoff, *A Handbook of Sociology*, Eurasia Publishing House, New Delhi, 1964.

Parsons, Talcott, *Essays in Sociological Theory*, The Free Press, Glencoe, Ill, 1954.

Parsons, Talcott, *The Social System*, The Free Press, Glencoe, Ill, 1951.

Pavitt, K.L.R., 'Harnessing development to specific objectives,' *The Times Higher Education Supplement*, London, 12 August, 1983.

Piddington, Ralph, *Social Anthropology*, Oliver and Boyd, London, 1957.

Popenoe, David, *Sociology*, Appleton Century, New York, 1971.

Pound, Roscoe, *Law and Morals*, The University of North Carolina Press, 1924.

Prabhu, Pandhari-Nath, 1954, *Hindu Social Organization*, Bombay: Popular-Book Depot. 1954.

Pritchard, E.E. Evans, *Social Anthropology*, Routledge and Kegan Paul, 1972.

Pritchard, E.E. Evans, *The Institutions of Primitive Society*, Blackwell, Oxford, 1954.

Queen, S.A., R.W. Habenstein and J.B. Adams. *The Family in Various Cultures, Lippincott*, 1961.

Radcliffe-Brown and Daryll Forde (eds.), *African Systems of Kinship and Marriage* (Oxford, 1950), Introduction.

Radcliffe-Brown, A.R., *Structure and Function in Primitive Society*, Routledge and Kegan Paul, London, 1976.

Ralf Dahrendorf, 'Uber einige Problems der soziologischen Theorie der Revolution,' *European Journal of Sociology*, Vol. 2 (1961); Hannah Arendt, *On Revolution* (New York, 1963); Carl J. Friedrich (ed.), 'Revolution,' *NOMOS*, Vol. 8 (1967).

Robinson, John A.T., *Honest to God*, S.C. M. Press, London, 1969.

Rogers, E, M., *Social Change in Rural Society*, Appleton Century, New Yrok, 1960.

Ross, Arnold M., *Sociology*, Alfred A. Knopf, New York, 1957.

Rostow, W.W., *Politics and Stages of Growth*, Cambridge University Press, 1971.

Samuelson, Paul A, *Economics*, McGraw-Hill, Tokyo, 1980.

Schrag, C.C., O. N. Larsen and W.R. Catton, *Sociology*, Harper and Row, New York.

Seligman, C.G., *Races of Africa*, Oxford University Press, London, 1961.

Shibutani, Tamotsu, 'Reference Group as Perspectives, *American Sociological Review*, 27: 19--30 (February 1962).

Simmel, George (translated by K.H. Wolff and R. Bendix), *Conflict and the Web of Group Affiliations*, The Free Press of Glencoe, New York, 1955.

Smith, E.C. and A.J. Zurcher, (Editors), *New Dictionary of American Politics*, Barnes and Noble, New York, 1949.

Smith, Marion B., *Survey of Social Science*, Houghton Miffin Co., New York, 1945.

Spencer, Metta, *Sociology,* Prentice-Hall, New Jersey, 1979.

Sterling, John (Editor), *The Bible* (Authorised Version), Micah, Chapter 6, Verse 8, The British and Foreign Bible Society, Oxford University Press, London, 1966.

Stevenson, Jim, 'In the privacy of their own homes,' *The Times Higher Education Supplement,* P. VII, London, 9 November, 1984 (Information Technology).

Stewart, E.W. and J.A. Glynn, *Introduction to Sociology,* Tata McGraw-Hill, New Delhi, 1976.

Strong C.G., *Modern Political Constitutions,* Sidgwick and Jackson, London, 1975.

Thomson, J. Arthur, *Science and Religion,* Methuen & Co., London, 1925.

Timasheff, N.S., *Sociological Theory,* Random House, 1967.

Tonnies, Ferdinand, (translated by C.P. Loomis), *Fundamental Concepts of Sociology,* American Book, New York, 1949.

Toynbee, A J. (abridged by D.C. Somervell) *A Study of History,* Oxford University Press, 1947.

Toynbee, Arnold, *Industrial Revolution of the 18th Century England,* Longmans, Green and Co., London, 1912.

Trevelyan, G.M., *English Social History,* Orient Longmans, Bombay, 1970.

Turner, Ralph H. and Lewis M. Killian, *Collective Behaviour,* Prentice Hall, New Jersey, 1957.

Von Borch, H., The *Unfinished Society,* Hawthorn Books, 1962.

Voskuyl, Roger V. and others, *Modern Science and Christian Faith,* Van Kampen Press, Illinois, 1950.

Walker, J., *The British Economic and Social History,* Macdonald and Evans, 1979.

Wanlass, L.C., *Gettell's History of Political Thought,* George Allen and Unwin, London, 1956.

Webb, Sidney and Beatrice, *The History of Trade Unionism,* Longmans, Green and Co., London, 1935.

Weber, Max, *The Sociology of Religion,* (Translated by Fischoffs), Beacon Press, 1964.

Westermarck, Edward, *A Short History of Marriage,* Macmillan, New York, 1926.

White, Merry I., as quoted in Boyer, Earnest, 'What the country wants from Dr. Bell's Successor,' *The Times Higher Education Supplement,* London, 18, January, 1985.

Wilds, Elmer H. and Kenneth V. Lottich, *The Foundations of Modern Education,* Holt, Rhinehart and Winston, Inc, New York, 1961.

Williams, Burce, 'Technology's Social Consequences,' *The Times Higher Education Supplement,* 12 August, 1983.

Young, Kimball, *Social Psychology,* Appleton-Century, New York, 1946.

Index

M

N

O

P

R